MW01094423

*"When we, for whatever reason, have the opportunity to lead an extraordinary life, we have no right to keep it to ourselves."*

- Jacques Yves Cousteau

AIM Group LLC
Houston, TX
USA.

xtra ordinary
LEADERS

# XO LEADERS
## VOLUME I - USA

**Creator of the Book & President**
Gustav Barcelo Juul

**Editorial Director**
Natasha Iglesias Aznar

**Editorial Coordinator**
Maricela Montes de Oca

**Graphic Design**
Laura Pavón Rodríguez

**Front page Design**
Alexa Xanat Rodríguez Noguez

**In collaboration with:**

**Customer Service**
Comments about the book are welcome
founder@xoleaders - 802 500 5151

**ISBN:** 978-13-12-22098-0
**Printed in USA.**

All material appearing in this book is protected by copyright under U.S. Copyright laws and is the property of XO Leaders or the party credited as the provider of the content. You may not copy, reproduce, distribute, publish, display, perform, modify, create derivative works, transmit, or in any way exploit any such content, nor may you distribute any part of this content over any network, including a local area network, sell or offer it for sale, or use such content to construct any kind of database. You may not alter or remove any copyright or other notice from copies of the book. Copying or storing any content except as provided above is expressly prohibited without prior written permission of XO Leaders or the copyright holder identified in the individual content's copyright notice. For permission to use the content on the University's website, please contact pr@xoleaders.com

# Co-Authors

Alejandro Kasuga · Alejandro Dabdoub · Ana Laura Arias Reza · Andrew Pollard · Ann Ravel · Ben Vaschetti · Bob Orsi · Bruce Cohen · Christine M. Wallace · Cristina Riveroll · Daniela González · David J. Whelan · Deven Nongbri · Eduardo Rosales · Edvard Philipson · Emilio Aragón Sánchez García · Eric Abensur · Erik Huberman · Espree Devora · Frank Kasnick · George Montgomery · Gustavo Lomas · Hans Guevara · Héctor Ventura García Flores · Ian Christopher Figueroa Schmehl · Jack Laskowitz · Javier Lattanzio · Jennifer "Jaki" Johnson · Jennifer Lahoda · Jeremy Hochman · Joel Primus · Juan Carlos Lascurain · Juan J Gallardo · Ken Bassman · Liliana Remus · Luis Diego Loaiciga V · Luis Silva · Maria I. Zepeda · Mario E. Moreno · Mark Hebner · Martin Cabrera · Nadim Jarudi · Natalise Kalea Robinson · Nick Jiwa · Nicolas Hauff · Omar Soto Sepúlveda · Omar Flores · Omero Flores · Paula Haza · Rachael M. Kim · R. Lee Harris · Roberto Bonelli · Roberto Litwak · Salvador H. Avila Cobo · Sandra Lilia Velasquez · Swati Valbh-Patel ·

# Acknowledgements

Every year I am amazed by the enormous generosity and good-will of the people who support and participate in this work. I am amazed that the success of this concept can cross borders and cultures and still find such an incredible audience. Our stories might differ, but as we read the stories, experiences, and anecdotes, we find that we are not so different after all. It is the first time we have published XO Leaders in the United States of America, and we have found such incredible people that we can wait to see how far it takes us.

I am deeply grateful to everyone who contributed to this book's making. It is through their support, encouragement, and expertise that this project has come to fruition. I would like to express my sincere appreciation to the following individuals:

First and foremost, I would like to thank my family for their unwavering love and support throughout this journey. Their patience, understanding, and belief in me have been instrumental in bringing this book to life. They gave me unconditional support, no matter how much time I sometimes spent on this project, allowing me to launch this great book again this year in a new country.

I extend my heartfelt gratitude to the extraordinary co-authors who, with the success of this new edition, show me once more that a dream followed up by action does become a reality. I am grateful for their generosity in sharing knowledge and experiences. I am the first to admit that I have a lot to learn and that I am a better person for the inspiration and knowledge I have received from the hundreds of co-authors who have participated through these many years. It has been a transformative journey.

I am indebted to my friends and colleagues who provided feedback, offered valuable insights, and motivated me during the writing process. Your enthusiasm for this project and willingness to lend a listening ear made this endeavor all the more rewarding.

A special thanks go to my Partners and individual team members of AIM Group for supporting me with their time, dedication, follow-up, and effort, without which this project would not have been possible.

I also want to acknowledge the readers who have supported me on this writing journey. Your enthusiasm, engagement, and kind words have motivated me to continue pursuing my passion for writing.

Lastly, I want to express my gratitude to the many authors and organizations who have bought books (undoubtedly many more than they actually needed) and made direct donations so that we may support extraordinary university students.

To all those mentioned above and to anyone else whose name may have inadvertently been omitted, please accept my sincere apologies. Your contributions have not gone unnoticed, and I am truly grateful for your involvement.

Writing this book has been a labor of love, and I am humbled by the support and encouragement I have received along the way. Without the collective effort and generosity of these individuals, this book would not have been possible. Thank you from the bottom of my heart.

If you hold a copy of the book, please know that we donate 100% of the profits and donations to students. You are making a significant difference in the lives of students eager to learn and grow, so I have but to thank you for purchasing this book and welcome you to **XO Leaders USA - Volume 1.**

Sincerely,
Gustav

*Dear Board of Trustees,*

*As I bring this book to a close, as President of the Board of Trustees, I would like to express my deepest gratitude for the valuable contribution of each and every member of the Board of Trustees, Anthony Dovkants, Richard Azera, Roberto Gonzalez, Yann Audebert, Juan Carlos Rojas and Nicolas Hauff towards the creation and publication of this book.*

*Your unwavering support and belief in XO Leaders have been instrumental in turning my dream into a reality. I am truly honored to have had the opportunity to work with such an esteemed group of individuals who are dedicated to fostering knowledge and advancing education.*

*The generosity you have shown through the time you have invested in presenting and the difficult task of selecting the right authors, has not only allowed me to bring my ideas to life but has also opened doors for countless readers to engage with the content and concepts we have explored within the book's pages. Your contribution has made it possible for this work to reach a wider audience, and I am humbled by the impact it has already had.*

*Moreover, your trust and encouragement have inspired me to push my boundaries and strive for excellence throughout the entire writing and publishing process. Knowing that I had the support of the Board of Trustees behind me gave me the confidence to work harder to present a work we all can feel genuinely proud of.*

*I would be remiss if I did not express my appreciation for your guidance and expertise throughout this journey. Your collective wisdom of such a distinguished group of individuals and your experience have been invaluable in shaping the direction of this first volume of XO Leaders in the United States of America, and I am grateful for the constructive feedback and suggestions that have enriched its content.*

*Please accept this heartfelt thank you for your contributions. Your belief in the power of literature and the importance of spreading knowledge has made a lasting impact, not only on me but on the readers who will benefit from the insights and ideas presented in my book.*

*I am truly honored to have had the opportunity to collaborate with the Board of Trustees, and I am forever grateful. Your generosity and* support have played an integral role in bringing my vision to fruition, and I am excited to see the impact it will have on readers far and wide.

I look forward to the future endeavors we may undertake together.

With sincere gratitude,


Gustav Juul

# *Index*

# Introduction

**T**his is not just another book that deals with leadership issues. We feel that it is a book with a novel style and format, in which founders and directors of leading companies within their sectors share with us part of what has made them achieve such remarkable results.

The business world is constantly changing, adapting, and evolving. On many occasions, this change has to be forced by social, economic, and technological contexts. The leaders participating in this new 2023 edition have taken on the task of expressing, based on their experience, some of their experiences and decisions they have had to make to face this adjustment in the most positive way for their organization.

In all the articles of our co-authors, you will find a human and warm side, never losing the strategic and corporate approach that made them achieve so much success and position themselves in the place they are today. This is a work that will provide you with focus, determination, advice, and strategies to achieve your goals. XO Leaders covers different business sectors, offering you a broad panorama that demonstrates the great difficulties and successes of the most important companies in the corporate world in the United States.

After eight editions, **XO Leaders** has positioned itself as one of the best business reference books, offering not only corporate strategies but the real and tangible experiences of all our leaders. That is why this is not just another book about leadership.

In this eighth book, we discovered the willingness and generosity of our participating leaders, this time addressing topics such as change, making the impossible a reality, leadership, challenges, and how to find balance, to mention a few. The companies that participated in this book, through their executives, understood that the objective of the book is to serve as a stimulus for people and companies that seek to innovate, grow and undertake.

This book also has an altruistic background. It is not-for-profit. We neither charge companies for their participation nor do any of the co-authors get paid for their contributions. We give 100% of the profits to extraordinary students or XO Students as we like to call them.

As a result of the previous years, we have been able to donate scholarships to young university students who needed this economic support to continue their dream of furthering their education. We are very grateful for the money raised from the sale, and we hope that in our eighth edition, which you are reading now, we will achieve even grander results.

It is for all of the above that I hope, with all my heart, that you, our readers, will once again find the inspiration and the necessary ideas that you can apply in your daily lives to grow as people and improve the level of companies.

I invite you to learn about the real experiences of our leaders and to contact me in case you would like to participate in the next edition. Our websites are:

**XO Leaders: www.xoleaders.com**

**AIM Group: www.aimsmg.com**

# Gustav

# Juul

**Founder y CEO**

*AIM GROUP*

**Alejandro**
Kasuga
*A. KASUGA
CONSULTORES*

**Joel**
Primus
*NAKED REVIVAL INC*

**Ken**
Bassman
*BASSMAN
BLAINE*

**David**
J. Whelan
*BIOSCIENCE LA*

**Emilio**
Aragón Sánchez García
*ASOCIACIÓN DE EMPRESARIOS
MEXICANOS CAPÍTULO THW
WOODLANDS*

# 1. Moonshots

**Alejandro**
Dabdoub
*ALLIED-ORION
GROUP*

**Mark**
Hebner
*INDEX FUND
ADVISORS, INC*

**Omero & Omar**
Flores
*THE J. FLORES
COMPANY*

**R. Lee**
Harris
*COHEN
ESREY*

**Nick**
Jiwa
*CUSTOMERSERV*

# Learning to Dream, again

**Gustav Juul**
Founder & CEO
*AIM GROUP / XO LEADERS*

*"All men dream, but not equally. Those who dream by night in the dusty recesses of their minds wake in the day to find that it was vanity, but the dreamers of the day are dangerous men, for they may act out their dreams with open eyes to make it possible."*
  – T. E. Lawrence

S ince my early adulthood, I knew I wanted to get married, but I didn't imagine having children would be such a blessing. There is something wonderfully simple about the way young children see life. They see life through a different lens in which anything is possible. When she was about three years old, I remember how my daughter transformed into a princess the moment she put on her dress and the hundreds of shiny bracelets I had bought for her at the dollar store. There was no shame, only pride when we walked down the main streets in full gala. It brought a few smiles from people that recognize the endless possibilities of a child's mind.

Similarly, my son becomes the real Spiderman, a magician with incredible powers or a knight in shining armor in the blink of an eye, sometimes even a combination of every superhero ever created. At least once a day, it is *"our duty"* to go out into the garden and slay all the *"bad guys"* in the world.

I remember a time when I truly believed that I would grow up to be Superman. As I grew older, this dream changed to being a Top Gun fighter pilot. Somewhere along the line, this dream faded, and for a long time, I never replaced it. For some reason, I stopped dreaming. Actually, that is not entirely true; I really never stopped dreaming; it was just that I stopped believing my dreams were possible.

### We All Dream

*"Only she who attempts the absurd can achieve the impossible."*
-Robin Morgan

**33**

I think most people dream, but our dreams change throughout life. They become more measured, less challenging, and more common. As I look around each day, I don't think I am the only one who has experienced this. So why is it that our incredible, colorful childhood dreams become bland small, gray, and small?

Someone that doesn't settle is not mature; they are called in-mature. We are told how complicated life is and how we need to find a purpose in life, but we should not stray too far from the path others have walked before us. We are recommended to dream, but to dream small, manageable, realistic dreams of a nice house, a steady job, and saving up for our pension.

We are brought up to give up our dreams; for some, that is just fine, although is it really? Are we true to ourselves if we only let ourselves dream at night, under cover of darkness, only to convince ourselves when we wake up to fall back in line and that it was all just a passing lunacy? Is it reasonable that men that decide to act on their dreams are seen as crazy and lost?

Let me take a step back which I hope will explain where I am going with this and why I guess I have *"dared"* more than most. My first contact with depression was in high school. One of my best friends' dads was a teacher, and I was a lot at his house because he lived close to the school, which was convenient. Still, there was something sad about his dad: he seemed subdued and melancholic, and he was one people didn't talk much to other than the typical *"Hi and goodbye."* One day the conversation turned to our parents, and I asked my friend why his dad was like that. His answer stuck with me. He told me that his dad wanted to be something else and hadn't; he had given up on his dream and now felt that he had wasted his life.

Now, who is more lost, the person who followed his dreams and failed trying, or who didn't even try? I remember that from that day, I have always had, in the back of my mind, the worry of becoming old with a feeling of not having followed my dreams.

### Let go of the need to know how

*"The future belongs to those who belive in the beauty of their dreams."*
— Eleanor Roosevelt

Since I turned 40 a few years ago, became a father again, and started my own business, I began to let myself dream as I did as a child.

Through this, I came to a powerful realization. I needed to let go of the need to know how. You see, when I put my dreams to the test of how to implement them, I found the problem was that I would quickly discard them as mere fantasies because I could not immediately imagine how these dreams would become a reality.

What I have come to realize since I started to dream again is that just because I can't immediately see how I would be able to accomplish it, it doesn't mean it's impossible.

At first, it was difficult to let go of having the certainty of knowing exactly how because it, frankly speaking, makes you feel vulnerable. Still, I also realized that if I was going to let myself fully live out my dreams, I needed to be able to let myself go and have faith and believe in my abilities. My motto is:

*"Dream big, think hard, act swiftly, be strong, stay focused, and win."*
-Gustav Juul

To me, this means literally that I let myself dream wildly without trying to know how these dreams will become a reality. To a large extent, I let the final outcome in the hands of The Almighty, and since I am not quite sure where dreams originate, maybe that also is in God's hands. During the process, there certainly is a time when I have to develop a plan, but I let myself enjoy the beauty of dreaming and the excitement of the unknown, and I trust that there must be a way to realize them.

## Exploring The Unknown

Thich Nhat Hanh, a Vietnamese Buddhist monk, said, *"People have a hard time letting go of their suffering. Out of a fear of the unknown, they prefer suffering that is familiar."*

So, if you feel *"stuck"* like I did, it could be that you have become addicted to the predictable flow of what *"feeling stuck"* entails. Indeed, psychologists have argued that the fear of the unknown is the fundamental fear of all. Put this way, *"feeling stuck"* and predictable suffering is, to many, the better choice over dreaming of something new, something unknown. Because that's really what the future is, a big gigantic unknown full of change and uncertainty. However, if you remove the anxiety of the unknown. You start to use the future for something else: its endless potential. In the future, everything could potentially happen.

You don't know. And so, when you tap into that, by dreaming and visualizing your future, you can start to shape it as you want it to be with hope and optimism.

## Change is Life-confirming

I had the fortune of first knowing Dr. Adizes, the founder of the Adizes Institute, which carries his name, and then later being invited to work with him, holding the second largest stake in the Adizes Institute at that time. One of our firm's objectives is, in many ways, to make medium and large companies reach far beyond their current capabilities and stretch them to reach entirely new levels of excellence. For some companies, typically family-owned businesses, we help professionalize others we support in re-vitalizing and finding new dreams to chase with incredible success. The foundation for this methodology was developed over 50 years ago and has been polished by the thousands of companies we have worked with. My favorite book is probably *"Managing Corporate Lifecycles,"* which will make you discover a completely new world of Corporate Management.

What not only worked for me but now also for the many companies I have helped, is realizing that change is a constant and that the rate of change is accelerating. The faster we are able to understand what is changing, the faster we can take decisions about how to deal with it and ultimately be more successful. Not taking a decision, by the way, is also a decision. A big part of adapting to change is letting yourself dream and allowing yourself to act out your dreams. This is wonderfully life-confirming because the alternative is falling into decay and eventually ceasing to exist.

## Making dreams reality

As an entrepreneur, you are bound to see things others don't. You have accepted to take risks that most people simply won't. But every now and then, you need to remind yourself how to make the impossible possible and how to stretch the organization. Instead of copying the past, it's important to focus on what you dream the future could be. Your brain is a powerful tool for overcoming obstacles.

## Dreams

What we believe is possible, and what is not, is a matter of perspective. Think of the pharaohs that built the pyramids, the Chinese that built the great wall, or in more recent times, the Wright Brothers and JFK.

When you think of the first airplane, Orville and Wilbur Wright must come to mind, and December 17th, 1903, is the day to remember. That was the day that Orville won the toss of the coin. He made the first successful powered flight in history! The place was Kitty Hawk, North Carolina, and there and then, the Wright Brothers' dream of inventing a flying machine came true. It all started when Orville was 7, and Wilbur was 11 years old. Their father, Bishop Milton Wright, gave them a flying toy helicopter. That toy made them dream of flying, and they made the dream come true.

John. F. Kennedy announced at Rice University on September 12th, 1962, that he wanted to land a man on the moon before 1970. In his speech, Kennedy characterized space as a new frontier, invoking the pioneer spirit that dominated American folklore. He infused the speech with a sense of urgency and destiny and emphasized the freedom enjoyed by Americans to choose their destiny rather than have it chosen for them. That is dreaming, big time!

This incredible dream was achieved less than seven years later. Apollo 11 took off on July 16th, 1969, with its destination "The Moon." On July 20th, Neil Armstrong and Edwin "Buzz" Aldrin became the first humans ever to land on the moon. About six-and-a-half hours later, Armstrong became the first person to walk on the moon. As he took his first step, Armstrong famously said, *"That's one small step for man, one giant leap for mankind.".*

It is true that looking forward feels different because you must take a leap of faith in order to accomplish anything that is a breakthrough, especially things that are giant leaps forward or what we now call *"moonshots"* in memory of JFK. Just because something hasn't been done before doesn't mean it's impossible. Sure, there are laws of physics, such as gravity, that we must obey, but the more we open our minds to new possibilities, the more we can see paths forward, some of which have never been walked before, and we need to create.

**Know Your Why**

Before you dig deep into how you make the impossible possible, you must first focus on your why. Why is it that this must happen? The more you can paint a clear picture of why what you're doing is important, the deeper a seed you will plant in your own mind and influence those around you. If your reasons are important, then you will find a way to make it happen.

## Know Your How

When turning your vision into reality, it can be helpful to understand why people tell you it can't be done. Listening is not the same thing as believing. If you believe that your vision is critically important, then you can listen with confidence to all the people who believe what you're looking to do is impossible. What they are actually telling you are the hurdles that you will face and must overcome in order to be successful. Instead of obsessing about what you can't do, it's important to focus on how you could accomplish your vision.

## Know Your What

When you ask questions, you get better results. By thinking deeply about what you would need to make your dream a reality, you can start to see the possibilities that most people are closed off from seeing since they already dismissed the idea as being impossible. Get really specific so that you know precisely what you'd need.

## Know Your Who

Once you know what you need to do in order to make the impossible possible, then it's time to get leverage by asking others to help you. When you tell them you need their help on something they don't believe is possible, they will be reluctant to agree. However, when you have broken down what you need into individual tasks and simply ask for their help with a specific task, it doesn't feel overwhelming, and therefore they are more likely to support you.

Gather enough support from enough people, and you can do just about anything. The bigger your vision for the future, the more likely you are to inspire others. So dream big, listen to those who doubt your vision, and then lead confidently as you show those around you how to make it happen.

# *Alejandro*

# Kasuga

**President**
*A. KASUGA CONSULTORES*

## Kizukai, the democratization of continuous improvement

It is a fact that today's world is increasingly changing and requires that both individuals and organizations have a focus on the formation of a culture of continuous improvement that allows us to anticipate the new needs of the environment. We generally focus on improvement projects such as quality circles, kaizen, lean, six sigma among many other methods which have a great impact, however they are top to bottom schemes where engineers and top management manage continuous improvement relegating lower positions who also have a lot of knowledge and are not taken into account as they should be.

The key problem in the formation of a culture of continuous improvement is first of all, the definition of organizational culture. From my personal point of view, organization comes from the Latin ORGNAUM, an organ is a living being that has to adapt according to the changing environment. All the cells of the organ have to communicate towards the same objective, otherwise they are cancerous cells that have to be eliminated. My body is made up of many organs and cells and the reality is that my right hand does not care much about what my liver does. My liver doesn't care

much about what my lung does, my lung doesn't care much about what my tongue does, but together they make my body work. In the same manner in many companies the person who recruits doesn't care much about what the purchasing department does, the person who works in sales doesn't care much about whether or not the production objective was achieved, the employee at accounting doesn't care much about whether there was a problem in logistics. So what is organizational culture?

Organizational culture is the blood and veins that unite all the organs and cells of our body at all times, in all places and by everyone.

It is a fact that today's world is increasingly changing and demands that both epmployees and organizations have a focus on continuous improvement as part of our DNA in order to anticipate the new needs of the ever changing environment. If we fail as company leaders to create an organization focused on improvement as a culture, we will become dinosaurs; perhaps very large companies with a lot of strength but very slow in the way we move, and the reality is that we have to transform ourselves into chameleons. Constantly seeing how the environment changes and adapting to it as quickly as possible to survive.

In my experience as an entrepreneur and consultant I have had the opportunity to see continuous improvement from different points of view and in different work cultures and this cultural mix that formed me from the beginning of my professional career was what influenced me to develop what is now known as Kizukai®, my continuous improvement methodology.

After having completed my studies in business administration at UC Berkeley and a specialization at Hitotsubashi University in Tokyo, I started collaborating in Yakult Japan and had the opportunity to learn all the benefits of a Japanese working culture in which there is a wide respect for issues such as punctuality, efficiency and always seeking maximum customer satisfaction. Later I moved to the consulting firm Deloitte, where employees are more individually focused on obtaining results, this being the basis of their working style.

Having two different working culture as my professional background, I returned to Puebla, Mexico. here I began to manage the leading company in the probiotics industry with the objective of blending the Japanese discipline with the Latin creativity and the results-oriented approach of the American.

As part of my cultural transformation strategy, I decided to change the mission and vision of the company. I spent hours and hours selecting the correct words and meaning; and I made sure that all my employees knew them by heart, the result was not what I expected, although everyone could recite it without error, the culture remained the same.

I decided to use another strategy by applying the theory of communicating vessels. In which if you pour water into a single glass the other vessels are filled. I decided to focus on pouring water in the vessel of order and cleanliness since it is a visual and tangible change and there is a methodology named 5's recognized worldwide. It was thanks to this that all employees began to develop new positive habits such as punctuality, respect for rules, teamwork, and empathy. I could say that this change was what laid the foundations of our organizational culture, it took us years to achieve it, but thanks to the fact that order and cleanliness are visual and tangible we were all able to experience the benefits gradually. In other words, order and cleanliness was the blood and veins that united all the organs of the organum.

After consolidating our organizational culture, we won the National Quality Award and the Ibero-American Quality Award. However, despite all the awards, we still made *"silly"* mistakes inside the company. Those mistakes such as rework, reprocessing, and errors that everyone knew about, and no one does anything to solve them.

I decided to set myself the task of finding the formula that would allow me to mix the creativity that characterizes Mexicans, the discipline and attention to detail of the Japanese and the focus on results of the Americans.

Kizukai is a Japanese term to describe to be concerned about others. In my point of view unless you care about how your daily work impacts internal and external clients, it is difficult to come up with good ideas. This is a methodology that is composed of four K's. Starting with the K1, which is the name given to the basic functions that each employee must fulfill, that is to say, what he/she is paid for and what gives his/her job its raison d'être, then we have the K0, which is the deficient state of a job, in other words, when the employee is performing his/her job badly, then we have the K3, which is the final objective of what we do as employees, that is, the impact that our basic activities have on the external and internal customer, and finally we have the K2, which are all those ideas for improvement that as an employee I can contribute so that in a methodological way the impact of my position is increasingly profitable for the objectives set by the company.

The objectives set by the company, in my methodology we call them guidelines, and with these guidelines is that we focus the improvement ideas of the people, these guidelines can be; reduction of costs, reduction of times, reduction of accidents, sales increase, customer satisfaction and so on.

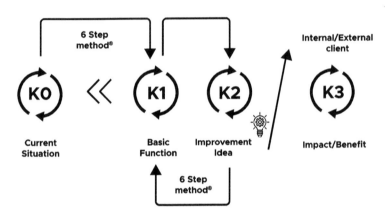

To break with the power and egos that exist in every organization, I decided to create the Kizukai committee. The members of this committee have the responsibility of being mentors or coaches for improvement. The employee, knowing that his idea does not go to the boss and that he/she has a mentor, makes it emotionally easier to give ideas for improvement. Additionally, I developed a web application that collects and manages all the information to follow up on all the ideas, so that each employee knows in which management process their idea is in and that it is a transparent and objective process. This helped to change the work environment by giving empowerment (voice and vote) to all employees based on their expertise.

Within the Kizukai® methodology, each improvement idea generated by an employee is managed us9ng the 6 step method: approval, implementation, verification, measurement, evaluation and documentation, which facilitates that all the company's knowledge is managed and talent is not wasted.

Unlike other continuous improvement methodologies, with Kizukai we seek improvement from the bottom up and not otherwise, and we help the organizations that implement it to obtain objective results. In this methodology the last word is in the results, since an improvement idea is neither good nor bad until it is measured.

Kizukai, has been implemented in companies at the highest level and in all sectors, such as; Tajin, Honda, Enel, Suzuki, Hi-Lex, Keken, among others, and that has allowed me to verify that the greatest value of organizations is still their people, because thanks to their talent, openness and focus we have implemented disruptive ideas with verifiable results both in the industry and in the service sector.

Although continuous improvement is a concept that emerged in the 80's, it is more valid than ever, now everything evolves faster than it did years ago and while everything continues to change in our environment, companies cannot remain inert in this scenario, we must move with the environment and the best way to do this is by teaming up with our people, listening to them and giving them tools to channel all the experience and proactivity they possess.

Without the involvement of employees, it will be very difficult for organizations to grow or even survive, so for those who read these lines, I hope you give yourselves the opportunity to bet on new methodologies that reduce the gap between managers and employees and bet on the potential that an idea for improvement can have.

# Alejandro

# Dabdoub

**Partner**
*ALLIED-ORION GROUP*

## How to dream big and achieve our goals

We humans tend to underestimate our own power. For instance, we all possess immense capability to influence others with our negative attitudes or discouraging words.

We're too often programmed this way, perhaps subconsciously, by formidable external forces – parents, school teachers, social media, to name just a few – to believe that we can only achieve a certain amount in this life and no more. We're too frequently discouraged from dreaming, and when we yield to that discouragement, we only wind up limiting ourselves.

By the same token, we also have the power to encourage others – as well as ourselves – with our positive thoughts and productive behavior. Toward this end, the most powerful muscle we can develop ... is our own mind. Because in reality, our enormous potential is usually much greater than our current circumstances, and our limiting beliefs are the only obstacles holding us back.

# ALLIED ORION GROUP

Each of us has the power to achieve any goal we can imagine – IF we adopt a mindset of committing ourselves to following just a few basic steps which, in my experience, have proven effective time and time again.

## SET CLEAR GOALS

*"Setting goals is the first step in turning
the invisible into the visible."*
~ Tony Robbins, Motivational Speaker

Like many college students, I had no idea what line of work I wanted to pursue while I was studying at the University of New Orleans. What I did have, however, was a dream. I wanted to build hotels or similar grandiose structures.

This dream remained just that – a dream – until one day after I graduated. My godfather introduced me to a real estate group that did exactly the kind of work I wanted to do. Today, I am a partner in that same company. What once was only a dream is today my reality in part because I made it my goal.

By setting goals – even if we don't know right away how we're going to achieve them – we create a desire and enthusiasm within ourselves that helps us prepare for our preferred future while becoming more aware of all the possibilities around us that can help us achieve those goals.

## VISUALIZE YOUR DESIRED OUTCOME

*"Luck is what happens when preparation meets opportunity."*
~ Seneca, Ancient Roman Philosopher

Throughout my life, I've heard it said that some people are lucky for being in the right place at the right time. But I don't believe in luck. I believe, based on my experience, that when we are attuned to our surroundings, we become more poised to take advantage of favorable situations and opportunities when they present themselves to us.

For example, as a business leader, I always want to grow every company I'm involved in, but when the COVID-19 pandemic hit, I faced a new challenge. During this time, like many companies, we started to suffer from supply chain disruptions that either prevented or severely delayed our construction projects. I started talking with friends and imagining new and different ways to continue construction.

Along the way, I encountered many people who were unwilling to understand or accept where the future was going, but I didn't allow their negativity to become a roadblock. Instead, I stayed true to my vision and used each person who declined my offer as a learning experience. I just kept proceeding to the next opportunity, becoming more aware of the possibilities that would open up us. Today, we not only survived the pandemic, but our company also imports more than four different brands all related to construction. I visualized the outcome I wanted and found a way to make it happen.

## CULTIVATE YOUR DETERMINATION

*"Never give up. There are always tough times, regardless of what you do in anything in life. Be able to push through those times and maintain your ultimate goal."* ~ Nathan Chen, U.S. Olympian

After setting my goal to be in the construction business and enjoying some early success in it, I had the chance to venture into new businesses. So, I decided to open a restaurant in Mexico City that eventually became very well renowned, featuring one of the top wine cellars in the whole country. At our height, we had a reservation waitlist of up to six months.

Our restaurant team was amazing, but after seven years, some political issues started to hurt the business. Several months later, we were forced to close – one of the toughest business decisions I've ever had to make in my life. But I was determined to learn from this painful lesson and refused to let it deter me from taking new chances in business and in life.

Following the restaurant experience, I reevaluated all my goals and made decisions that will change the rest of my life. I moved my family to Houston, Texas, where we now live and where I base most of my businesses. We are happy and thriving here.

Sometimes, life teaches us hard lessons that we don't understand immediately. In hindsight, though, we usually come to discover that our hard times were merely uncharted paths leading us closer to our ultimate goals.

## WHAT IS YOUR DREAM?

*"If one advances confidently in the direction of his dreams, and endeavors to live the life which he has imagined, he will meet with a success unexpected in common hours ...*
*and he will live with the license of*
*a higher order of beings."*
~ Henry David Thoreau, 19th Century Naturalist & Philosopher

Today, I am living my dream of helping other companies better their businesses and helping my employees pursue better lives. I have quite an ambitious mind, though, and am dedicated to bringing even more new opportunities to our company.

My main goal is to better the lives not only of my employees but also of the people who rent from us in the buildings we construct and oversee. To this end, I am focused on reducing costs for our renters while increasing our company's profitability.

I've learned that, when you set a goal, you have to be open to possibilities and accept that failures are just lessons that will take you to the next step. Persevering to reach those goals is crucial to achieving anything you want in life.

Determination can be a powerful motivator that helps us conquer fears, overcome obstacles, and continue pursuing our visions even through difficult times. To be determined, however, we must first know where we are going and maintain a strong desire for what we want. When faced with challenges, we can recall lessons we've learned along the way and use them to become more aware of new possibilities.

Perhaps you're still unsure what your goals might be. That's okay. Try this quick and simple exercise that's worked well for me.

Think about something you've always wanted. Each morning for the next three weeks, spend just 15 to 20 minutes visualizing it as vividly as possible, using all your senses to make the association as real as if you were already living it. You will be amazed at how your goal will form and your mindset and determination will begin to shift toward accomplishing that goal.

Also keep in mind that earning respect and making a name for yourself in any industry can be time-consuming and difficult, but they can be lost very quickly and easily. So, remember the importance of your personal values and never deviate from them, especially when this seems like the easy way out.

And don't forget to enjoy the process. Connect all the dots in your life that brought you where you are today, then start a new cycle with a new goal. It can be easy to become complacent once we've achieved one goal, but if you were able to do it once, you just might be able to do it over and over again. So, always have a new goal toward which to strive.

It doesn't matter how big or small your goal may be. What matters is that you have a clear vision of what you want and the determination to see it through to the finish.

But I've found that small dreams and big dreams often require the same amount of time and effort to accomplish. So, my final piece of advice is simple. Dream big! Because the power to accomplish anything lies within you. If you believe in yourself and your ability to achieve your dreams, anything truly is possible.

# Emilio

# Aragón Sánchez García

### President
*ASOCIACIÓN DE EMPRESARIOS MEXICANOS*
*CAPÍTULO THE WOODLANDS*

## It is a matter of trust

*In my opinion, trust is one of the most valuable things in the world. It takes years to create and only an instant to lose. According to the dictionary, trust is the assured reliance on the character, ability, strength, or truth of someone or something. Muinín (Irish), Confianza (Spanish), Fiducia (Italian), 信頼 (Chinese), Tillid (Danish). No matter the language, trust has the same meaning. However, people don't seem to recognize the enormous weight and value of trust. Mostly, it is simply taken for granted.*

### Start by trusting yourself

Mexico, Early-February 2011 – It had been months since I had an income. The balance on my bank account was $0. I was trying to keep my head above the water. Problems seemed to be popping up left and right. I had been sending out resumes to everyone I knew and a bunch of people I didn't know that well either and barely had any response, to the point where I didn't know who to write to anymore. Everything looked grim. I felt that I was going from one failure to the next.

Mid-February 2011 - I received a call. Finally, someone had actually read my CV, and I was finally being invited to an actual job interview! I only got 2 hours' notice to meet an Entrepreneur, who, for the purpose of this article, we will call Mr. X. He had found something in my resume that caught his attention; not sure what it was, but I trusted that it was something good.

I still remember walking into his fancy office. I was already daydreaming about Mr. X offering me an amazing position, a solid salary, maybe even a company car to go along with, at the very least regional manager, or perhaps even a Vice-Presidency of something or other.

After a short introduction, he explained his business to me and told me what he needed from me. He said, *"I need a translator." that is where reality hit me right in the face.*

Swallowing my pride and being out of options, I gratefully accepted the position. I had nothing to lose, and I trusted myself to do everything I could to show my capabilities and someday be offered a more senior role.

**Finding Trust through Death**

After a few months of working for him, we went on a 5-day trip to Houston. The idea was to scout the area and evaluate if it would be an excellent area to open a new division. This was to become the trip that would end up opening incredible doors for me.

We arrived on a Friday at about 11:00 pm. The moment we landed, Mr. X's phone rang, and someone told him that they needed his help. An influential Mexican businessman had died at the hospital in Houston, and the family was having a challenging time getting all the paperwork together to get their father released and transported to Mexico for his funeral on Sunday.

If you think it's difficult to get a healthy person out of a hospital, try getting a deceased person out, especially if you want them flown out of the country. It is a nightmare! My challenge was to help the family members make all the arrangements and have the gentleman's body reach Mexico in time.

At that moment, I didn't know who the grieving family was; they certainly didn't know me either. My first challenge was, therefore, to earn their trust in something so emotionally charged as organizing the transportation of the remains of their loved one.

Saturday morning, I woke up early to meet with Mr. X., who already had a hectic agenda. He gave me a computer and a cell phone and asked me to solve this issue, and so my journey began. Call after call, trying to find a way to help the family and feeling that doors kept closing on me. After a large part of the morning had flown by, making what felt like hundreds of calls, I started to think that it might be impossible to help this family in the timeframe they were hoping for. Just then, one of the people I had talked to called me back and suggested that I speak to a specialist who handles VIP funerals for international clients. I didn't think that someone like that existed, but I felt that if there was anyone in Houston that could help me, it would surely be him.

You cannot imagine my excitement. I immediately arranged to meet him and reached his office in record time. Together we cleared all the paperwork, and 12 hours later, the family was on their private plane flying to Mexico for the funeral. After that experience, I know that 90 percent of the things we think are impossible are actually possible.

This difficult and fantastic experience turned into a job, and I was soon after living in Houston.

## Selling Trust

We are all in the business of selling trust. Everyone all the time!

Every product has its own beauty and performance, but the buyers need to trust that they are getting what they are expecting. There is a direct relationship between a client's excitement and the trust they have in what they are going to receive in return. It can be anything, from a 1-dollar toothbrush to a multi-million-dollar item. It is all about trust and not so much the product.

In personal relationships and even within our families, I have experienced that it is much the same. We all seek the trust of our sons and daughters, wives and husbands, fathers and mothers, and friends and neighbors.

Living in Houston, I met the owner of a magazine directed to the very rich and famous and especially to the Hispanic market. Through him, knowing of my racing background, I got the chance to meet the owners of the Rolls Royce / Bentley Houston dealership.

We got to talking, and that's where trust again plays an important role in my life. I met the Director of both brands, who had identified a great potential market in The Woodlands, TX, but they had difficulty reaching it without building a full-blown dealership here. After much thought and creative discussion of the different options, we agreed that I would become their Brand Ambassador for the area.

I was so excited! Imagine that, a Brand Ambassador. What a cool title for a job. My mind was going at a million miles an hour, but after a while, there was a question that was begging to be asked: What is a Brand Ambassador? Is it the valet who brings the car around, is it the one who explains the features to the customers, or is it something more? Well, I discovered that the Brand Ambassador is all that and much more. As a professional race-car driver, I can not only explain the features but show the sometimes extreme capabilities of a top-of-the-line car. Through that, I gain their trust.

So yes, I became a car salesman, but through the understanding of trust, both the interaction with the people I met and the results became completely different. When Rolls Royce / Bentley introduced me to a possible client, three out of four times, what I was sending back to the dealership was a check instead of the car.

There was also a fun factor in the Brand Ambassador job; I started taking the cars to local events, galas, etc., and got to keep the car for a few days. It also led to a lot of interest from my dear neighbors. Imagine this, at that time, I was renting a lovely little house worth much less than the cars I had delivered to my home on a very regular basis. Physically I fit the Mexican stereotype much better than that of a Swiss banker. So I think that more than one started to think that I was a mobster, definite cartel material, and maybe even a Drug Lord who was horrible at hiding his mountains of cash. Needless to say that my landlord got more than a few calls.

I had a blast for three years and then slowly started my consulting business supporting various other brands such as Lamborghini, Ferrari, and Mercedes. I now offer the complete organization of VIP experiences on different tracks.

My business grew through trust, and so did I. I can now say that I have come full circle and am happy doing something I love.

**Go for a, Yes!**

There is a history behind that phrase. In Latin countries, there is a saying that goes something like this: You already have the "no," so you might as well go for the *"Yes."*

Having *"no"* as your starting point, every effort, every action that takes you closer to getting a *"yes."* So at a young age, I decided to trust myself; I decided to *"Go for the, Yes!"* and honestly, although I have had a few setbacks in my life, I feel that I more often than not make the impossible possible through trust.

# Ken
# Bassman

**President/CEO**
*BASSMAN BLAINE*

## Challenges

Just hearing the word *"challenges"* evokes so many emotions. As a leader, employer, athlete, adventurer, entrepreneur, father, husband, son, brother, and friend, challenges are quite simply a part of my everyday life. I love a great quote or cliché, and so many come to mind as I think and begin to write about this. A few of my favorites are *"that which does not kill you makes you stronger," "smooth seas do not make skillful sailors," "challenges are what makes life interesting; overcoming them is what makes life meaningful,"* and perhaps my very favorite *"we don't grow when things are easy, we grow when we face challenges."*

Looking back at my life from the vantage point of being almost 60 years old and wanting to believe that my experiences (good and bad) have made me the person and leader that I am today, I cannot help but to think that one specific life changing challenge has had the biggest impact. I tend to remember and focus on way more of the good than the bad, but there is no sugar coating what happened 47 years ago on May 31st, 1975, as a twelve-year-old boy. I will never forget answering the phone on this Memorial Day afternoon, handing it to my dad and standing next to him when he was told that my mom had suddenly died. It took about a week or so to learn how, but at 39

BASSMAN
BLAINE

years old, my mom had a massive stroke. There were no warnings, no chance to say goodbye, and life as I know it was never going to be the same.

I have always prided myself on being someone who enjoys a challenge, the bigger the better. Not that it is always fun when you are in the eye of the storm, but coming out on the other side, whether successful or not is where the growth is. Challenge and change are inevitable; there is just no staying still, you are either growing or dying. I choose growing, and challenges and overcoming them are the fuel to the growth.

I have certainly made my very fair share of mistakes, both in life and in business. As a serial entrepreneur, I have started fourteen companies (and counting); it is from the failures and challenges and the process of overcoming them where the real growth and education has come from. In fact, one of the main reasons why I enjoy leadership, coaching and mentoring as much as I do is that the lessons learned from the countless challenges that I have faced have provided so much perspective and an ability to help others not make the same mistakes. I look forward to new challenges and new mistakes and only hope that I practice what I preach and not repeat the same ones. So far, so good, at least for the most part.

I grew up in the Los Angeles suburbs of the San Fernando Valley in the city of Northridge. Looking back on my childhood with the benefit of experience and hindsight, it was probably not nearly as idyllic as I like to remember it. But I like this about myself; a bit Pollyanna-ish, I tend to remember the good and let the not so good and/or the bad just fade away. I grew up in a typical (slightly just above) middle class neighborhood with my parents and one brother who is 13 months older than I. My dad was a travelling salesman, and although a genuinely nice man, not an overly engaged father. From losing my mom at 12, my brother and I were left largely to our own devices.

I often say that in my early to mid-teens I was a Straight A juvenile delinquent; nothing too bad, just finding trouble. I have often wondered how different things might have been had my mom not died so young. Tony Robbins, who is one of my mentors, says and teaches that *"life is happening for you and not to you."* I have spent a lot of time contemplating and thinking on this and I absolutely love it. From an early age, I became extremely independent and self-sufficient. I learned how to advocate and look out for myself, how to plan, how to budget, how to motivate myself, how to get things done and how to make things happen. My mom was a doting and hands-on mother, and I'm pretty sure that she would have been doing most things for me through most of my teens, but obviously that was not the case.

Of course, many others have had similar circumstances, and many have been through far worse that losing a parent at 12, but this was my reality, and in reflecting, the first very major challenge of my life.

Another impactful challenge that I have contended with is one that I share with many Americans, and many all around the globe for that matter. As I reflect on my career, the biggest professional challenge that I went through was the great Recession of 2008/2009. I live in Newport Beach, CA, and in 2001, my family stepped up to a bigger house in the beautiful neighborhood where we have lived since 1999. All was going well, we were enjoying a growing business and a growing family, and in 2008, things came to a standstill.

My wife had left a great corporate career in 1998 and was the full-time mom to our three (amazing) daughters. We were not necessarily living beyond our means, but it was close. When the recession hit, it hit our business and industry extremely hard. Quite vividly, I remember staring at my ceiling for several hours most nights from about 1:00 or so in the morning. My thoughts were usually relating to our expenses; we had cut out all non-essential expenses at home and for the first time in my post college adult life, were living on a strict and no-frills budget.

On the business front, we tightened some screws, and I went without a paycheck for over six months, but instead of leading from the fetal position and stopping to spend or invest, I decided that this was exactly the time to expand. Three opportunities presented themselves which led to three new business channels. Thirteen/fourteen years later, two of these are some of the best and biggest things that my company does. This was quite the balancing act, as our cash flow was tight and I was not taking a paycheck; we had payroll, commissions, rent and expenses to pay, but not enough coming in to get a good night's sleep. Especially with the benefit of hindsight, I am so glad that I faced this huge challenge with a forward-looking attitude and mindset. Had I frozen (like a deer in the headlights) to wait out the tough times (of the recession) and did not create and follow up on opportunities, I am certain that my business would not have survived. Although I am not sure that this would have worked at the time as we were teetering on the edge, again, with the benefit of hindsight, I do like the idea of pay yourself first.

Years later, on my ever-expanding quest for personal and professional growth and development (thank you to my wife, Teri, for starting me on this), I have learned so much more. Tony Robbins calls this (or significant challenges) *"Winter."* The truth is that winter is always coming; preparing for winter is something that I am always thinking of and constantly doing. Winter is where Kings and Queens are made. To me, this is facing challenges head on, almost relishing them, looking at them as opportunities and having the mindset that life is happening for me and not to me, as it is for you.

As Covid made its way to the US in March of 2020, and almost overnight, the country and the economy shut down, there was no panic. I was practiced and prepared to make tough decisions and take swift and massive action. Once again, the cash flow faucet was turning off, and we, like everyone were in unchartered waters. I am so proud of the fact that we acted with tremendous integrity as well as respect and understanding for our employees and did the right thing by our business and customers as well. We faced the challenges (winter) head on, found ways to reinvest in our company, shortened the necessary furloughs as much as possible. made key strategic hires and were ready to pursue and create new opportunities for growth. I am so proud to say that we were well positioned to have our best year ever in 2021, and of this writing, just over halfway through 2022, this will be our best year ever, or at least so far, as I like to say. If the country falls into recession, we will react from a place of Teamwork, Integrity, Growth, Excellence and Respect (our company's core values), and take the challenges that come our way head on. As Winston Churchill said, *"when you find yourself in hell, keep going."*

Wishing you much success and satisfaction overcoming (and appreciating) your challenges.

Sincerely,
Ken Bassman

# David

# J. Whelan

**Chief Executive Officer**
*BIOSCIENCE LA*

## Why *"Impact"* Is My Personal Moonshot

Growing up in Central Pennsylvania, where nothing exciting ever happened, I spent my youth dreaming of getting out. My life was a 1980s nerdscape of D&D, arcades, and watching VHS movies in my friend's basement. Basically, if you've seen *Stranger Things*, you know what I mean. That was me, minus the Upside Down.

The entry under my high school yearbook photo reads:*"Future plans: 'name' college, grad school, science research, never returning to PA, breaking the land speed record, still listening to old music."*

While I've always enjoyed reading and writing, I was very much a science, math, and tech guy. I was inspired by Douglas Hofstadter's *Gödel, Escher, Bach: An Eternal Golden Braid and Silicon Valley* tales like *Fire in the Valley*. I idolized godfathers like Hewlett and Packard, gurus like Minsky and Winograd, and entrepreneurs like Jobs and Wozniak.

So, I did what any self-respecting kid with good grades and SAT scores would do: I packed up my Beatles records and headed to Stanford.

Majoring in Symbolic Systems, my plan was to reinvent intelligence – of the artificial variety. When I graduated in 1992, the job market for AI just wasn't there yet, and I didn't think I had the resources to head to a graduate program at MIT's Media Lab, so I found myself running IT for a small biotech incubator. I didn't have any real mentors there, but I did learn the phrase *"doing well by doing good,"* which would return to my life many times, often when I least expected it.

While those stock options are worthless to this day, I felt that I was starting on my dream track. Recently, I recalled this as thinking I would start a dotcom in my 20s, start a VC in my 30s, and retire in my 40s. Those were my personal moonshots – or so I thought.

Contrary to those aspirations, I spent my formative years as a retained executive search consultant, helping founders and venture capitalists build successful teams. It was an incredibly rewarding experience, recruiting executives, often decades older than me, into new roles, which would change their lives, change their families' lives, and sometimes change companies, industries, and the world. My boss and mentor, Conrad Prusak, taught me so much, especially how to listen, but also how to be a humble leader.

Yet still, I told myself I was on that personal moonshot track. Having worked with numerous telecom and technology companies, when I moved to Los Angeles at 30 to start an MBA program at UCLA Anderson School, my retooled vision was to become a telecom venture capitalist. I could do that in my 30s and still retire in my 40s, right?

What happened instead is that I found my way into a consulting project with a subsidiary of 24 Hour Fitness, where I fell in love with the passion of those in the fitness industry to transform people's lives. Things got even more exciting when we partnered with a technology company (coincidentally, founded by a Stanford classmate and based in, of all places, Pennsylvania) to launch what turned out to be one of the first consumer activity-tracking wearables. We were too early for the market, so while the immediate business impact was not there, the possibilities of healthcare data excited me.

Those possibilities returned to the forefront several years later, when a three-month consulting gig turned into a three-year journey to plan, fund, and launch New York Genome Center, an innovative not-for-profit research institution. Living in Los Angeles and commuting across the country, sometimes weekly, was inspiring, tiring, and rewarding. We were building something that would change lives, that would save lives, that would impact the world. I was 40, I was not a VC, and I was not retiring any time soon, but I was having fun making a difference.

Seeing the potential in healthcare innovation, I developed a personal brand phrase, *"building businesses and inspiring entrepreneurs at the intersection of technology, health, and wellness,"* and set out to do just that. The most eye-opening part was realizing that I had been doing aspects of this all along.

When I edited my high school newspaper and designed a Soviet-American student journal at Stanford, I was questioning the world, telling stories, and inspiring others. When I taught computer literacy to middle schoolers in my school district, or taught Macintosh skills to college students at the Tresidder Computer LaIR at Stanford, or led presentation and communication workshops to Boeing engineers, I was helping give leaders the tools they needed to communicate, to build their products and their businesses, to make an impact. I co-founded an alumni group called Stanford Ideas & Connections Network. I served on the UCLA Anderson School Alumni Network Board. I volunteered with Business Volunteers for the Arts and joined the board of San Francisco Shakespeare Festival. I've been a mentor, coach, and advisor for organizations like Larta Institute, Women Founders Network, and Cedars-Sinai Accelerator. The common thread is helping both myself and others to make an impact on the world around us.

New York Genome Center led to numerous other opportunities at the intersection of technology, health, and wellness – including steering a multi-year strategic and financial plan for a leading synthetic biology organization, launching a cancer diagnostic spinoff from a leading hospital, and developing a market assessment and strategic plan for an innovative integrative healthcare research concept. I also found time to work on some start-ups of my own, from nutritional products to wearable healthtech to digital health and media. None cashed out for me, but all of them taught me lessons, introduced me to some amazing people (many of whom I've worked with multiple times over the years), and allowed me to continue to make a difference in people's lives.

More than that, a funny thing happened on the way to JFK. When we launched New York Genome Center, it was a critical part of an inflection point in New York's life sciences community. Without realizing it at first, I was part of a group of people helping to build a business ecosystem.

Without those experiences, I am not sure that I would have found my way into the non-profit world. I am not sure that the *"intersection of techno-logy, health, and wellness"* would mean anything to me. And I am almost certain I would not be leading an organization like BioscienceLA.

Founded in 2018, BioscienceLA is the innovation catalyst for life scien-ces in the greater Los Angeles region, accelerating the growth of funding, space, and talent. The independent not-for-profit organization was see-ded by LA County and has backing from Amgen, PhRMA, Richard Lund-quist, Richard Merkin, City of Hope, and Cedars-Sinai, among others. I was named the first permanent CEO in 2020, with my first day being Monday, March 16, the day that LA and much of the world locked down in the early days of the COVID-19 pandemic. I challenge anyone to think of a more appropriate moment to go all in on healthcare innovation.

As a catalyst for innovation, BioscienceLA seeks to enable diversity, amplify science, and accelerate collaboration. Every day, I get the chan-ce to work with scientists and physicians, researchers and entrepreneu-rs, investors and advisors, to help build companies and communities that will save lives, create jobs, and redefine Los Angeles. Some of those days, I can measure my impact directly, through investment dollars, new hires, or busy lab facilities. Other days, a CEO will share with me how my work has put his company on a path to success. Once, I met someone who had been part of New York Genome Center years after me. He told me that not only did he owe that job to founders like me, but because of that job, he was able to help improve the quality of life of a child born with a rare genetic disorder.

Today, I am in my early 50s. I never started a dotcom, and I probably won't start a web3 company. I'm not a venture capitalist (although throu-gh my work today, I am proud to be an LP in a prominent VC firm, where I am helping create a successful portfolio of healthcare companies). I am not sure if I will ever retire, and likely not with Fire in the Valley wealth. Nevertheless, I wake up every day excited to be doing well by doing good. I am blessed to be part of the leadership of a diverse ecosystem, which requires a healthy dose of humility. In a post-pandemic world of advanced diagnostic tests, remote patient monitoring, and telehealth, I can think of nothing as impactful or meaningful as building businesses and inspiring entrepreneurs at the intersection of technology, health, and wellness. My moonshot is helping others achieve theirs.

I am not exactly who I set out to be. However, I feel like I am so much more. Some days, I help founders to move their science research forward. Other days, I help entrepreneurs break their own personal land speed records. Every day, I find ways to make an impact – on Los Angeles, on life sciences, on people's lives. And, every day, I am still listening to old music.

# Harris

**President/CEO**
*COHEN ESREY*

## Mars or Bust

Elon Musk wants to go to Mars during his lifetime. Talk about Big Hairy Audacious Goals (BHAG)! But I can relate. My whole adult life has been all about moonshots. Fortunately, Mars has never been on my radar. Many other different BHAGs have, however.

I graduated from Kansas State University in 1975 with a degree in economics. I knew beginning in the eighth grade that I wanted to be a real estate developer. I jumped into the commercial real estate world right after college as the property manager for a 234-unit apartment complex in Topeka, Kansas. The first few months were miserable, but I persevered and used it as a steppingstone to learn the business. Oh, and I'm still with the same company today. The Kansas City-based firm was only five years old when I joined, and I convinced my boss (the owner) that we should expand our management presence in Topeka. He said, *"Have at it, but make sure to do your main job at the same*

*time."* The first third-party assignment we won was an 18-unit property; then we picked up a 63-unit apartment complex; then 66-units; then 120-units, and we were rolling! In 1979 we assumed the management of a 1,385-unit property in St. Louis which to this day is the largest apartment property in the history of our firm.

I must confess that while building a property management business was bread and butter, it certainly wasn't shooting for the stars. The good news is that I learned what was needed over the course of the first 20 years of my tenure to put me in a position to begin pursuing the development and acquisition of apartment communities in the mid-1990s. We began building some smaller apartments, then renovating several historic structures. Eventually our development activities involved much larger complexes – 150 to 300-units in multiple cities across the country. For many years we had managed tens of thousands of units for third party owners – and made them a lot of money in the process. In 2015, we began acquiring larger existing apartment properties – generally ranging from 300 – 600-units – and did so on a programmatic basis. Today, we have amassed a portfolio that we own valued at more than $1.6 billion with a solid plan that we expect will take us to $5 billion in apartment assets by the end of 2026. Never in my wildest dreams!

Here's an example of another moonshot. I was invited to serve on the board of the Kansas Bioscience Authority, formerly the venture capital initiative for the state of Kansas. The KBA made Series A and B investments in companies engaged in agriculture, animal health, and human health. I realized that such funding did not exist at the time for even earlier stage companies in those verticals. So, we started a separate business unit, brought together domain experts as investors, and along with a professional team began identifying companies and investing in the space. To date, we have made 28 investments (including follow-on) in 20 companies and expect to have a portfolio of 60+ companies by 2027. Never in a million years would I have dreamt this could be real.

There are many ingredients that factored into the massive success we are realizing. My formative years were filled with possibility. Thanks to my parents and teachers pushing me to use my natural-born potential, I never bought into any notion of lack and limitation. I started a firewood business in high school; got a real estate license in college and sold a few houses as well as launching a small development deal. When someone suggested that I couldn't do something, I simply ignored them.

As time passed, I became more and more focused on always maintaining a positive attitude. When something didn't go right, I learned to look for silver linings. And that mindset led to my current philosophy that if something doesn't happen the way I want, it simply means that something even better is in store. Sound Pollyanna-ish? I can point to countless examples of how this has been true for me. And believing this way has allowed me to remain open and receptive to the good that comes to me.

I learned to think big and taught myself to then think even bigger. It's amazing how easy this can be when one doesn't buy into the *"I can't"* mantra. Someone once asked me if I see life as a glass half empty or half full. I chose neither by responding that I'm a multiple glass guy and they are all overflowing. Many people work a job. Some people pursue a career. I consider myself blessed that I am one of the few who have been able to live my passion every day of my life. True confession – early on I chased the almighty dollar, and I was often frustrated that the dollars were just beyond my outstretched fingers. Fortunately, I eventually shifted into passion mode and stopped focusing on the money and guess what? The financial rewards began coming bigger and better than I could have ever imagined. It's been more than 20 years since I took a salary. Why? Because it was way too limiting.

Have there been failures? Of course, there have! But I see failure as simply an unfinished experiment in the laboratory of life. In fact, I developed a risk mitigation exercise called, *"Opportunities-to-Fail."* Does this sound negative? It's not. This concept has served me well in my quest to think big and even bigger. Here's how it works.

When considering a major development project, we assemble the entire development team and conduct a brainstorm session to inventory everything that could go wrong. A simple Excel model has been created in which we ascribe a numerical value (one through ten) to both the probability of the negative event and its impact. We weight the impact 25% higher than the probability and derive a composite score for each item. Then we sort the items – sometimes as many as 40 or 50 – from the highest to lowest scores. Finally, we set the list aside for a few days to give each team member some reflection time.

Next, a second team session is scheduled to determine how to mitigate each of the downside elements. Specificity is the byword here. We don't want to get caught in the trap of being too general or *"broad brush"* in the methods for mitigation. We mitigate all the higher-scored risks – generally 50% to 75% of the list. A contingency plan is also identified for as many items as possible – should our mitigation efforts be unsuccessful. At the end of the Opportunities-to-Fail exercise we can decide whether to move forward with the project based upon a solid risk management plan that includes a healthy margin-of-safety. There's no question that this approach has contributed mightily toward my ability to think big and even bigger, knowing that there is always a way to measure and protect against the downside.

For years I was asked about my vision for our family of companies. I pooh-poohed this for a while – after all, I knew in my head where we were going. But in 2016 I sat down and pretended that I was writing an article for the Wall Street Journal. I mocked up the masthead and used the name of a real WSJ reporter. The theme was the state of the company as of December 31, 2026 – sort of a *"back to the future"* perspective. I shared this with our team and the light went on for many people. There's no doubt some heads were shaking over some of the BHAG achievements I was affirming, but it was clear to everyone what it was going to look like when we got there.

How does this all sum up? First, moonshots take a great deal of vision, creativity, and planning. Strong foundations must be laid requiring patience and perseverance. A great leader surrounds himself or herself with other members of the team who are smarter than he/she and have a myriad of different strengths and skills. A mindset of thinking big and then thinking bigger is an absolute must. Failure is expected and embraced, but risks should be managed and not taken indiscriminately. Remaining positive even during the darkest hours is mandatory. Some might say that achieving the loftiest of goals requires an element of luck. If luck is the combination of all the aforementioned factors, then I believe we make our own luck. The way he's going, Elon Musk has luck in bushels, and he'll bypass the moon on his way to Mars.

# Jiwa

**Founder and President**

*CUSTOMERSERV*

## An Immigrant's Perspective of the American Dream

One of my greatest fears in life is working for someone ever again. I had to overcome many fears and obstacles to achieve my goal of becoming self-employed. This is my story about turning that dream into reality, and I sincerely hope it inspires others to believe in making the impossible happen.

My family emigrated from Tanzania to New York City in 1974, when I was five, in pursuit of the proverbial American Dream. Resettling in the U.S. was a success itself, only to face the harsh realities of having to restart from the bottom. Jobs were scarce, money was scarcer, and my family was crammed into small living spaces.

We were immigrants trying to assimilate in an unforgiving, crime-ridden, decrepit city which was New York in the 1970s. To top it off, I was an underprivileged asthmatic who didn't speak English being raised by a single mother. The deck was stacked against me—but then again, millions of immigrants share my plight, many of whom overcame the impossible to achieve great things.

### A Journey Begins—The Discarded Kid

Life in the big city is daunting, especially without means. I was often mired in self-doubt because society profiled me as "one of those kids." By that, I mean a kid from a broken home who will probably underachieve and become a burden on society. I was often grouped among the discarded who lacked confidence and hope because of the tall barriers blocking us from realizing our full potential.

I hope my experience gives others faith that the less fortunate have a path forward regardless of their circumstances and that the seemingly impossible task of lifting yourself up to achieve the highest heights is realistic and possible. I am that one-in-a-million chance—a clichéd phrase we often hear—but the term takes on a different meaning to those who embody it.

### Education

From elementary to middle school and high school, I lived a typical unremarkable life of a kid from a struggling NYC family. Despite the challenges, I wouldn't trade my New York upbringing for anything in the world. I was fortunate to grow up in Queens, having learned street smarts and the importance of loyalty and accountability, blessed that I lived within an incredible melting pot of a community, teaching me the vital importance of cultural diversity.

I graduated from high school in 1986. While my friends got accepted to *"popular"* universities with sprawling green campuses and dorms, I ended up attending the City University of New York (CUNY)—Baruch College. I was accepted through a program called SEEK (Search for Education, Elevation, and Knowledge), designed for underprivileged kids.

Baruch's campus is in the heart of Manhattan, so I could work full-time and take on a full credit load. I completed my undergraduate degree in four years and graduated among the top of my class. I thought about an MBA but needed to fast-track an income stream and start my career.

### The First 'BIG' Decision

Sometimes in life and business, an ordinary decision can be your most fortuitous one. The concept of self-sufficiency was taught to me by my late grandfather, and because of him, I got my first job at age 12 and always had a part-time job as far back as I can remember.

My motivation to work led me to a milestone decision when, at age 17, I took a job as a call center agent. At the time, I did not know and could not possibly predict that this one small step would lead to something much greater. A part-time summer job turned into a 36-year lifelong passion and career for me in the Call Center or Business Process Outsourcing (BPO) industry, which today is a high-growth $300 billion global marketplace.

## The Second 'BIG' Decision

After graduating in 1991 with a BBA, I was recruited by an outsourcing firm in Houston, Texas. I took the job, hesitantly headed out west, constantly second-guessing myself. Having worked for a top-five call center outsourcing agency, I was initially hired for an operations role. However, upon my arrival, the CEO moved me into business development, bringing in clients who needed outsourced call centers, something I had never done.

So, here is me, at age 22, thrust into an unfamiliar role at a new company in a nascent industry, adjusting to a new city with little money and no security. I was terrified and quite unsure of the future, but I saw the possibilities. I quickly realized that I was given an incredible chance to be a leader in my field. My fate was staring me in the face, challenging me to seize the moment—and I did.

## Career Pivots and Challenges

After my first big break, I never looked back. I worked for several other outsourcing firms, was promoted multiple times, and built my CV, network, and knowledge base—all while making a positive impact, generating millions in new client revenues for my employers, creating new jobs, and scaling the corporate ladder with each opportunity.

While my dreams and hopes were palpable, I had no financial cushion, security, savings, and nothing to protect my family from falling back into the abyss I worked so hard to pull us out of. I had one nice suit and a belief in the greater good. I was ridiculed by the more experienced, successful, and older sales guys who worked for competing outsourcers. I was young, inexperienced, naïve, atypical, honest, and just looking to make something of myself in one of the most brutally competitive industries in the world.

## Early Career Success

I attribute this drive to my underprivileged roots, humility, and appreciation for people from all walks of life. I was able to cut through corporate barriers, make human connections, and communicate with my clients on a grassroots level. They did not see me as a prototype, aggressive, self-serving, one-liner-obsessed, name-dropping sales person.

I wasn't interested in the wine-and-dine, glad-handing approach. I was more serious, grounded, and laser focused. And because I started in this industry at the entry level—a call center agent who worked his way up—I was able to make genuine connections with people who saw my authenticity. Competing against more experienced sales executives, I carved out my niche, achieved the highest milestones, and laid the building blocks for my future as an entrepreneur.

## Entrepreneurship Begins—the American Dream Personified

I do not hail from a family with an entrepreneurial pedigree. Throughout my professional career, I envisaged business ideas, often struggling to come up with a winner. Over time, I toyed with startups and investments, some mildly successful and some face-plants, but I always kept the dream alive.

Finally, in 2006, I found my calling when I created my company, CustomerServ, an outsourcing ecosystem that helps corporate brands select the right call center or BPO outsourcing providers. Vendor selection in our industry is central to successful outsourcing, yet too many client-vendor relationships fail, so we created a more predictable way to solve this problem. The genesis of CustomerServ coincided with a personal discovery of my inner entrepreneur at the right time in my life and professional career.

## Transition to Entrepreneur

I enjoyed corporate life until I didn't. I had grown weary of bureaucracy and analysis paralysis, which are anathema to people like me who thrive on creativity, solutions, and unbridled action. While the excitement and newness of working for oneself is a great feeling, it takes an adjustment. The high pressure of being your own boss is stressful because you must answer to your worst critic: **you**.

Even with the broadest of shoulders and sharpest of minds, entrepreneurship can be a grueling yet rewarding way of life. I used to stress about everything about the business in the early days. I attribute this to the normal lifecycle of a new company and my perfectionism coupled with over-reliance on too few clients. My mentors often advised me to control the controllable, but I did not always know how.

## The Start-up That I Almost Didn't Start

Every entrepreneur needs resilience to overcome start-up fears. I recall sleepless nights worrying about the transition from employee to business owner. I had come to realize that being my own boss is, in fact, in my DNA, but I still had to overcome the fear of leaving the safety net of a high-paying position. Job security has a strong gravitational pull, and it nearly prevented me from entrepreneurship, but my allergy to failure resulted in CustomerServ succeeding.

In our infancy, it never occurred to me that I was a disruptor. But, over time, once the industry started referring to us as revolutionary, difference makers, and my favorite— outsourcing thought leaders—it dawned on me that we are a unique and transformative company. We are saving organizations $millions while creating new jobs and revenue streams for our BPO vendors by facilitating lasting business marriages based on our authentic process, proprietary vetting, high integrity, and matchmaking expertise.

## Learning and Earning Selectivity

You have heard the phrase *"control your destiny or someone else will."* To control my company's destiny, I had to become more judicious, especially about the opportunities I chose to invest in. You cannot be all things to all people. Therefore, my company and I earned the right to be selective over time. Selectivity comes from consistent, successful outcomes. As you and your organization mature, you will naturally lose your appetite for lower-hanging fruit and phantom *"opportunities."*

More importantly, you must become an expert at deflecting time- and resource-draining situations.

As much as I love people and networking, there is a fine line between benevolence and practicality. It is imprudent and impossible to allow everyone into your tent, so you must carefully choose your network, service providers, and clients. The ability to decide where you invest your time and effort is a sign of a responsible, well-balanced, diverse, and healthy operation. Discernment, not arrogance, can drive positive outcomes. It takes years to develop the right professional and business maturity formula to achieve this milestone.

## My Company Today

If you had told me when I was younger that one day, I'd be the CEO of one of the most successful companies of its kind, I would have asked you for the punchline of your joke. But it happened for me, just like it has for many immigrants who traversed their way to the United States, full of hopes, dreams, and beliefs. Today my company CustomerServ is responsible for creating over $3 billion in successful outsourcing contracts for Fortune 100 companies and brands of all sizes. We've created over 100,000 call center outsourcing jobs globally and, in the U.S., including jobs and careers for disadvantaged individuals in emerging countries.

I am the poster child for those who come from humble beginnings only to scale the corporate, then entrepreneurial ladder against unbelievable odds. I am fortunate to be one of the bricklayers who built the foundation of the BPO industry as we know it today. As a pioneer and *"founding member"* of BPO services, I will continue giving back to an industry that has enabled me to achieve the American Dream of professional and personal success and, ultimately, entrepreneurship.

## Final Words

- **Risk and fear:** As much as the corporate world is not for everyone, neither is entrepreneurship. Employment and entrepreneurship have inherent risks, but entrepreneurship requires a certain risk tolerance. It calls for the ability to convert fear into energy, then channel this energy into successful outcomes.
- **Don't panic:** No matter what highs and lows you experience, never panic—even in the darkest of times. Irrationality is panic's best

friend. Experience has taught me to be patient and prescriptive.
- **Path of least resistance:** Pretend that it does not exist.
- **Embrace change:** Always be open to criticism, never stop in your pursuit to be better, and do not allow complacency to enter your realm unless you enjoy stagnation.
- **Be obsessive:** If you do not obsess over your business or work, you might be in the wrong profession. Anything less than perfection is tantamount to failure. That is why my personal commitment and effort are indefatigable. I have an undying devotion to my clients, vendors, and close network, and I am an advocate for them.
- **Learn:** Bob Ross, the late famous painter, referred to mistakes as happy accidents. Yet, I lose sleep if we do not get it right. I take it personally if a client is ever unhappy with a vendor match. Fortunately, this rarely happens. In fact, the outsourcing relationships we create usually result in unprecedented success, and there is no greater satisfaction than knowing that we delivered on our commitments.
- **Define your own success:** We are pre-programmed to measure success by financial milestones, but monetary accomplishments alone should not define success. Success is relative and it requires initiative, awareness, selectivity, and accountability, not advanced degrees, or higher intellect.
- **Instinct is your best mentor:** Looking forward is wise, but only if you learn from the past. You can draw on experience and gut instinct to help you. Your instinct is an asset and can be more valuable than your best business ideas. Even if your instincts are more right than wrong, arrogance will drive good karma and opportunities away.

## Summary

I take inspiration from people who have experienced a similar journey as mine and I hope to inspire others to stay on course. I am a once disadvantaged kid who became a champion for independence, entrepreneurship, and paying it forward. No matter your background or struggles, never stop dreaming. Believe in the greater good, visualize your dreams becoming reality, build your career, grow your business, be bold, let your fears motivate you, have courage and faith, do the right thing, and great things will happen.

# Hebner

### CEO and Founder
*INDEX FUND ADVISORS, INC*

In late 1998 I was contacted by a recently widowed friend. She asked if I would accompany her to her investment advisors to interpret what they were telling her. She had been very confused in previous meetings where they tried to explain their investing strategies.

I agreed to her request, but then realized I better read up on investing so I would be well versed to make the translations. I visited the local Barnes & Noble and bought 22 books on investing. That was the beginning of what is now a 2,584-book library of financial books going all the way back to a book titled A Way to Wealth from 1648.

As I read through my initial purchase of books, I was shocked to discover that both professional and individual investors weren't beating the market, the market was beating them. How could this be? How could mutual fund managers charge billions of dollars to beat their respective benchmarks when the only winners were those who just got lucky! This meant that no managers are *"expected"* to beat their appropriate benchmarks in the future!

The answer was hidden away in academic research about markets that started in 1900 and culminated in the late 1960s. Virtually no firms in the financial industry wanted to share this information because it would destroy their business model, which was based on investors trading securities. There are many opportunities for brokers to earn fees on trading and if investors decided to become buy and hold investors instead, the whole industry would have to change their revenue models.

Trading is the service offered by most of the securities industry for either a fee or a share of the trading price. On the other hand, registered investment advisors typically charge a percentage of assets under their management and therefore don't rely on trading as a source of revenue.

After I finished my research, I realized that most of the industry was not maximizing the expected returns for their clients and therefore doing them a tremendous disservice.

My moonshot was to try to fix a broken industry and to do so utilizing an online investment education and offering a wealth management service that was fee based and utilized a passive management approach, as opposed to an active management approach.

I am a scientist by training and more specifically a Nuclear Pharmacist. So, my first inclination was to look for evidence and data to support my education. In fact, today this approach to investing is referred to as evidenced-based investing.

For the 2 years prior to my discoveries about index funds and passive investing, I had been an angel investor in several internet start-up companies, and I learned what was working in new dot com companies and about the interactivity of software tools like flash. Flash would allow me to create charts and graphs that would be dynamic and provide buttons that would change time periods and the display of moving data depending on options selected. It was a game changer for the visualization of large data sets and that was exactly what I needed to educate investors about the history and benefits of passive investing. But I was told by just about everyone that there was no way that people would trust their money to an online investment advisor. Instead, they wanted a face-to-face meeting because money is so personal.

But way back in 1999, I thought if I could do a Zoom like video conference utilizing Microsoft's Netmeeting, I could show them my face and make it personal enough. Also, I planned to provide them such a high-quality investor education that they would develop an online trust for me and my firm. The video conferencing didn't work until recently because the prospective clients did not have the technology to do it, but the online education did. Slow but sure we started receiving emails and calls from people who were blown away with our educational content and felt safe hiring us to manage their wealth.

Index Fund Advisors, Inc. started in March 1999 and by year end we had about $5 million in assets under management (AUM). About 23 years later we ended 2021 with $5 Billion in assets under management and 50 employees. I developed a survey that identifies each person's risk capacity and directs them to a portfolio of index funds that has a matched risk exposure. I published my book in 2005 and have made 8 revisions since then. I then utilized the book as the basis for a script to make a documentary film. I also developed a series of indexes and index portfolios and took the data all the way back to 1928. This hypothetical back tested performance data provided risks and returns that was useful for investors and still are not available anywhere on the internet. Our website, ifa.com, is a cornucopia of knowledge about how markets work and how investors can maximize their expected returns given a certain level of risk.

My moonshot turned out to be a very long shot, but with lots of hard work, money, passion, creativity, and relentless persistence I was able to pull it off. Not many people encouraged me along the way. I had to rely mostly on my own entrepreneurial instincts that these Nobel Prize winning ideas would revolutionize the way people invest and that I, with a team of dedicated employees, had the skills and determination to pull off a nearly impossible achievement.

My mission is to change the way the world invests and every day I get a little closer to my goal.

# Omar Flores & Omero Flores

**Teammates**

*THE J. FLORES COMPANY*

## New beginnings

As I nervously drove up to my childhood home, searching for the right words, my father approached me. Lines of worry were deeply etched into his 75-year-old face. He had been observing as we sold off assets and shut down offices. It had been 22 years since he last worked, and he was well aware of his age, too old to be considered for employment anywhere. He asked if he should brace himself for a drastic change in lifestyle. He contemplated selling goods at a flea market and was even willing to relocate to San Antonio, if necessary, to evade the shame of our failure.

For the first time in my life, I stood there, paralyzed, unable to find the right words to explain our predicament to my father. Eventually, he just walked away, leaving me to grapple with the consequences of my decisions and the crumbling business we had so painstakingly built.

Why was this happening??? This question plagued my mind, gnawing at me incessantly. Why? Why were we being punished after years of hard work and sacrifice? Why was the universe conspiring against us,

The J. Flores Company

pulling the rug out from under our feet just as we had started to find our footing? We had given our all to this business, dedicating countless hours and pouring our hearts into it. And yet, it felt like everything was falling apart, slipping through our fingers like sand.

## My father's story

In order to explain what my father felt, I have to trace it back to the origins of his story. As a young boy, he undertook a perilous journey, crossing the Mexican border illegally in search of a brighter future. He traveled with his mother, his younger brother Pancho, and his sister Lidia. Their existence must have resembled the lives of the children you might encounter on the streets of a developing country, hawking chewing gum and trinkets under the vigilant supervision of their mother. This was their humble beginning.

Their pursuit of a better life left them no choice but to embrace relentless labor. As the eldest male child, my father naturally slipped into the role of protector and provider. He toiled away at odd jobs, from shining shoes and collecting cans to working in the fields—anything that would contribute to their survival.

Throughout our childhood, my brother and I had limited insight into our father's past. He was a man of few words who largely kept to himself about his childhood. If you met him, you would likely find him open and jovial, a persona he had perfected during his years in sales. Yet when it came to his personal life, he remained a closed book.

The story I'm about to share is a patchwork of fragments, pieced together from rare moments over the years when he'd let his guard down. One particular incident stands out, something that occurred very early in his life and that, I believe, profoundly shaped the man he became. As I've mentioned, my father worked tirelessly, as did his mother in her role as a housekeeper. Their minimal earnings were what kept the family afloat.

One day, when I was around 22 or 23, we were sitting in a doctor's office. As we waited, my dad's attention was caught by an old magazine ad featuring Pancho Pantera, a brand of chocolate milk popular in Mexico similar to Quik. Seeing that advertisement sparked a memory, prompting him to share a story from his childhood, an unusual occurrence for my typically reserved father.

He began to reminisce about how Sundays were a special day for him and his siblings. It was the only day of the week when he didn't have to work. Every Sunday, as far back as he could remember, his mom would buy them a "mollete dulce", a type of Mexican bread that has a bit of butter and sugar on top. She would divide it into three pieces, and each child would get one.

He was probably about seven years old at the time. They each had little plastic cups into which they would pour a generous serving of Pancho Pantera chocolate milk. That advertisement had triggered these sweet memories, and for a few moments, he opened up to me, and he spoke fondly about how on Sundays, they had the liberty to be kids and play. Seeing my dad light up like that, brimming with childlike excitement, was a rare sight. As he recounted these memories, his eyes sparkled with the same excitement a child would exhibit while narrating their playtime adventures.

Then, as he continued his story about the *"mollete"* his mood got darker as he recalled the memory of a particular Sunday. It was the first time each of them had their own "mollete" — one for him, one for his brother, and one for his sister. He seldom shared personal stories. But that day, he was living through his past, reliving each moment in vivid detail. It was as if I was seeing a side of him I never knew existed.

He recounted how that particular Sunday would always live in his memory. After they had eaten their *"molletes,"* his mom gathered them, and they began walking down the street. Their destination? A monastery for nuns. Upon arrival, he, his little brother, and his sister continued to play. I was sitting there in the doctor's office, engrossed in his narration, when all of a sudden, I noticed a shift in my dad's facial expression. His eyes, once shining with joy, were now staring blankly into the distance, tears streaming down his face. I had never seen my dad cry before. This was not just a few tears trickling down; it was uncontrollable sobbing. We were in a crowded waiting room, people all around us, and I was desperately trying to figure out what had triggered this sudden emotional breakdown. He couldn't articulate his words, but as he tried, I began to understand the story he was trying to tell.

He was reliving the heart-wrenching memory of when they had to leave his little brother and sister at the monastery because they couldn't afford to take care of them anymore. The weight of the guilt he carried was immense. He blamed himself because he hadn't earned enough money to keep his little brother and sister with them. His grief stemmed from the fact that he never wanted anyone to experience the pain and sorrow that he had felt on that fateful day.

Already as a child of seven or eight, my father carried an unimaginable burden. I have a son who's now eleven, and it's inconceivable to think of someone so young shouldering such responsibility. But I believe this was one of the experiences that fueled my father's drive. He never wanted to relive that painful moment, and from then on, he worked relentlessly, always striving to stay ahead.

His life didn't get much easier. He spent his days working in the fields where his mother dropped him off each morning. During the periods of the year, like harvesting season, when he had to sleep on the farms, he even had to worry about things like hiding a knife under his pillow to protect himself from the older men.

He couldn't attend public school because of his undocumented status but got a break from another group of nuns who ran a private school. They knew of his situation and let him attend without charging any tuition. His mother would help clean the place up in return. I seldom talk about this, but there's another incident that had a profound influence on him.

Once, he shared a story about his time at the school. When you're dirt-poor and pretty much known as an orphan, it's a tough situation to navigate. He found a pair of nice shoes in the trash that someone had discarded. The soles were pretty worn out. But in his youthful optimism, he thought that if he tore off the worn-out soles and walked carefully, no one would notice. He did just that, and it turned into a deeply embarrassing situation at school. The other kids found out, and, as kids do, they made fun of him for essentially wearing shoes without soles. I believe it was experiences like these that molded him into the man he became and spurred him on in his relentless pursuit of a better life.

As he advanced in his career, he found himself drawn to sales. Through the late 60s and early 70s, he honed his skills as a floor salesman in a local electronics store. His talent didn't go unnoticed even by big-name companies. They must have started to see that a Spanish speaker who excelled in sales was an asset. I also imagine he must have felt a huge sense of accomplishment knowing that.

## A beginning

In those days, when you needed to buy a TV, you'd go to a mom-and-pop shop, and if it needed fixing, you'd have to return to the store you bought it from. My father asked: *"What if there was a repair shop that would fix it no matter where you bought it?"*

By 1974, my father had successfully launched his business. Growing up, our father was a constant worker. He was seldom around, but somehow we never felt deprived of his presence, and he made sure that we never wanted for anything. During the little time he had with us, he made sure it was meaningful.

At the time, I didn't understand what he was trying to do. But he would impart some serious life lessons on us. *"Don't ever trust anybody in this world. Nobody. If we're ever at war, don't turn your back on me."* I had no clue what he meant then. *"Mistrust people, be cautious," "Keep your business to yourself," "Always pay cash."* Despite his cynical outlook on life, his heart was always filled with compassion, and his values were centered on caring for others.

Not long after us graduating from high school, my father fell seriously ill. Like many small business owners, he had pushed himself to the brink for the sake of the family. The result was that he became incapacitated, unable to move or communicate.

There was no way around it my brother and I had to find a way to keep the company afloat. My brother was 20, and I was still in my teens. The only thing I knew was that we had to ensure people got paid on Friday. That was the extent of our knowledge of our father's business. We tried to decipher his business operations based on our recollections of accompanying him to banks, visiting various stores, and observing his collections process. He had a box at home where he kept everything organized and a small card file with names. We began scrutinizing everything, studying his notes, attempting to comprehend his shorthand.

That week felt like it stretched into infinity. Somehow we managed to assemble the payroll and ensured everyone was paid. It felt like an incredible feat, but in an instant, it was Monday again, and we had to restart the whole process. It was like emerging from a nightmare only to discover you're still trapped within it. The second week was no easier, nor was the third. It was an endless cycle of weeks flowing by. For years, we lived with the anxiety that we might not make it to the next week.

MOONSHOTS

I took up station at the same desk my dad had once occupied. Stretched between two filing cabinets, a piece of plywood covered with stacks of paper, bills, and envelopes served as the desk. Sitting there, a surge of emotion overwhelmed me. I was occupying the same space my father had, mere feet away from where I used to impatiently wait outside, bitterly complaining about his perceived selfishness. Now, I was navigating through his personal hell. All those instances where he picked us up late from school, the countless errands he ran with us in tow, even the moments spent in the sweltering car outside his office, now my office. I was awestruck by the enormity of pressure and stress one person would willingly endure for their loved ones.

The relentless nightmare persisted; it didn't abate. Fast forward three years, and I was about 21 or 22. I remember carrying a persistent knot in my throat, an ever-present sense of dread. It was my companion as I drifted off to sleep, and it greeted me as I awoke. It clung to me every hour of the day, seven days a week. Tears often streaked my face each morning upon waking. I yearned for an end to it all. My dad had recovered by then, but we refrained from reintegrating him into the business, knowing it was a slow poison to him. I lacked the courage to admit to him that I no longer wanted to carry on because that would mean he'd have to step back into the fray.

**Struggling**

One day, my brother approached me with a suggestion. He recommended that I read a book. In my entire life, I had never read a book — not in high school, not anywhere. However, I decided to take his advice and read the suggested book, 'Rich Dad Poor Dad.' The book prompted me to read another and then another until a cascade of knowledge opened up before us. We quickly grasped that acquiring knowledge is akin to embarking on a journey. Reading books is like walking to your destination, attending seminars is like driving there, and finding a mentor is akin to flying. We determined that we needed to go to seminars and find mentors, individuals who could guide us and invest their knowledge in us. This became a cornerstone of our belief system.

Fast forward to 2008. My brother and I had made money in several different sectors, such as real estate, land development, the stock market, and precious metals, and all our earnings from our side businesses were put back into our father's business to keep it afloat. It had been evident for years to anyone that we should have closed down the original business. Still, it was like attempting to bite off your own tongue; we just couldn't bring ourselves to do it. I think it was a mix of pride and the fact that it was my father's legacy.

We were, therefore, turned to anything that would help us find the magic bullet that would help us sustain the business. This search led to two events that fueled a rage so potent within me that it consumed every bit of me for years to come.

The first event took place at a global seminar in Arizona, attended by intelligent people from around the world. We were confident in our ability to hold our own in any conversation. We were well-rounded, well-read, and it was right after the aftermath of 2008. Many attendees were discussing the future, speculating about what was going to happen and where the opportunities lay.

At the after-party, we found ourselves on the outskirts of a circle of people. My brother and I tried to nudge our way in, but one influential individual, a wealthy man, locked eyes with my brother. He began collecting plates from everyone around him and handed them to my brother. In his world, there was no other reason for two Latino boys to be there except if it was to help clean up. It wasn't overtly racist; he was just immersed in his own worldview, and in that perspective, that was our role. He might not have realized it, but everyone else did. The embarrassment was intense.

I was silenced by the humiliation. To be looked upon and know that no matter how hard I worked, no matter how much I read, no matter how much I knew, I was always going to be seen as just a Latino. For my brother, it was no big deal. He shrugged it off with a laugh. For me, that realization cut me deep.

This incident, along with others of the same sort, filled me with a seething internal rage. At that moment, it was like a bomb went off inside me. I found a new clarity about what I wanted to do with my life. I wanted to build the biggest business I could as a form of retaliation. I wanted to leave a mark. I wanted to carve a path across the earth, and when people would ask: *'How did you do it?' I would know exactly what to say to them: "Because of a WB."*

## Drive

That drove me. I lost interest in real estate, stocks, and precious metals. I wanted to learn everything about business. In my mind, I needed to become the best businessperson in the world. And that's exactly what I set out to do.

When I returned from that seminar, and I cast everything aside to dive headfirst into business. I sacrificed my social life, my weekends, everything. While others were out at the movies or drinking, I was at home, reading and honing my skills in every spare minute I had. During this period, I got married and had a child, but I was scarcely present for either. Despite our efforts, we could never make a breakthrough. Every year, our revenue hovered around $900,000 to $1,000,000. Invariably, there would be some setbacks.

My brother Omar is just a year older than me, and we have been inseparable since childhood. One day, we were in our office building, and he said to me: *"Hey, bro... I want to see if I can skip lunch from now on and leave a bit early every other day. I want to spend some time with my kids. They're growing up, and I want to pick them up from school."*

Omar's shift in focus sent me into a panic. I realized time was slipping away from us. Everything we wanted to achieve seemed to be falling through our fingers as time caught up with us. This realization only drove me to make more aggressive moves, behave more assertively, and push even harder.

## Success

Around this time, a gentleman entered our office during one of our ambitious Friday company meetings. Intrigued by our discussions, he wanted to meet with us after hearing us speak.

The man had arrived in a decrepit pickup truck that seemed barely roadworthy. According to him, his air conditioning company had been a remarkable success, starting from a garage and eventually reaching a turnover of $35 million. He narrated the whole saga of its rise and fall. There wasn't much reason to believe his claims, but as was my habit, I decided to verify his story online. The company did exist and had indeed seen success. However, they had run into legal trouble.

This discovery sparked a heated debate in my family. They wanted no part in this venture but propelled by a blend of ego, anger, and a growing fear of time running out, I was resolute in my decision, and he started growing our sales team. He was good.

At first, it was just him. Then, he brought in another person, and they would huddle together, strategizing their daily tasks. We observed them from a distance. Gradually, two turned into three, and before we knew it, they had attracted a crowd. That crowd continued to grow. They began to occupy more space in the office, the lower level of the building, and even the parking lot. Our revenues grew from 1 million to 2 million, then to 3 and 4 million.

We began hosting lavish quarterly meetings, renting out venues, flying in motivational speakers, inviting vendors, and showcasing our progress through charts. We compared our current position with our humble beginnings, using Apple as an inspirational reference, and outlined our future ambitions. Our air conditioning business, once considered the company's laughing stock, now accounted for 95% of our total business, completely overshadowing my father's business.

At this stage, we were financing 99% of all our air conditioning sales. However, only 2 out of every 10 customers had good credit, and we knew we were missing out on 80% of the market. Reflecting on the knowledge we had acquired, we devised a plan to find default insurance that we could purchase for customers with higher credit risk, thus making it attractive for investors to buy our contracts.

With the plan in place, all we needed was to approach an insurance company, but everyone brushed us off. They were utterly perplexed because this concept was unheard of on such a small scale. Despite making countless calls and enduring repeated rejections, it seemed like we were hitting a brick wall. They kept insisting, *"You're out of your depth,"* and *"That's not a thing."* I knew what we were proposing was viable, even though I felt like I was buried deep in Google search results, endlessly scrolling, dialing, and getting nowhere.

## Moonshots

Still, it pays off to work hard. After a long and winding road, we ended up getting a meeting with the CEO of Redstone. Upon arrival at their offices, we stepped into a vibrant space filled with rows of individuals engrossed in their monitors, engaged in phone conversations, and the buzz of the place was palpable. We were escorted to a glass-encased conference room situated in the heart of the action. As we commenced our presentation, I started to outline our business plan as I had practiced for days on end in the hopes of getting a meeting like this one.

As soon as he comprehended the crux of my discourse, he was able to anticipate the remainder and interrupted me by saying: *"What else?"*. It was a humbling experience, to put it mildly. After fast-paced, intricate discussions, we managed to walk out of the meeting with a letter of intent for $60 million. On that same day, we got another promise of $10-$15 million from Flexport Capital.

After an exhilarating day, we went out for dinner, ready to indulge in one of the most expensive steaks we had ever eaten. Over dinner, Omar turned to me and said, *"Hey, dude, it's unfolding exactly as you predicted. I don't know how you do it. Everything you described, from negotiating with hedge funds to orchestrating all of this just as you envisioned."* To his remark, all I could respond with was an overconfident, "I know. This is nothing." Looking back, that exchange is one I deeply regret. Rather than celebrating our collective triumph, I arrogantly hogged all the credit.

## Crossroads

Fast forward to July 2018, Omar and I walked into one of our sales offices, where we were met by a secretary we hadn't directly worked with. She explained, *"Yeah, it's just my time. My sister has an awesome opportunity, and I'm going to join her."* I didn't give her announcement much thought, but Omar did and stayed behind. After about 5 minutes, he came out and said, *"Guys, we need to go back inside. Something's off."* Confused, I asked him what he meant. He couldn't quite articulate it, but he had an uneasy feeling. We returned inside and started talking to the secretary, who, by that point, was visibly nervous and kept her conversation brief and vague.

At the rear of the office, we could hear our sales director's booming laughter filtering into the space we were sitting. He was the same person who had once arrived in a beat-up pickup truck and the one who had been the result of building our incredible sales results.

We had recently promoted someone to an HR role and decided to consult with this new HR manager. As we began to recount the strange interaction we had with the secretary, we were abruptly interrupted, and she said: "I already know what's happening."

She then started to describe the sales director's interactions with women in the office after hours. She asked, *"Don't you remember so-and-so?"* *She listed several names, all women, who had left the company.* *"That's why they're not here anymore,"* she stated matter-of-factly.

This revelation brought everything to a grinding halt. Back then, I didn't have a daughter as I do now. The only woman I could think of was my mother. The thought of someone treating my mother the way this sales director had treated those women was too much to bear.

My brother Omar and I stepped outside. Despite the sweltering heat of July, I felt a chill run down my spine. I stood there, trembling, my body convulsing with shock and wrestling with what to do next. The architect of our well-oiled sales machine, the man who had helped build a company that efficiently churned out products, was also the same man who had exploited women in the most abhorrent way.

We could have confronted him, demanded he stop his behavior, and likely, no one would have said a thing. But deep within, I knew that if we turned a blind eye, we would cross a moral line we could never step back from, so Omar and I made a tough decision. That very afternoon, we drove to the sales office and confronted him. Without resistance, he collected his things and left the office.

The aftermath was brutal. We witnessed our once-flourishing company crumble before our very eyes. Our workforce shrunk from a robust 80 to a meager 18 within three months. As we exposed the rot at the heart of our organization, it seemed that those who had thrived under such corrupt leadership scattered like roaches under a harsh light. We tried to steady the ship, but it was as if we were grasping at sand – everything slipped through our fingers.

**Crash**

The descent into financial chaos followed rapidly thereafter. Foreclosure notices started piling up, and banks grew impatient. Frantic, I brokered deals to offload properties we owned. We sold off an office in McAllen, a building that held a special place in my heart. It was the first property my father and I had ever bought together. As a teenager, I sat with him and watched him sign the papers with gleaming pride. Back then, it was a triumphant milestone. Now, it was just another casualty in our desperate scramble for liquidity. One by one, we let go of our properties and buildings, even our vehicles. Each time a vehicle was sold, it brought a temporary sense of relief – we could afford to make payroll a little longer. One of the hardest moments was letting go of one of our first technicians, a man I'd known since childhood, but our situation left no room for sentiment.

This is where I started my story. My father braced for the worst and worried that he might have to go back to the misery he had grown up in.

Just months prior to this upheaval, my brother had sold his house, planning to build a new one with his wife. They were temporarily residing in a rental, dreaming of the day they would move into their newly built home. Those dreams were now ashes in the wind. In my desperate state, my thoughts turned to the money from my brother's house sale. Perhaps I could borrow it to keep our sinking ship afloat a bit longer…

I found myself sharing a desk with Joe, one of the many individuals I had steamrolled on my ascent to power. Now, we were equals, making desperate phone calls side by side, fighting to keep our heads above the water. By this point, November had descended, and the biting chill of winter was setting in.

## Brotherhood

The dreary weather outside was a mirror of my inner turmoil – cold, desolate, and stormy. I was in a state of morbid anticipation, awaiting the inevitable downfall. I remember one particular Saturday morning when I accompanied my brother on an installation job. He picked me up in the wee hours of the morning, a flicker of hope dancing in his eyes. He turned to me, his voice ringing with conviction, *"We're gonna make it, man. We've done it before. We'll do it again."* But the circumstances had changed dramatically since the first time. We were now ensnared in the throes of millions of dollars of debt. He was oblivious to this detail, and I didn't have the heart to shatter his optimism. I met his hopeful gaze and echoed his words, *"Yeah, man. I know."*

Our financial condition was alarmingly precarious, leading to our employees' checks bouncing back. The staff lived in constant trepidation, rushing to cash their checks at the earliest opportunity, dreading the moment when the funds would dry up. There were establishments that flatly refused to accept our checks.

Amidst this chaos, there was Bob, who had willingly accepted a pay cut, relinquished his hard-earned commissions, and was commuting long distances to the office every single day. His unflinching commitment in the face of such adversity was profoundly moving. Despite the dwindling resources, despite the uncertainty surrounding his pay, Bob was a steady presence in the office. He tirelessly made phone calls, resolved customer queries, and upheld his duties with remarkable resilience. I was at a loss to understand his motivation. Why was he subjecting himself to such duress? Yet, his unwavering loyalty lent me a sense of solace. For the first time, I felt the warmth and support I'd only felt from my brother. His silent solidarity seemed to whisper, *"Don't worry, I got you."* I never voiced this to him, but at that moment, I knew that I wanted to inspire the same sense of reassurance in someone else, just as Bob had done for me.

I had spent my entire professional journey with a single-minded focus on ascending to the top. Now, for the first time, I was beginning to grasp the true essence of *"we."* We were confronted with what seemed like an insurmountable challenge, yet everyone around me was pouring their heart and soul into their efforts. I was ready to throw in the towel, but they were not. They relentlessly pushed forward, striving to keep the ship afloat. January yielded to February, and we managed to make small sales here and there, just enough to keep going. Despite the persistent issue of bouncing checks, everyone showed up, their spirits inexplicably buoyant. Gradually, our somber, silent office began to resonate with muffled chuckles, then laughter, and eventually a pervading sense of camaraderie. I found myself witnessing the forging of unbreakable bonds between teammates, a camaraderie born of shared struggle. This collective resilience was drawing us closer together, imbuing us with a newfound sense of hope and determination.

### New beginnings

Turned out the universe wasn't against us. Rather, it had been guiding us through a crucial learning process. It was teaching us that success wasn't solely about making money or building a business empire. Maybe it was about building a community, a family, a tribe that stands shoulder to shoulder, supporting each other, that earns and learns together.

And so, we started to look at our situation differently. We stopped asking *'why us?'* and started asking 'what now?'. We realized that we still had a choice. We could let our circumstances define us, or we could define our circumstances. We could give up and admit defeat, or we could rise from the ashes, stronger and wiser.

With this new perspective, we began to see light at the end of the tunnel. We saw a path forward, not an easy one, but one that was worth walking. We saw a future where we could rebuild our business, not just as a money-making entity, but as a force for good, as a platform for creating shared wealth and fostering a culture of respect, dignity, and mutual support. We saw a future where we could make a real difference, not just in our lives but in the lives of all those associated with us.

And with that vision in mind, we started our journey anew, armed with lessons from the past and hope for the future.

# Primus

## CEO Founder
*NAKED REVIVAL INC*

## Making the impossible happen

*Lao Tzu's "A journey of a thousand miles begins with a single step."
Or, Stephen Covey's "Begin with the end in the mind."*

Once the buzz of these pithy didactic saying and stories wears off, do you actually believe them?

We'll come back to these quotes in a few pages.

Baseball is arguably America's most iconic sport; in the game, a moonshot is a home run hit that reaches a great height and distance.

In the world of entrepreneurship, and most notably tech, a *"moonshot"* is an extremely ambitious and innovative project. Much like how we can visualize a heroic home run sending the crowds into a frenzy, we can hear the Nasdaq bell ringing or see Time magazine's cover about an entrepreneur reaching the zenith of their pioneering pursuit.

This chapter is about entrepreneurial moonshots, with two crucial/ parallels to baseball.

# NAKED REVIVAL

What comes before that apex of glory?

How many strikeouts, hours of practice, lost games, injuries and meltdowns must one endure and learn from before that one big moonshot is achieved?

How close does an entrepreneur come to burning up in the sun, so to speak, on the way to the moon?

And what is the foundation that guides them on that journey?

It starts, indubitably, with an idea.

As one of rock's most ambitious, innovative musicians, Peter Gabriel, once said, *"All of the buildings, all of the cars, were once just a dream in somebody's head."*

Making or doing what others believe impossible begins as a wisp of thought conjured up in the deep cauldron of one's mind. Maybe as a dream that awakens one in the middle of the night, maybe as a thought that strikes like lightning, or maybe as inspiration captured through our senses as we observe the world around us.

Elizabeth Gilbert puts it perfectly:
*"I believe that our planet is inhabited not only by animals and plants and bacteria and viruses, but also by ideas. Ideas are a disembodied, energetic life-form. They are completely separate from us, but capable of interacting with us — albeit strangely. Ideas have no material body, but they do have consciousness, and they most certainly have will. Ideas are driven by a single impulse: to be made manifest. And the only way an idea can be made manifest in our world is through collaboration with a human partner. It is only through a human's efforts that an idea can be escorted out of the ether and into the realm of the actual.*
*Ideas spend eternity swirling around us, searching for available and willing human partners. (I'm talking about all ideas: artistic, scientific, industrial, commercial, ethical, religious, political.) When an idea thinks it has found somebody — say, you — who might be able to bring it to fruition, the idea will try to get your attention.*
*Sometimes — rarely, but magnificently — there comes a day when your defences slacken, your anxieties ease, and you're relaxed enough to receive the magic. The idea, sensing your openness, will start to do its work on you. It will send the universal physical and emotio-*

*nal signals of inspiration (the chills up the arms, the hair standing up on the back of the neck, the nervous stomach, the buzzy thoughts, that feeling of falling in love). The idea will organise "coincidences" to tumble across your path, to hold your interest. You will start to notice all sorts of signs pointing you towards the idea. The idea will wake you up in the middle of the night and distract you from your everyday routine. The idea will not leave you alone until it has your full attention.*

*And then, in a quiet moment, it will ask, "Do you want to work with me?"*

An entrepreneur, a pioneer in any medium, has two choices. *"No, I don't want to,"* is an option, but *"yes, I'm going after this moonshot,"* is often where we unlock our deepest lessons and potential as a human being. For when we say *"yes"* our spirit makes a choice to *"sign a contract"* of which only we know the terms and can hold ourselves accountable to.

The rest of world will not care about our contract; if they even know about it, they may criticize and doubt us until we've made the impossible possible.

Which means, of course, that it was never impossible to begin with, and the only limitations were of the mind and zeitgeist.

Which brings us back to the proverbs shared at the beginning of this chapter. With no real road map to guide us, we have to meet ourselves where we are right now — knowing what we know (and don't know) about our pursuit, believing in it and ourselves, knowing where we want to end up, and taking the first step.

In Start-up Land, nothing is ever a straight line. It's critical that you have some basic principles in place before you start your moonshot — because things don't always go as planned. If your guiding principles are solid and clear, they can act like a compass to help you navigate the inevitable surprises and sudden changes.

If you envision a house, these principles are the foundation on which the house is built. If the foundation isn't properly established and solid, the house won't survive shifts in the ground or bad weather. Over time, your house will deteriorate. In a moonshot this foundation include:

1.  Establish your visions – *"Why"* and the Why behind your Why

2. Establish your guiding principles and core values
3. Establish your objectives
4. Establish what is essential—personally and professionally
5. Mindset

The first thing to get crystal clear on is: Why are you starting this moonshot in the first place? This underlying *"why"* is rooted in your emotional make up. It is part of understanding who you are and why you do the things you do. For instance, your motivations can be rooted in insecurity, feelings of not being enough, and/or the need to prove someone wrong. Insecurity can be a powerful motivator, but if not managed and understood, it can lead to self-destructive behaviour.

As Tim Glover, author of Relentless, says:
*"Being the best means engineering your life so you never stop until you get what you want, and then you keep going until you get what's next. And then you go for even more. Relentless is about never being satisfied, (it has) a dark side... They get what they want, but they pay for it in solitude. Excellence is lonely."*

Knowing the why behind your why will help you be objective in your decision-making so as not to be victim to your own blindspots, so you are doing things that support the main *"Why"* of your moonshot and not your ego.

What's the reason for your company to exist? What is its singular purpose?

Your *"Why"* is true north on your moonshot compass. It keeps you focused on what is essential so as not to get distracted along the way.

## Establish your Guiding Principles and Core Values

When you're launching a moonshot, just like building a house, understand that it's going to take longer and cost more (maybe a lot more) than you originally thought. To paraphrase Prussian Field Marshall Helmuth von Moltke: *"No plan survives first contact with the enemy."*

Of course, I don't view launching your business as akin to facing an *"enemy,"* but the point is still powerful. You'll face many different and unexpected scenarios as you build your moonshot. In order to navigate the challenges and make the best possible adjustments for each scenario, your Guiding Principles and Core Values should be established early and understood by your entire team.

Values are qualities or standards that act as the foundation for our principles and guide our behaviours.

Principles are the rules that lead to our actions.

Establish about a few key Core Values and Guiding Principles to help guide your decision making early. Add new ones over time.

Here are two Core Values and two Guiding Principles:

**Core Values:**

- Continuous improvement
The desire for continuous improvement in everything we do. We're all on individual journeys personally and professionally.

It's important to find peace and acceptance wherever we are in any given moment, and with whom. Simultaneously, we must focus on continuous improvement — to be the best that we can as individuals and as a company. This includes our personal lives, our relationships, our goals, products, customer experiences — everything.

-Action
Seek knowledge and feedback. Reflect. Apply the lessons you've learned. Do better next time.

- Gratitude
We practice gratitude daily.

We must have a commitment to gratitude and allow it to guide our thoughts and actions. Let us be grateful for those who host us in their beautiful cities when we travel; those who cut the grass, take out the trash and make the coffee; those who raised the people who are responsible for our freedoms today. Let's be radical about our gratefulness every single day.

**Guiding Principles**

- **Action:** Say, *"Thank you"* regularly. Check yourself when you're fee-

ling negative about a situation and count your many blessings.
- **Always Follow the Process.**
Following the process keeps team members accountable and reduces errors. When there's a process to follow, and people follow it, it helps you address issues as they arise; you can correct your course and get the desired result.
Focus on the Most Important Task First.
Even if it's something you don't want to do, you should always do the most important task first.

## Establish your Objectives

Everyone needs Objectives (even the founders and CEO) and everyone needs to know what they are. Objectives are usually simple, easy to define and measurable.

An objective doesn't have to include how it's going to be accomplished. Moonshots are usually new territory and the how may not be clear at the start. The person assigned an objective still has a lot of freedom to figure out the best way to achieve it, as well as the flexibility to try creative solutions if their first plan doesn't work.

Making objectives public (at least within the team) allows everyone to know what everyone else is responsible for, and creates a sense of accountability. With public objectives, everyone can rest assured that everyone else is working as hard as they are; it's the ultimate accountability.

Objectives that are anchored by realistic and agreed-upon timelines keep your team focused on required tasks. Team members will feel much better about the company and their day-to-day work when goals and objectives are clear. Establishing fewer objectives will increase the possibility of success.

At my first company, Naked, we established objectives very early on. We borrowed from Entrepreneurial Operating System® to define our key objectives as *"Rocks"* according to four distinct parts:
- **The What** — What is our goal? It should be easily understood by all.
- **The How** — What do we need to do in order to accomplish the objective and what do we need to do to get there?
- **The Results** — Are there measurable steps we can take along the way that lead to successfully reaching the objective? Establish

relevant KPIs (Key Performance Indicators) to measure results that will lead to success in the objective.

- **The Reflection** — Afterward, we reflected on what went right and wrong with our steps, KPIs and process. We'd discuss this openly as team members and assess what we might need to change for the next set of objectives.

Setting objectives is a foundational pillar of building a business but it's important to approach objectives with an open and, dare I say, flexible mind. The Marshall Goldsmith expression — "What got you here won't get you there" — comes to mind. Factors change and you need to be able to pivot and adjust your objectives as needed to propel the business forward.

## Establish What is Essential

Essentialism, to focus on what matters most so you can give your best to it, is paramount when it comes to striving for your moonshot.

Your moonshot Essentialism is established by your *"Why"* and your Objectives, and it's personal as much as professional. Choosing to focus on what's essential provides us with the time, creativity and clarity to execute our business and maintain a healthy balance in our lives while doing it. But our time at the office isn't all that needs to be accounted for. Time spent with family, friends, extra-curricular activities, health, dating, etc., all factor in. All the things we do affect us mentally, emotionally, financially, socially and physically.

As entrepreneurs building a business, we need to prepare for this by understanding that:

A. We can't do all the things we want and give our business the amount of time it needs to be successful;
B. The time we spend on non-business-building activities should relieve and refresh us, not create additional stresses that then carry over into our business.

We can't control every single thing that happens, but we can certainly make choices about what and who is essential to us and build a structure into our life that focuses on that. Organise your personal life, establish work routines that optimize your performance and focus, and learn to say *"No."* Opportunities will come up all the time.

If it's not a *"Hell YES!"* then it's a *"No."* *"If I do this extra thing now, can I do it as well as I could two years from now? Will I be present while doing it?"* There will be time down the road to do other things and give more of your talents and effort to others.


## Mindset

Part of the moonshot foundation is mindset. Our inner judge, sha-dowself, or inner critic is an ever present voice often taunting and stri-king down our noblest thoughts. How you interact with your own thou-ghts is the true X-factor of your moonshot. Can you listen to your inner critic, allow its concerns to be voiced, but choose the best possible thou-ght instead? Can you practice self-compassion in the face of self-judge-ment? Can you embody grace and reverence for the process in the face of hardship and let down? What about acceptance of your moonshot's worst nightmares and darkest days? Can you push forward trusting that you are on the right path? Can you be open to the possibly of landing in a different, better place all together?

The answer of course is yes, you most certainly can. By following your why and principles, doing what's essential, and keeping constant watch over yourself. Through the practice of radically accepting what is and has been and letting go of that which does not serve you, as you move forward. Through consciousness meditation practices to clear your mind and detach from incessant negative thoughts, by having positive honest mentors, and by continuing to cultivate your personal development.

Although you can change the world for the better with your moons-hot, it's ultimately a journey of self-cultivation with no destination. As Tony Robbins says, *"It's not about the goal, but becoming the person capable of achieving that goal."* It means that much about you will chan-ge along the way...that red hot sun will burn up a great deal of you, and you'll be reborn, again and again. You will ascend to the *"impossible"* heights of your potential in a world of infinite possibility.

**Omar**
Soto Sepúlveda
*FOUNDERS ENTERPRISES INC./*
*TRANSPORTES SOTO E HIJOS*

**Christine**
M. Wallace
*KETTERING UNIVERSIT*

**Héctor**
Ventura García Flores
*GRUPO GARFLO*

# 2. Leadership

**Luis Diego**
Loaiciga V
*AMERICAN TALENT JOBS*

**Eric**
Abensur
*ABENSUR CONSULTING*

**Bob**
Orsi
*FIRST CLASS INVESTMENTS*

# Perfect leader

**Gustav Juul**
Founder & CEO
*AIM GROUP / XO LEADERS*

*"The pursuit of perfection often impedes improvement." – George Will*

Some people think a leader should have the complete set of skills, characteristics, and abilities to single-handedly handle any problem, challenge, and opportunity that comes along. To me, the *"perfect leader"* is a myth. I certainly don't fit into that category. I am definitely not a perfect leader. Most of the time, I am not even a leader. I'd describe myself as someone who strives to be a well-rounded person who makes decisions through the support of a great team. Over the years, this has enabled me to take many more good and average choices than bad ones.

Almost right out of college, I was responsible for leading a team with people thrice my age and decades of experience. I had a deep-seated feeling of being an impostor. To say the very least, I was immensely underprepared for the responsibilities I had been given, and I only had a minimal understanding of the challenges I would face. Furthermore, my boss felt it was better for me to learn through *"trial by fire"* than for him to waste time teaching me. Fearing being exposed as a fraud, I overcompensated with a know-it-all attitude, only half-listening to those who offered their advice. What I should have done was to tell them that I desperately needed their advice, but I didn't.

Here is a shout-out to you: I thank you for your patience and for never making me feel less, accepting the flaws I tried to hide but which must have been painfully apparent to you. Thank you for saving my ass more times than I can count, for guiding me without making it too obvious, and for giving me time to build my skills as a leader.

To you, who have taken the time to read my article, I would like to share a bit of what they taught me.

### Trust, Respect, and Imperfection

**Trust–** I work the hardest on gaining people's trust. I stand up for my team. I never blamed them for something I was responsible for. We share our successes. I let them know I don't have most of the answers and show them I need them more than they need me. I am not perfect in my score, but in most cases people have rewarded me with their trust.

**Respect–** Through this trust, it gives us the ability to create. It is empowers us to dare try new things and, through that, do incredible things together.

**Imperfection-** I show them that I don't have all the answers. I want them to know that I have made more wrong decisions than most. It is up to me to teach them where I failed, and it is up to them to make their own wrong decisions... and live with it. That is evolving. In recent years I have even become very explicit when I tell them that I want them to make mistakes. My reasoning is that it's only teams that never push themselves are the ones that never screw up. Striving to be perfect fosters micromanagement, criticism, and stalls change. Going for greatness is only achieved through accepting that we will never be perfect. I want them to reach for the stars.

I have found that the organizations that I've led and the many companies I now Mentor, just work better when there is Trust, Respect, and an acceptance of imperfection.

## Organizational Fairness

CEO's are paid to decide on the organization's strategic priorities, such as resource allocation, investments, client care service levels, employee compensation and wellness, promotions, profit margins, and as a result, shareholder dividends. What I have learned is that for an organization to be successful, it is just not possible to base decisions on short-term win-win for everyone. Long-term win-win is much more feasible, but because of the lack of trust and an ever more impatient society, people seem predisposed to expect to get the short end of the stick.

Organizational injustice is in the eye of the beholder, and leaders are scrutinized for needing to be *"fair"* in ways that seem unfair to me. As a young leader, I honestly worried too much about pleasing everyone. I contorted to find ways to do what was impossible to do, i.e., pleasing everyone, and I, therefore, did worse because of it. While everyone wants to be treated equally, not everyone is equal, and not every contribution holds equal value.

Comparing the first team I had with the next, the people who reported to me were my junior in many ways, including experience, executive seniority, and education. I went from a team needing very little of me to a team needing much more time than what I could possibly give. In the beginning, it felt great to be *"needed,"* then quite quickly, I became unable to do my own job. I had a couple of disastrous quarters and had to learn to set clear boundaries. I implemented team meetings and almost completely canceled all the one-on-one conversations.

I learned a lot from that experience too. Any team that you head should know that you are there in two aspects alone. The first thing I am always going to help them with is to make suggestions in case they encounter something they can't make sense of. That is sharing my perspective. It is not the same as taking the decision for them. If they are responsible for the outcome, the decision is theirs to take. If they want someone else to make the decision for them, when they report to me, they will quickly find out that they are wasting their time and mine. The second is to help get cooperation flowing in case of internal unwillingness to act.

I might not be a perfect leader, but I don't see myself as an incompetent leader; I am just an incomplete leader. I know I don't have the intellectual capacity to make sense of everything. I don't have the capability to foresee all the repercussions of my decisions. I am not always able to create a vision of the future that everyone wants. More often than not, I lack the experience to translate my dreams into concrete actions. Last but not least, my interpersonal skills are not always able to foster the commitment necessary to get people to give everything they've got.

## The 4 C's

After learning to apply different management theories and reading hundreds of books, I have arrived at the conclusion that there are four important roles that together make up a successful management team. These roles are: Creator, Champion, Custodian, Caregiver.

What I find interesting about the management roles is that I believe that no one can fill these four roles simultaneously, as they have contradicting objectives. In very general terms and only to give you a few examples: If you are quick to act, you can't be slow as well. You can't be creative and go *"by the book"* simultaneously. Some look for effectiveness, others for efficiency. There is long-term versus short-term. Perfecting my understanding of it, I feel, has made me a better support for my teams. I can now predict where I'll need the help of others and how to better support each member of my team individually. Through this, I have learned to form successful diverse teams.

That said, I don't feel like I am a flawless leader who has figured it all out. The more I know, the more I know what I don't know, but the moment I figured out that it was all right to be open about both my strengths and my weaknesses, I was able to allow myself to start really relying on others to make up for my lack of perspective on certain aspects of the business. I became a better leader for it and certainly a much more successful business owner. As they say, *"numbers don't lie"*.

Most leaders I support in my consulting business call me because, to some degree, they feel trapped in the myth of needing to be a perfect leader, and it's a heavy burden that only leads to becoming a bottleneck for the business. I don't swap them out for a *"professional"* management team; I teach the people already working in the company how to support the owner and the owner how to be a leader.

How many times have you felt uncertain about what the results of a decision you've taken will be? Have you ever felt uncomfortable because the IT or the Marketing person was using concepts that were unfamiliar to you? Would you dare to admit that you don't have a full picture of what is going on in the organization? Do you even know the names and birthdays of all your employees, if they have children or are married? You probably did when you started your business, but do you know it now? If you recognize any of this, please send me an email (gustav@aimsmg.com). We might have a good basis to talk. It's time to put that myth to rest and take action, not only for the sake of frustrated leaders but also for the well-being and continued growth of your organization.

Well, I am not Superman. There is only one of those around, I am not him, and he probably wouldn't know the first thing about running a successful business.

What I do know is that it is not possible for a person to single-handedly handle any and all problems. That being so, it takes a mature leader to realize that people need each for the business to grow.

In business 1 + 1 is not 2, it often is less, but it can be so much more.

# Abensur

**President**
*ABENSUR CONSULTING*

## Introduction

I'm an anarchist.

As wikipedia tells us: *"Anarchy is a society being freely constituted without authorities or a governing body."*

Doesn't this sound like the web3 world? Web3 promises to create a social universe built on the pillars of decentralization, transparency, where everyone is empowered and accountable. And this is a wonderful promise.

This promise for a better world to be realizable, its members should possess certain qualities and skills. However, I believe we remain very young human beings, and we have not yet mastered the virtues required to build such a world. And it is quite understandable: they are very hard to learn.

Let me share with you an insightful story.

London. April 2003. For the first time in my life, I was a CEO. I had been at the head of a telecom business for 6 short months. It was one of those foggy rainy days, and I was meeting with the corporate coach of my company. She was there to debrief my first 360. Just so you understand, during a 360 exercise, the coach had interviewed several members of my team and key stakeholders, asking them to share their opinion on the quality of my leadership.

To start off the meeting, she asked me: «*Eric, what do you think your employees view on your leadership?*». With a fake confidence, I said: «*A collaborative, conscious leader. A servant leader*». She answered: *"Eric, you are perceived by your team as... a dictator"*.

My first reaction was: I wanted to fire my entire team. She responded with kindness: *"Sure that is an option. But let's discuss option B. What changes can you make?"*.

I asked her to observe me during meetings. She noted my tendency to always give my opinion first before asking for my collaborators' views. And this had a disastrous effect. When you lead a team or an organization, if you give your opinion first, you kill the conversation. Since you are in charge, people will generally not dare contradict you, even if they have a constructive thing to say. This was what we call a « blind spot ». I lacked the sufficient self-awareness to understand why I needed to compulsively give my opinion before anyone else. Looking back now, I knew I did it in order to appear in charge, because deep down, I actually doubted myself. It was the expression of a typical impostor syndrome.

However, of course, my employees did not see that. We judge others by observing and interpreting their behaviors, we cannot see through to their real intentions. We spend our time guessing other people's intentions, when we barely understand our owns'.

Therefore, they saw me as a dictator. As a result, they were less engaged in their work, they did not feel empowered, and information was not shared. There you have it: we lacked decentralization, engaged workforce and transparency. My telecom company, which was part of the web2 movement, failed to achieve the promises of the internet.

This is my key message: if you want to live in a decentralized and transparent world where everyone is empowered and accountable, you need to master some critical skills, such as self-awareness, active listening and how to give feedback. These are the tenets of a coaching culture which I believe is the secret ingredient that might help web3 entrepreneurs to successfully address their goals.

Today I'm a 58 years old executive coach who still remembers the promises of 30 years ago.

## Unfulfilled promises

In the early 1990s, the internet arrived and everything changed. Forever. Or dit it really? When today you type these 5 words on Google: *"the promises of the internet"*, the first result that pops up is: *"How The Promise Of The Internet Was A Lie"* (Sean Clarke, article in Medium, 2021). Back then, we all heard the words of decentralization, empowerment, freedom, endless opportunities, autonomy, connections and transparency.

Then, Web2 arrived. Its revolutionary quality laid on the opportunity it gave each and every one of us to create our own content. And we thought this would guarantee the fulfillment of the goals web1 failed to achieve.

Yet again, these promises were not fully delivered. And giant, hierarchical, centralized organizations were created, controlling transactions, owning identities, influencing behaviors for the good and less good, and most of the time without our knowledge.

Today, web3 is making the same promises as web1 and web2.

I ask you these two questions: why would this time be any different? And why did it fail?

At the heart of a revolution, the mindset of its creators should reflect their ideals.

In the same way, I believe the dreams of web1 and web2 were not fulfilled because their values were not translated into their organizational structure and management philosophy.

So, what would such structures look like?

## Management revolution

On a regular basis, Gallup surveys millions of employees, worldwide. For the year 2020, they disclosed that 20% of employees are engaged at work. Engaged meaning motivated, inspired, enthusiastic, driven. So as of today, 80% of the global workforce is either neutral or disengaged. Obviously, something is not working.

Even before the 31st of October 2008 when Nakamoto published a white paper titled *"Bitcoin: A Peer-to-Peer Electronic Cash System"*, a number of organizations started implementing radical changes in their way of working. They had grown frustrated by the lack of innovation, accountability, and empowerment they internally observed, the lack of engagement of their employees.

In his book Reinventing Organizations (2014), Frederic Laloux studied these avant-guard companies. Their vision was founded on three pillars:

1. The absence of a hierarchical structure,
2. A high-level of transparency
3. The employee's great freedom to make decisions and express their opinions.

Those three pillars are concrete applications of the web1, web2 and web3 promises.

These organizations are engaged in the journey to self-management.

Managing teams has never been so difficult. Employees are more demanding, ready to switch companies on a whim. It is so easy to compare companies and their benefits. Managers must always be at their peak: managing up, managing down, influencing their peers, using more and more numerous tools to stay always on: slack, WhatsApp, emails, telegram, Zoom or Teams...Unsurprisingly, burn-out among managers is not uncommon. According to a BCG study, only 9% employees are willing to manage teams.

To achieve self-management is becoming a necessity and, a number of changes are recommended. Decisions need to be more collective. Therefore it signifies sharing more information and educating the employees so they can properly contribute to the decision process. In addition, specific conflict resolution is required. Performance review could also be revolutionized with peer-to-peer feedback. Bit by bit, we remove some key tasks from the manager's responsibilities. The organiza-tion becomes flatter. Laloux compares them with a living organism that can perfectly adapt to the never ending changes we all observe. And evidently, Web3 is the most unstable of all industries.

But those changes are difficult to implement and many of those companies, albeit their sincere intention of aligning their work culture with their ideals, have failed. They failed because we, as young human beings, are not prepared and trained to embrace these radical changes.

The necessity of a coaching culture

As human beings, we make up stories and act out on them without ever questioning their accuracy.

We are wired, coded, to be binary.

When we first meet someone, within the first 200 milliseconds our brain has made an unconscious decision on whether this person is safe or a threat to us. A blink of an eye. And this « survival » decision will lay down the grounds of this future relationship. If, for whatever unjustified reason, our decision was to feel threatened by this person, then we make it very difficult to build a transparent, horizontal relationship. We need to feel safe.

As my imposter syndrome story reveals, so many unconscious pro-cesses get in the way of implementing the changes required. Those ins-tant decisions we make, those fictitious stories we create are influenced by:

- – Our personality traits
- – Our education
- – Our life experiences
- – Our first bosses

And it's even worse today. Our capacity of creating stories on how others perceive us just got out of control with remote work: why does she not involve me in her decision?... Is he really working or watching Netflix?... His slack message was insulting!... Does she want to take my job?... They don't like me!...

We are creating more miscommunication, frustration and unnecessary conflicts.

We must master critical skills and transform our work culture before even considering getting into the self management journey.

This is a culture where :

- I and everyone else are crystal clear and on agreement on what is our mission, what are our values, and what success looks like
- I and everyone else are fully aware of the impact, both positive and negative, we have on others, and we are committed to address the negative ones
- I and everyone else feel heard
- I and everyone else feel safe to give and receive feedback
- I and everyone else are ready to ask what we need, to be vulnerable
- I and everyone else are sincerely committed to walk the talk

If those requisites are met, a climate of safety and confidence will be created. And I and everyone else are safe to be who we are, safe to ask questions and learn, safe to make mistakes, safe to contribute, safe to challenge. Everyone learns to behave like a coach. And this starts to resemble a coaching culture.

## Conclusion

If we want to deliver the promises of the web3 movement, we need to create an organization that is more decentralized, more transparent, more autonomous, where everyone is more accountable, more empowered.

I believe it is still possible.

We must learn and master self-awareness, active listening, how to give feedback and create a coaching culture. Then we can change the way we work to self-management, or we will fail. Again.

This is the opportunity of a lifetime, I should say a century-time.

You can start today, now.

After reading this article, you may join a friend, a colleague or a loved one for a casual conversation. Just be a better listener: stay focused, don't interrupt, suspend judgement, ask open ended questions to clarify, summarize back what you heard to them and then you can share your thinking. They will feel heard!

This may not guarantee the success of your web3 project. But I guarantee it will make you a better human being. And if that is not a start to build a better world, what is?

# Luis Diego
## Loaiciga V

**CEO**
*AMERICAN TALENT JOBS*

In the 90s, Antony had a job as a sales representative for a major transnational logistics company and was recently appointed responsible for a coastal area of the thriving Costa Rica. For Antony, it was a big step in his budding professional career, and being honest with himself, he had no idea how to achieve the exceptional results that were required of him in that remote tourist town. The first two months were a complete failure in terms of results. His bosses were not known for their patience, and Antony was aware of this.

One afternoon, absorbed in his thoughts, Antony walked from his small bungalow to do some basic shopping at the local store. Already in the store, standing in the cashier's line, he observed another customer, an older man, who was trying to juggle his purchases and his daughter in his arms. Suddenly, logic prevailed; the purchases rolled around the small store amidst the distress of the sorry father, who made a huge effort to ensure that his daughter did not suffer the same fate. Without thinking twice, Antony put his own purchases aside and quickly went around the store, retrieving what had fallen, which had conveniently landed in every corner of the small store. After the tense moment, and with most things recovered, the situation turned into a pleasant conversation between

the young executive and the mature father, who received Antony's business card *"in case he ever needed to send any packages."* Both went their separate ways. Two days later, Antony received a call at his office. That father turned out to be the director of a huge hotel group, who was visiting the development of a six-star hotel in the area, and who, grateful for the help received, scheduled a meeting to coordinate all the logistics of moving anything needed for the hotel, as everything had to be moved from other areas or countries since it is a small coastal zone. From curtains, furniture, kitchen equipment, and everything else, needed to be moved to the hotel under construction. Antony got tired in the next 24 months of receiving recognitions, bonuses, and awards from that day on for his sales achievements. Why that anonymous customer decided to contract such a contract? Antony asked in one of his meetings, and the answer he received was: *"because you showed me respect without knowing me, that made me trust you."* Respect and trust are values that are born individually, but one is the result of the other. Thanks to respect, we begin to generate relationships. And established these, we begin to believe and feel secure. This is trust. Respect generates trust and trust generates long-term relationships. Today we are witnessing a reality in personal and professional environments with a deep crisis of values. And we forget that, just as primary colors are the basis of the beautiful spectrum of colors that surrounds us, values were, are, and will be the pillars of more, better, and more solid relationships between human beings. Back to the roots! When we instill respect in our families and companies, especially in the new generations, we are planting the seed of people who will know how to be reliable and therefore successful. If in our personal environment there is an atmosphere of responsibility, within which each member knows their rights, and they...

If in our personal environment there is an atmosphere of responsibility, in which each member knows their rights and their duties, we create the ideal environment for trust to flourish and bear fruit. When we trust someone, we assume beyond any doubt that that person will be consistent in their actions and words, uncertainty can be eliminated because there is certainty in predicting their behavior in the most complex situations. In business environments, adding team members who give and receive respect, and therefore become trustworthy, will have a positive impact on the organization's results. Volkswagen - 87 billion in losses -, Enron 638 million in losses, World.com 107 billion in losses, FTX - 32 billion in losses - remind us that even the most reliable and praised companies can collapse in a matter of months or weeks. Why? Because to live values, we must learn to maintain them in our day-to-day lives so that they become part of our lives. It has been shown that 80% of internal frauds are committed by employees at medium and low levels, 20% by executive level employees. However, this 20% is responsible for 80% of the total losses, that is, the smaller number of frauds carried out by the executive level has an economic impact four times higher than that carried out by the other levels in the organization. Aren't those executive positions in which we usually have the most trust? In 1962, the Nobel Prize in Economics Milton Friedman, in his book *"Capitalism and Freedom"*, stated that companies should not have any social responsibility, and that they should only be accountable to their shareholders. What an impulse he gave to many of that generation of managers! These ideas gave legitimacy to business management based on disrespect for colleagues, suppliers and customers, the results we saw there in the great crisis of 2008. That collapse forced us to rethink the way things are done, and today we advocate for leadership based on respect for all components of the ecosystem. Mahatma Gandhi said: *"Keep your values positive because your values become your destiny."* Trust (which arises from respect) is the basis for decision making and action of individuals and groups within a society or company. They promote positive action for the improvement of each person and coexistence. The recipe for respect is a little simpler than it seems: it has three basic ingredients: tolerance, consideration, and recognition. And it must be applied to collaborators, suppliers and customers, the ecosystem does not allow half measures, if you apply it partially you are guaranteed failure.

We're going a little deeper. Respect is related to social intelligence and is linked to emotional intelligence. It requires being aware of the motivations and feelings of others, observing what makes us different with respect and acting accordingly. This in turn helps us to better understand and guide our behavior.

Many times, you have probably seen someone demand respect, or you have demanded respect yourself. It is important to understand that respect is not something that is demanded. It is only through our respect that we can earn the respect of others (also knowing that this does not guarantee it).

And how do we convert that respect into trust?
- When respect has been established as a way of interacting with others, it is easier to trust them.
- When trust is established, it is easier to work together to achieve common goals.
- Trust allows for open communication, which leads to better understanding and problem solving.

- Trust creates a positive environment where people are motivated to do their best.
- Trust allows for risk-taking, which is necessary for innovation and growth.
- In summary, respect and trust are closely related, and they are essential for a positive and productive environment in personal and professional settings. Building respect through tolerance, consideration, and recognition will naturally lead to trust,

When you establish respect as a way of interacting with your peers, you are creating a safe emotional space. In that environment, people will feel comfortable giving their opinions, and that's where trust begins to be built! Clear rules! Play fair. In any relationship, there will be differences of opinion, how you handle them will determine whether you strengthen or destroy trust. An old saying goes, *"Better an bitter truth than a sweet lie."* Be brutally honest without exception. No one will respect someone who usually lies to achieve their goals. Few things have as positive an impact on people as the certainty of feeling trusted. Phrases like *"I believe in you and I'm with you, I'm on your side, and you have my support"* strengthen the bond between people, feed the survival instinct and the limbic system, generate commitment and obligate reciprocity. Lastly, be consistent in your actions in any situation, small concessions in your actions break the trust someone may have in you. It is a basic survival skill to have the respect and support of our loved ones, that environment of psychological well-being and mental health fills us with oxytocin, the hormone of love, happiness, and ultimately social connectivity. Lastly, we should not misinterpret and assume that needing the trust of others makes us dependent on external affirmation, quite the opposite! It is a basic pillar of human relationships, the child needs it from their parents in their growth and development of autonomy, self-esteem and security, couples need it to solidify their relationship, companies need it to achieve their goals. The causality consists in that it has a universal character, and the law of causality is the universal law of the material world. This means that there is no single phenomenon that is not subordinate to this law, The law of causality knows no exceptions. If something has happened, look for the cause: without it, nothing arises in the world. Do you want causality in companies? If you nurture the value of respect, you will see the value of trust in its fullness.

# Orsi

**Founder/CEO**
*FIRST CLASS INVESTMENTS*

## Building a Great Team

It took me years to realize that I could not do everything myself and that I needed to build a great team. It took trust and a bit of exhaustion in order to relinquish full control. I did not wake up one day a team builder. I gave up management control in stages. I learned slowly the power of culture and team building. The rewards were many fold.

I had three stages of my business career. In the first stage, I spent twelve years in the public schools including ten years in administration. In the second stage, I became a business owner when I opened my first preschool. As that business grew, I had other owners join me. First my wife at the time and later a former school district colleague joined me in running the company. In seventeen years, we built that company to thirteen locations and earned a place in the Top 50 companies in the industry. The third stage of my career was buying a preschool company out of bankruptcy court and building that business with a friend from the Young Presidents Organization. We started with sixteen locations of which we owned none of the real estate and grew to thirty one locations, of which we owned twenty two of the school properties. This company ended up as the thirteenth biggest child care company in the country.

When I opened my first preschool, I knew a great deal about educating young children and running a school but I knew nothing about running a business. I visited other preschools and saw them through the eyes of an educator. Most of these schools had very weak educational programs. I spent two years editing and writing a detailed early education curriculum of two thousand lessons which were used in my schools for thirty years.

In the eighties, there was great growth in the preschool industry, as women became more engaged in the workforce. When I had two schools, I could do everything myself: manage the managers, be a face to the public, deal with licensing, market the schools and supervise instruction. It was tiring but it could be done.

In the late eighties, I had an opportunity to buy several schools from a company that expanded too fast and ran out of money. I bought their four newest and most cash negative schools and two schools under construction. A former colleague from the public schools bought into our venture and joined me. I now had a competent educator and manager as my partner to share the load. Even though I completely trusted her, I had a hard time letting go.

After about six months of underutilizing my partner and over extending myself, I knew that I needed to change things. I then started a long journey of building a strong team. In stages, I continued to see the value of the organizational strength that comes from building a strong team.

First, we invested in a Regional Manager. Then we divided our ten schools between my partner and the new Regional Manager. Second, we began regular staff meetings with the site managers. The site managers that we inherited with our business purchase, did not share our values. The next thing that we did was to develop a formal management training program to bring our own people up through the ranks. This involved extra expense to pull potential managers out of their classroom and train them with our best site managers. Virtually all managers and workers in the child care industry are women and we gave them a chance to advance. It was a great investment in people.

Next we opened our books to the managers. Every manager got a simple report of her weekly child count and her labor costs. Each month she got her school's financial report. We started giving bonuses to our managers based on their efficient use of labor. We found that this made our schools more profitable.

Additionally, we started to pay bonuses to our managers on enrollment growth and school profit. It is much easier to run a school at about 2/3 full. It is much less work but much less profitable. After all the fixed costs are satisfied, a preschool really starts to make money. Sharing that profit and rewarding the hard work that it takes to fill the schools, made our company much more successful. Now every manager had the financial information for her operation and every manager could share in the prosperity of their school.

The next big step was the evolution and clarification in our management meeting rules. Our Golden Rule was that the best idea wins not the idea from the most senior person speaking. Everyone was encouraged to defend their proposals and listen to others. Our debates became spirited but respectful and we discussed until a consensus was reached. It was not a complete democracy because I still reserved the right to decide what was the *"best idea."* However, that option was very rarely utilized.

As our team strength built, my role changed. I focused on real estate, marketing and government relations. My partner who was now president, ran the management meetings and eventually, I only came to the Management Meetings when requested.

In the late 1990s my partners and I sold that company. The acquiring company undid all of our management, training and compensation programs. They cut out all our performance bonuses, management training programs and management meeting rules. Within two years the profit margin was down to 40% of what we produced. This experience reinforced my desire to build even better team management, if I got another chance.

After I sold my preschool company, I went looking with a friend for business to buy. I was not looking for a preschool company, but one found me.

Another of my friend was in the turnaround business and he was hired by a cradle to grave education conglomerate to stave off bankruptcy. When he started, he called me six to eight times a day asking questions. Over the ensuing months, the calls dwindled to two or three per week. Three weeks later, he called and told me that the company had filed for bankruptcy. He told me that the preschool business, Sunrise Preschools, was the only profitable part of the company and I should buy it.

Every big childcare company in the country was looking at Sunrise. It took me two months of daily calls to the court appointed administrator to get in line. Sunrise had oversized inefficient schools with tons of deferred maintenance but it also had a highly recognized name and top quality senior management. It took persistence and excellent work by my partner to secure the purchase in the bankruptcy court.

My partner is a certified accountant and an experienced CEO, but he did not know the preschool business. We divided responsibilities. Among other great accomplishments, he developed the best and fastest financial reporting system in the industry. We both realized the great leadership and culture building acumen of the existing operations manager. We soon made her President.

The strength of the President and armed with timely financial measurement tools, we were in a position to empower and develop a great management team.

Sunrise had been drained of capital by the prior owners. The positive cash flow was taken to fund other failing company enterprises. There was deferred maintenance on the schools, no supplies, or instructional materials.

On the first day that we owned the schools, I sent a letter to every employee saying that we would live by three rules: We would 1. Invest whatever was necessary to build profitable enrollment, 2. Waste nothing, 3. Share the fruit of our labors.

We set up separate monthly meeting of directors and of assistant directors. These site managers developed lists of material and supply needs and as well as deferred maintenance at their school.

The Operations and Regional Managers prioritized the needs and we worked together to fulfill these needs. These managers then accessed the needs of their staff mangers and the Team set up monthly training for these site leaders. Preschool are open twelve hours per day and the site managers wanted better help running their schools, particularly in the hours that they were not on site. The Management team developed the Director in Training Program to train the captains and the lieutenants of the school site. This was so successful that the hiring of all of our managers was coming from within our ranks. Next the Management Team developed the Leadership in Training Program for the sergeants and corporals of school site management. Both of these programs elevated our people and our staff saw clear paths to advancement.

We did invest in growing profitable enrollment. We acquired eight schools from a competitor and improved their property and their operation. We also build twenty beautiful new schools and moved existing operations out of 30 or 40 year old buildings.

In order for our regional managers and school site managers to make meaningful decisions and to effectively operate their school, they needed information normally reserved for senior manager and they needed it quickly. My partner developed and continually refined a financial reporting system that was user friendly for site managers. By 10:00 AM on Monday, every manager had the revenue and cost by age level for the prior week. They got these numbers for infants, toddlers, three year olds, four year olds and school age. This allowed them to know very quickly what problems to fix and what opportunities to grasp. The director received the same information for every school. They knew how they were doing relative to ever other manager and who to ask for advice.

To fulfill the third element of our management creed, we rewarded performance. Regional Managers were reward on the performance of their school and about 30% to 35% of their total compensation came from bonus. School site Directors and Assistant Directors made bonus on enrollment growth, labor control and bottom line and bonus was 20% to 30% of their total compensation. Our base pay for site managers was below market but actual compensation was above market. We never lost a manager to a competitor.

The Senior Management Team was made up of the two owners, the President and the VP of Finance. Our group rules were the same as the Management Team rules: the best idea wins. Our decision making standards remained the same: invest in profitable growth, waste nothing and share the benefits. These two Management Teams managed an operation of 5,000 children and 600 employees.

My partner and I knew that we were not perfect and we did not know everything. Empowering people, giving them the training to grow and the resources to succeed set the stage for success. We gave our management teams the responsibility to solve problems and aligned their rewards with the company's success. A supportive culture, transparency and collaboration built great team spirit and an effective and successful company.

# Soto Sepúlveda

**CEO**

*FOUNDERS ENTERPRISES INC./ TRANSPORTES
SOTO E HIJOS*

## I am not a Perfect Leader, but a Leader with Team Vision

*"To be a leader, you must first have the courage to admit your mistakes, choose to learn from them, and have the maturity to correct them."*

In this article, I would like to share how I have learned to overcome hardship and created a company that has a life of its own, which will survive, with or without me, for many years to come. I am, and it is, still a work in progress, but I firmly believe that to achieve this goal, my primary function within the company is to be a transformational leader and promoter of change. I will stress during my article how important it is for a leader to learn how to communicate and motivate our team members to allow them to become *"the innovators"* and thereby set a culture of a company that evolves independently of its owner.

To give you a bit of background, I think it is important to share with you that this has been a long journey that started with my father buying and restoring a burnt-out truck that my family restored. You might ask why a burnt-out truck. Well, because that was the only truck on the lot we could afford. There were no frills, bells, or whistles but a means to start a trucking business.

LEADERSHIP

We have come a long way since then. Today we have hundreds of trucks and three logistics terminals. Our operations span from the USA well into Mexico. Although we are growing furiously and work in many different sectors, our most precious cargo will always be our drivers.

## What it takes

Transformational leadership is all about helping our team members on every single level of the organization realize that they are the leaders of tomorrow. I have seen that this transforms their level of commitment because they are part of what we are doing, not a means to what the organization wants to achieve. This, in turn, generates two things; for one, in a low practical way, a much better economic situation for them and their family, but also an increase in the welfare of their communities far beyond what they might be making in our company.

We all have seen companies transform their business models out of need; when they have encountered challenges, some do it successfully others fail. We have all seen the example of Kodak. Time will tell what ultimately happens to this company that changed late and did not take advantage of its privileged position in the market. I believe in a type of leadership that transforms the organization before it is needed through its team members.

One might call it qualities or abilities that the company's leader should have to initiate this transformation from within the company and for it to become part of the team-spirit character of the company. I feel the most important are:

**Enthusiasm:** The noun originates back to Ancient Greece *"enthousiasmos"* and comes from the combination of three words *"en"* (in), *"theós"* (god), and *"ousía"* (essence), meaning *"inspired by god's essence."* It was originally used in a derogatory sense to describe excessive religious zeal. Today both the religious and derogatory connotations are gone from enthusiasm, but the zeal has survived.

To me, enthusiasm springs up when the person passionately discovers his reason for being. I am fortunate to have seen it truly happen a few times. The result is that it makes the bearer of this *"enthusiasm"* capable of leaving a legacy that transcends generations.

> *"Be as enthusiastic about the success of others as you are about your own"*

**Empowerment:** To achieve a transformational company, team members need to be strengthened. One needs to give everyone in the company the confidence, autonomy, tools, and guidance for them to trust that they can make decisions and solve problems by themselves. The transformational leader empowers his colleagues to work for the success of the whole team, not just his/her own. This is an incredible enabler for each individual to reach their full potential, understand their purpose, and give themselves the opportunities to excel. As a team, the organization becomes extraordinary by everyone contributing to a common cause.

*It is placing trust in people capable of*
*generating the well-being of others.*

Sustainability: One needs to safeguard the current needs of the organization without compromising the needs of future generations within a company. It might seem simple, but I have found that the longest organizations typically think it is reaching the objectives of the next quarter but that the future, the real future, which is the next generation, is just an uncomfortable afterthought. By thinking *"real"* future, is the only way to achieve a *"real"* sustainable well-being for all.

*"The success of sustainable leadership is not measured by today's results. But for the ability to generate a chain of conscious and genuine leaders who are constantly committed to building a sustainable future."*

Vision: The leader must be aware of all aspects of the business, such as finances, technology, attitudes, people behaviors, and organizational culture. He is the Captain of the ship, but a transformational ship is a strange ship. It is really everyone around him who make the ship sail; he is just around to remind everyone that they need to work together to be on the best course and adapt faster than the competition.

Organizational transformation, creativity, and innovation are intimately linked and, in turn, are focused on proposing new ideas that can face a future that does not yet exist. This is where vulnerability comes in. Although vulnerable, the transformational organization needs to find the courage to face uncertainty by taking risks that facilitate innovation in a sometimes adverse political, economic, or social environment. Yes, to innovate, it is necessary to be brave to face uncertainty and take the risks that it entails.

> *"Without vulnerability there is no innovation,*
> *because only he who sees the invisible, can achieve*
> *the impossible.."*

Integrity: The person creating a transformational organization needs to be true to his life's purpose as well as that of his company. These cannot differ significantly and ideally not differ one bit. When they are aligned, it inspires people and positively impacts both the organization and the community. Only an organization led by a leader who is true to himself will be generous enough, will dedicate his time, can truly empower his colleagues them trust them with authority to achieve extraordinary results.

> *"Integrity is doing the right thing, even if no one is watching."*

As you can see, the challenges are great, and they are many. It is not easy for all these qualities to exist in a single person, so a leader must surround oneself with an intelligent team with different skills capable of solving adverse situations that help complement each other. In addition, to strengthen your work as a leader, it is crucial to understand the word *"Humble."* It is necessary to be honest with yourself and thus be able to identify your areas of opportunity, as well as have the ability to listen to others and trust points of view that become different from your own.

An effective tool that can help put these characteristics into practice is strategic planning in the company of your collaborators. One of the many functions that this tool has is that you will be able to identify your own strengths and areas of opportunity at the individual level as a leader and at the organizational level. That is why humility plays a very important role in accepting comments for the common good of Society.

Within my personal and professional experience, I have been fortunate to live through some difficult stages in my life that have shaped me to become the person I am today. To name a few, I would like to mention the difficult loss of my mother in my adolescence, very early on, having the responsibility of growing the family business, creating the structure it required to become a noteworthy company, suffering my father's illness and departure, becoming executor of his inheritance, restructuring the company's shareholding, reengineering the conglomerate of companies we had become, encouraging the culture change of a transformational organization, professionalizing the companies and lately being vigilant of the generational transition I am working on.

Given the experience of all these experiences mentioned above, I would like to recommend the following tips that have been of great support to me and that I consider can also be helpful:

1.  Reach out to the right people who have the experience to share with you to develop you and your team.

2.  Get involved in subjects that generate value and are aligned with what you seek.

3.  Meet people who have businesses that are different from yours and try to figure out how they overcame challenges.

4.  Create a council within your company and invite your colleagues to participate. When you do this, let there be people from all levels within the organization.

5.  Constantly learn about topics that help you envision the future as an agent of change.

6.  Finally, look for consultants and advisors in the areas in which you feel your organization requires support.

One of the biggest challenges I have faced in my career as a leader and as a General Manager of the Group has been the following:

1.  Delegate: Letting go of the reins and putting them in the hands of *"strangers"* is a difficult decision. However, with the passing of time, you will realize that there are people more capable than you.

2.  Gender Transition: In this era where there can be up to four generations working together, empathy and compassion are essential. Learning to work with people's changing expectations within quickly evolving generational gaps has been challenging for me.

3.  Transcendence: Without a doubt, the most cherished dream of someone like me is that the company exists for many generations to come. The only answer I can find is to create a culture of continuous autonomous transformation.

As you can see, there are many activities and challenges that someone who aims to create a transformational organization faces, especially in times when uncertainty and change are a constant, but without a doubt, these activities and challenges are part of the development and transcendence. It's clear that it's hard work and a long way to go, but to me, it's worth a try.

For your team to see all this development as a positive impact, it is vital to give them an approach in which they obtain a personal benefit as well as self-realization within the business environment. In this way, each of the members will find his raison d'être and contribute favorably to the common good.

Therefore, if this is the way you choose to go, I would recommend that you design a general plan and a few basic guidelines for what you want to achieve. Try to delegate all the activities you have been performing so far, yes, ALL. Your future focus should not be on the present but on visualizing the future.

I'll wrap up my article by saying that I am not perfect, but I try to be a good leader. What I do have is a strong will and the firm conviction to lead my company to a place that creates welfare for all my colleagues, their families and for our society. I know that I have an incredible team, that we complement each other, and that thanks to them, our company will be here tomorrow and for many generations to come. For the same reason, my pledge to God is the same as I have for my company: *"Serve to help, Learn to teach"*... So be it...

*"Never Let success come to the
head and failure to the head heart."*

Someone once asked me what I would like to be reborn as, and I answered: *"A truck driver."*

# Ventura García Flores

**President**
*GRUPO GARFLO*

*"I am not perfect and that is precisely why I have a great team" - The Importance of Collaborative Leadership in the Business World*

Collaboration and teamwork have always been essential components of success in the business world. A great leader not only acknowledges their own shortcomings, but also values and leverages the strengths of their team members to achieve common goals. It is said that a great leader does not need to be perfect, but rather needs to be able to lead and inspire their team to perform at their best. In this article, we will discuss the importance of collaborative leadership in the business world and how it can lead to success.

Collaborative leadership is a type of leadership that values input from team members, encourages open communication, and promotes a culture of collaboration. It involves working with others to achieve common goals by utilizing the strengths and talents of each individual. Collaborative leadership is particularly important in today's business environment, where diverse perspectives and inclusive practices are valued and seen as a key driver of success.

LEADERSHIP

## The Importance of Humility in Collaborative Leadership

Humility is a crucial aspect of collaborative leadership. Leaders who are humble are willing to admit their mistakes, recognize their limitations, and learn from feedback. This approach allows for open communication and a collaborative environment where everyone's ideas are considered.

In contrast, leaders who lack humility can be seen as unapproachable, uninterested in feedback, and rigid in their ideas. This can lead to a lack of trust and respect from team members, hindering collaboration and progress.

A humble leader not only acknowledges their own limitations, but also values the strengths of their team members. They recognize the importance of diverse perspectives and opinions, and encourage open communication and feedback. By being humble, leaders can create a culture of collaboration where team members are comfortable sharing their ideas and working together to achieve common goals.

## Fostering a Culture of Collaboration

Creating a culture of collaboration requires intentional efforts by leaders to value the input of team members, promote open communication, and foster an environment of mutual respect and trust. Leaders who prioritize collaboration over competition are more likely to create a positive work environment where team members are motivated to contribute their best efforts.

To foster a culture of collaboration, leaders can implement various strategies such as team-building exercises, regular feedback sessions, and collaborative decision-making processes. Additionally, leaders can encourage cross-functional collaboration by breaking down silos and promoting communication between departments.

Effective communication is also key to fostering a culture of collaboration. Leaders should establish clear communication channels and encourage team members to share their ideas and concerns openly. They should also provide regular feedback and recognition to encourage continued collaboration and team cohesion.

## Benefits of Collaborative Leadership

Collaborative leadership has several benefits for both leaders and team members. One of the main benefits is increased innovation and creativity. By bringing together diverse perspectives and ideas, team members are more likely to develop innovative solutions to complex problems.

Collaborative leadership also leads to improved decision-making. When leaders and team members collaborate on decisions, they are able to make more informed and well-rounded choices. This also leads to greater buy-in and commitment from team members, as they feel valued and heard in the decision-making process.

Finally, collaborative leadership creates a positive work environment where team members feel respected and supported. This leads to increased job satisfaction and motivation, which can result in higher productivity and overall success for the business.

Collaborative leadership requires a shift in mindset and a willingness to let go of traditional leadership approaches that prioritize hierarchy and control. It is a leadership style that values the strengths and skills of team members, and encourages them to work together to achieve common goals. Collaborative leaders prioritize relationships over tasks, and are able to inspire and motivate their teams to perform at their best.

One of the keys to successful collaborative leadership is creating a culture of trust and open communication. Leaders who prioritize collaboration create an environment where team members feel comfortable sharing their ideas and concerns openly. This leads to greater creativity and innovation, as team members are able to build on each other's ideas and work together to find solutions to complex problems. Collaborative leadership also leads to increased accountability, as team members feel a sense of ownership over their work and are motivated to perform at their best.

In addition to creating a culture of trust and open communication, collaborative leaders also need to be skilled at building relationships and working with diverse teams. This requires strong emotional intelligence and the ability to understand and respond to the needs of team members. Collaborative leaders need to be able to listen actively, provide feedback, and encourage team members to share their thoughts and ideas.

Collaborative leadership also requires a willingness to take risks and embrace change. Leaders who are able to adapt to changing circumstances and remain flexible in their approach are more likely to succeed in a collaborative environment. This requires a willingness to let go of control and allow team members to take ownership of their work.

Another important aspect of collaborative leadership is the ability to celebrate successes and learn from failures. Leaders who prioritize collaboration recognize that success is a team effort, and are quick to acknowledge the contributions of team members. They are also able to learn from failures and use them as opportunities for growth and improvement.

In conclusion, the importance of collaborative leadership in the business world cannot be overstated. By being humble, fostering a culture of collaboration, and promoting effective communication, leaders can create an environment where team members are motivated to contribute their best efforts. The benefits of collaborative leadership are numerous and include increased innovation and creativity, improved decision-making, and a positive work environment.

As famous philosopher Aristotle once said, *"the whole is greater than the sum of its parts."* This sentiment is particularly relevant to collaborative leadership, where the strengths and talents of each individual team member combine to achieve common goals that are greater than what any one person could accomplish alone. It is through collaboration and teamwork that great things are achieved, as noted by the famous basketball coach Phil Jackson, who said *"the strength of the team is each individual member. The strength of each member is the team."*

Collaborative leadership also requires a willingness to take risks and embrace change, as noted by the famous entrepreneur Richard Branson, who said *"if your actions inspire others to dream more, learn more, do more and become more, you are a leader."* Collaborative leaders inspire their teams to take risks and try new things, creating an environment where innovation and creativity can thrive.

Ultimately, successful leaders recognize that they do not need to be perfect, but rather need to be able to lead and inspire their team to perform at their best. As noted by former President Barack Obama, *"change will not come if we wait for some other person or some other time. We are the ones we've been waiting for. We are the change that we seek."* Collaborative leaders understand that they are not the only ones responsible for achieving success, but rather that success is a team effort.

In conclusion, collaborative leadership is essential for success in the modern business world. By valuing the input and strengths of team members, fostering a culture of trust and open communication, and being willing to take risks and embrace change, leaders can create an environment where everyone is motivated to work together to achieve common goals. As the famous football coach Vince Lombardi once said, *"individual commitment to a group effort - that is what makes a team work, a company work, a society work, a civilization work."* Collaborative leadership is the key to unlocking this commitment and achieving success.

# *Christine*
# M. Wallace

## Vice President Kettering Global
### *KETTERING UNIVERSITY*

*"I can bring home the bacon, fry it up in a pan and never let you forget you're a man..." (1980s ad for Enjoli perfume)*

That perfume ad, popular in the early 1980s was something that all women from my generation grew up hearing and can still remember. It featured a beautiful blonde woman going from business attire to a sexy negligee. Today, those images make me bristle. Growing up in a time when women still had limited opportunities, this advertisement seemed to tease, *"Yes, you can have it all!"* But was having it all reasonable or even something we should have aspired to obtain?

That generation of women grew up to think that we could *"do it all"* and do it all equally well. We got sold a bill of goods. It meant that we ended up trying to climb our professional ladders, be excellent wives and mothers, not to mention always willing lover, make cookies for school events and keep an immaculate house. Many of us ended up exhausted,

feeling like we were always failing and never measuring up to some invisible but palpable standard that was not achievable in the first place. We were often plagued with guilt. Guilt over not spending enough time with our children, not being present enough on the job and not being great partners. On top of all that, we felt very alone in these struggles with little *"sisterhood"* in the way of support from one another. After all, we were all trying to climb the ladder of success to the proverbial *"glass ceiling."* Sometimes that meant climbing over one another.

### How the world has changed, and yet remained the same.

Young men and women today inspire me with how they have written their own script for life and work balance from young fathers who choose raising their children over their careers, and young mothers who take less stressful jobs so they can be more available to their young children. I marvel today at women like my Executive Assistant who works from home three days a week to make it easier to spend time with her toddler daughter. My own daughter who earned her PhD from one of the best Universities in the country and gave birth to my twin grandchildren, managed to write a book and earn tenure, because she had a partner who supported her throughout the process. I see women who make the decision to stay in a job less demanding so they can spend time with aging parents, or more time with their children, or work on community projects. I see women who have designed who they are and who they love by their own rules and not those society has imposed upon them. At the same time, I see stress and mental health issues at an all time high and more and more young people exhausted and burned-out. So maybe things have not changed as much as we hoped.

After a 35-year career that has allowed me many opportunities. I have been lucky enough to learn a few lessons worth passing along. I was a not so rich little girl growing up in the inner city of Detroit who found her way to go to one of the best Universities in the country and buy my dream home on one of the Great Lakes in Michigan. Those were dreams my own mother not got a chance to realize or see her daughter finally capture. The main lesson I have learned is that *"having it all,"* it not what you think it means. My *"all"* is dramatically different from what I anticipated it to be nearly four decades ago. As a good friend once said to me, *"our problem is that you and I wanted to change the world, only we discovered our world was smaller than we thought."*

That is indeed true. I have changed the world, but the world I changed is dramatically smaller than I thought it would be. Yet, from my perspective, my life has been a resounding success! I have had a satisfying and interesting career, lived in some great places, traveled the world, raised two amazing children and have an enduring marriage. I have friends, a spiritual life and many hobbies. As an Online professional working in Higher Education, I have helped thousands of students achieve their academic and career goals by earning their degrees. I have mentored many young people to aspire to dream jobs and during my time as a counselor in private practice, helped many individuals through challenges in their life. I have learned a few things (sometimes not easily) that are worth passing along. Let me offer these items for consideration:

- Remember you can always change your mind. There are very few decisions that cannot be changed. You can start down a path and take a turn at any time.
- Take the time to love and enjoy your life.
- Find a hobby.
- Choose a partner wisely, both of you will change over time and finding someone who appreciates you and can always make you laugh is vital.
- If you choose to have children, understand they did not ask to be born and need to be a priority for at least 18 years. That is best example of commitment I can think of and it means you have to give up some things in your own life because you chose to raise another human being who depends on you for everything.
- Write your goals down every year. I use my birthday as a time to sit down, look at my accomplishments and plan the goals for the next 1, 3, and 5 years. You forget what you accomplished in 365 days. Keep this in a special bound book reserved for your plans. If you have a partner, be sure to do some of this together as a couple and create goals for you to achieve as partners in this life.
- Find a community that supports you and feeds your soul. Whether this is a group of people from your high school or college years, a church, AA group, a knitting group or LGBTQ community. Find a group that you trust and that loves you for who you are and make them an important part of your circle.
- Find a career that brings you satisfaction and that you enjoy. No one enjoys every minute of every day on the job but when you get to the point that you no longer get up with a spring in your step and joy for the day-CHANGE your job or career path.
- Start saving money early. No matter how small, remember to pay yourself first and invest that money, whether it is ten dollars or ten thousand. If you start young that money will compound over time

and it allows you more options at the end of your career.
- Do not waste time on regret, understand that it is our mistakes that truly help us grow.
- Learn to be humble. It takes practice.
- Give others credit.
- Work on listening with as much intensity as you speak.
- Exercise and take care of your body.
- Find a spiritual center in your life.
- Say thank-you, especially to those who do not often hear it.
- Give a hand-up to another person who is trying to find their path.
- Pay attention when others need support and be a source of that support when you can.
- Forgive often-but especially forgive your parents for maybe not being perfect human beings.
- Remember life is short, we have a limited time in this world and you should find joy, maybe not every moment of every day, but let the joy outweigh the bad and negative energy.

These are not only words of wisdom but lessons to strive to bring you balance and harmony in your life. These things have made a difference in my own life and career. Most of these take time, patience, practice and self-forgiveness to find a way not to be *"perfect"* but to make your life a never-ending journey of evolution. Finally, the most important thing to remember is to breathe. Breathe in and take in the world around you, holding your breath will make you miss a chance to smell the flowers that surround us every day.

And as for bringing home the bacon. I no longer eat meat... so bacon is pretty far from my universe.

**Ann**
Ravel
*FORMER CHAIR FEDERAL ELECTION
COMMISSION / CALIFORNIA FAIR POLITICAL
PRACTICES COMMISSION / DEPUTY
ASSISTANT ATTORNEY GENERAL IN THE OBAMA
ADMINISTRATION*

**Juan Carlos**
Lascurain
*LASCURAIN-GROSVENOR
AND GROSVENOR
SQUARE CONSULTING
GROUP*

**Roberto**
Litwak
*FEHER CONSULTING*

**Jennifer "Jaki"**
Johnson
*WELLMISS*

**Salvador H.**
Avila Cobo
*CONSERVELOPMENT INTERNATIONAL
CORPORATION/INTERNOVA INNOVACIÓN Y DESARROLLO*

# 3. Challenges

**Swati**
Valbh-Patel
*PROSPERA HOTELS*

**Ben**
Vaschetti
*MAISON BENJAMIN*

**Liliana**
Remus
*REMUS & ASSOCIATES CONSULTANTS*

**Espree**
Devora
*WEARELATECH/
WOMEN IN TECH PODCAST*

# Humble Leadership: Battling the Vices of Pride

**Gustav Juul**
Founder & CEO
*AIM GROUP / XO LEADERS*

*"Humility is not thinking less of yourself; it's thinking of yourself less."*
--- C. S. Lewis

When we think of the great qualities of leaders, the first things that come to mind are traits like charisma, bravado, and vision. Most people wouldn't immediately associate humility with leadership, but they should. To many, an ideal leader looks more like a superhero – strong and overflowing with confidence. But in my opinion, humility holds a not-so-silent power.

We have more than 50-year experience proving that humble leaders have more influence, they attract better people, their teams genuinely trust them, are therefore more loyal to them, and they earn more respect than those who rely upon ego and power.

Demonstrating humility speaks to the higher purpose of accountability within business and community. As such, it does not rob you of power but enhances your authority as a leader. These are the kinds of leaders that people will jump off a cliff for.

Still, it sure seems like humility is in short supply these days. I feel that the world has become a narcissist's paradise and that social media only serves to fan the flames.

As a young regional director, humility was not one of my core leadership traits. Along with having that word written on my business card, I figured I'd better have all the answers or at least act as if I did. Like many first-time executives, I confused humility with a lack of confidence and, therefore, chalked it up as a weakness, and I certainly didn't want to be seen as a weak *"leader."* I had arrived, arrived earlier than any of my friends, and I planned to stay there.

Just like I did at the beginning of my career, many confused being humble with other attributes such as modesty, shyness, or submissiveness. We often see humility as a trait that deflects praise from oneself and attributes it to others, but this is not accurate, in my opinion. Humility is an internally focused trait, and modesty, shyness, and submissiveness are externally focused. An internally focused leader, a humble leader truly believes that it is the work of the team, with its strengths and weaknesses, that achieves success, together. A humble leader will not shift authority, accountability, and responsibility but will empower the team with greater capacity without his or her ego getting in the way. Having a humble demeanor provides perspective, judgment, and an internal appreciation that things are bigger than oneself, so that the team can draw on the power of being valued.

In contrast, an externally focused leader will think he or she is the one responsible for the successful outcome but will redirect the praise to acknowledge others.

I have dedicated the last few years of my life to implementing Organizational Transformation by focusing on the value each individual has in an organization and creating a structure through which implementing change becomes second nature.

Is there a benefit to this, you might ask. Well, we have helped transform companies from a few million-dollar businesses to several billion-dollar businesses in a few years without the owners losing control. That means organic growth, people. Billions might not be what you are looking for, but it sure helps to say it out loud for people to start listening.

The best leaders have a realistic appreciation of their strengths and weaknesses. They are secure in knowing that they don't know everything, and they have no problem asking for help, learning from others, and, when they've made a mistake, they accept themselves for being imperfect. In the real world, CEOs don't have all the answers. What they should have is a system through which the right questions are asked and where implementation of the decision taken, whatever it is, is done flawlessly.

Only this degree of confidence and open-mindedness calls out the best in teams. They become participative and engaged and start taking responsibility on a completely different level. It levels the playing field for everyone you lead and nurtures a hunger for knowledge and transformation, thereby driving a culture of learning and ultimately being able to change and adapt to new opportunities faster than the competition. For me, such confidence is inextricably linked to curiosity and especially a mindset receptive to discovery.

So, how can we become more humble in our work and personal lives? Well, it sure didn't come naturally to me. Actually, I am still working on it a little every day. So for those who aren't blessed with being born humble, take me as your example. The good news is that humility is a skill that you can learn. So where to start?

Know yourself and seek self-improvement - Most who have read my articles know that I worked with the US Navy and Marines during the first large part of my career. In my experience, few organizations have as much experience in bringing out leadership behaviors and traits in young people. Their 11 Leadership Principles are full of good advice, regardless of whether the context is the government, a non-profit, or any part of the private sector. That is also why they make exceptional team members once they leave the service. They are as follows:
- Know yourself and seek self-improvement.
- Be technically and tactically proficient.
- Develop a sense of responsibility among your subordinates.
- Make sound and timely decisions.
- Set an example.
- Know your people and look out for their welfare.
- Keep your people informed.
- Seek responsibility and take responsibility for your actions.
- Ensure assigned tasks are understood, supervised, and accomplished.
- Train your people as a team.
- Employ your team in accordance with its capabilities.

I will not go into all of them, but I think it is noteworthy that the first is one of self-reflection and self-improvement. For me, this principle is fundamental to leadership for three big reasons.

- **Know yourself and seek self-improvement.**

First, if you want others to follow you, you must have a sense of your strengths and your weaknesses. You can then take that as the starting point to build a team around you that complements you. Second, seeking self-improvement is critical because a leader who thinks he or she knows it all is proof of plain and simple stupidity, and the holder of this belief is doomed to learn the truth the hard way. Third, attempting to know yourself and seeking self-improvement requires humility. Both parts of this principle demand that you're honest with yourself and that you open yourself up to the possibility that you don't have it all figured out yet.

Listen, like really listen. I think everyone, at one time or another, has caught themselves politely waiting for just the shortest gap in the conversation to cut in and deliver their *"golden nuggets."* I think it happens to the best of us. We assume we already know what the person is going to say, so even though the conversation is still ongoing, we tuned-off minutes ago.

There's a difference between listening and hearing. To me, listening is driven by curiosity, and it goes hand-in-hand with humility. When we are tuned into the conversation, we are present to learn, open to dialogue, and exchange ideas.

- **Employ your team in accordance with its capabilities.**

Use your team to the best of its ability. I've found that leaders who lack humility tend to be micro-managers. They're so focused on ensuring everything is done their way that they lose sight of the goal. This inevitably affects the entire organization's results because the employees are not able to perform to the best ability based on their capabilities. Forcing employees to cater to a *"my way or the highway"* leadership style is really the best way for the best people to leave and the worst to stay.

When a leader is humble, this just does not happen. This type of leader is confident in the fact that there is not just one way of doing things. They back off because they accept that they're not always going to be the ones with the answers; this promotes autonomy and accountability.

Just the other day, I was having dinner with one of my clients, and he was thanking me for having given him more time than ever to pursue his hobbies. He had just gotten back from his first family vacation to Europe and had been gone from his office for almost three weeks. He told me that he had doubted me when I had told him that I could help him triple the size of his business in two years, increase his profit by 250% and give him more time for himself. I told him that it had not taken us two years but almost three. He agreed, but then he said that he wasted almost a year by not being fully on board. He said: *"Even after I saw the results your methodology brought my organization, it took everything I had to become humble."* I asked him why he hired me in the first place, and he said: *"I figured that if only a tiny bit of what you said was true, you'd be well worth it. Also, it was that or sell the business. I felt like Gollum from The Lord of the Rings, remember? Stretched"*

- **Develop a sense of responsibility among your subordinates.**

Your team is not a threat to you. Humility breeds selflessness. Leaders like that are able to admire and support others. That's because humble people know their self-worth. They are secure knowing who and what they are, and since they don't need people to feed their egos constantly, they have the time and space to put others' needs in front of their own. Humility and selflessness indicate emotional intelligence, situational awareness, and empathy. Take the time to understand others, their capabilities, their needs, and what you can do to help them become greater.

- **Seek responsibility and take responsibility for your actions.**

Hold yourself accountable. I think I can think of very few things that bother me more than a leader who avoids or shifts the blame to preserve their own image. I was raised to be honest about what had happened when I messed up, and taught to own up to it.

Leadership without accountability is just a contradiction in terms, in my opinion. When the boss shows accountability, it leads to improved performance. It creates an environment of acceptance and inspires critical thinking: it's okay to make mistakes as long as we can address them, identify solutions, and move forward as a team. Leaders should serve as role models by encouraging accountability, starting with themselves.

In my case, I expect my team to make mistakes. Why? Because the only ones that don't make mistakes are the ones who stand perfectly still doing nothing.

Lighten up. If you have been in a leadership position for more than one day, I shouldn't have to tell you that there will be criticism and there will be jokes. Some of it is going to be deserved a lot of it is not. Deal with it and learn to live with it. In my experience, a little humility goes a long way.

Humble people see criticism as a valuable opportunity to improve their skills and address whatever they might have been able to do better. They also know how to take a joke. There is nothing that deflates criticism better than a person smiling and admitting that the situation was silly, funny, or embarrassing.

I won't lie to you; learning to be humble isn't going to be easy. It certainly isn't to me. It takes a great deal of restraint, openness, self-reflection, and emotional fortitude to better yourself as a person. The rewards I have gotten from my efforts are extraordinary. My business is better, and I am a better father and husband than I was before.

# Ann
# Ravel

-Former Chair Federal Election Commission
-California Fair Political Practices Commission
-Deputy Assistant Attorney General in the Obama Administration

Many young people decide what they want to be; how they will make a mark on society; and, what kind of job they aspire to early in their lives, sometimes even before high school. I have known people whose lives were so carefully planned that they have determined exactly what they have to do in order to get them to their goals. I thought that I would be such a person - that I would do what my father had been telling me most of my childhood - that I must make a difference in society. While it is not a bad thing to have a motivation, my experience in many different areas and in extremely different jobs has led me to believe that making precise plans and not experimenting with other experiences can actually stifle our ability to make change.

An example of this is my own high school experience. I became enamored with philosophy when of my teachers, in a public speaking class, used philosophy as a way to provide a topic for our speeches. Because philosophy could be about ethics, Justice, government, and analysis, and other arcane issues, I was certain that I would be a philosopher. When in college at the age of 16, philosophy was my major and I delved deeply into phenomenology, morality and political philosophy. I was firm in my desire to get a PhD in Philosophy.

## CHALLENGES

My father, who was a college professor in the sciences, and had a PhD in Physics and Meteorology, strongly dissuaded me from choosing that route. He said that I would end up teaching at a small college in the middle of the country, and would have to keep writing articles to be promoted. He knew that I would hate that, and encouraged me to go to law school instead. He was right. The legal profession was a great choice because it enabled me to do many different kinds of work in many different arenas- from teaching, to writing, to advocacy, and giving advice and mediating disputes.

My career as a lawyer began in a small law firm, representing ( and giving free legal advice to) clients who were in the trades, including carpenters and bricklayers. But what I found particularly meaningful was the pro bono (free) work that I did for immigrant farm workers who were working picking strawberries, which is back-breaking work, but they were not being paid fairly by the big corporate grower that employed them. I sued the company, and was able to get them to agree to increase the wages of the workers. After the settlement, the workers came to see me, driving a long distance to thank me with a tray of delicious strawberries to thank me for my efforts and to let me know what a difference the settlement had made for their families.

Another case that I handled for free was to against a Shopping Center owner for not allowing a group of high school students to ask people at the shopping center to sign a petition against a United Nations General Assembly Resolution. Although I lost the trial in the lower court, it was appealed to the California Supreme Court and then the US Supreme Court, which found that the private owner of the shopping center could be prohibited from excluding peaceful expressive activity to open areas of the shopping center. This case is now a standard throughout the country allowing  advocates to petition for their issues.

These cases made me realize that what I really wanted to do was precisely what my father instructed - to make a difference in the community and in people's lives. After a year at the law firm, I knew that I didn't want to be in the law to make a lot of money, I wanted to use the law for good, so I left to work in the public sector where I could make change for the community.

While a new lawyer at the County Counsel's office, I agreed to take on many different legal issues and cases in various aspects of the law - from arguing for conservatorships of the mentally ill, labor law issues, gender discrimination cases, and defending the county in medical malpractice cases, and more. Working on many different issues gave me valuable experience, and enabled me to be promoted to supervisor positions. As one of the very few women in the office, it was not easy to be a supervisor of men who had worked there for more years than I had, but I recognized that even challenging and difficult situations gave me important experience in how to respond to aggression and anger of other employees. And, it provided greater access to and insight into my own boss and how he made decisions. Although he was not a good boss, the insights proved helpful for me, by watching his dysfunction, to understand how to treat employees respectfully and to enable them to succeed. It taught me how to be a leader.

And I did become the head of the office. I was able to hire more women and minorities. And, I knew that the job at a government law office should not be just to defend the government in lawsuits against it, as had been the tradition. Because the job of the government is to serve the community, I thought that the lawyers in my office could use the law to help the community thrive. So I started a *"Social Justice Affirmation Litigation"* division, to help those subjected to immigration fraud, to ensure educational rights for children who were in juvenile facilities, to sue those who were defrauding seniors, and to sue companies that were injuring the health of members of the public - tobacco companies, and paint companies which knowingly sold toxic paint which had caused lead paint poisoning in children in mostly low income families. The lead paint case, the first in the country, settled for $305 million so several local governments could remove the paint. Because this was a ground-breaking case, I was asked by the new Obama administration to be the Deputy Assistant Attorney General in the US Justice Department, to oversee Consumer litigation. I also worked on the oil spill in the Gulf of Mexico, financial issues that had been caused by mortgage fraud, compensation for the responders to 9-11, and many other significant matters.

But being in Washington DC, away from my family took a toll, and I felt that I was not accomplishing enough. And, interestingly, as a woman who had previously had many important jobs, I nevertheless did not think that I was good enough. Most of my male colleagues had gone to elite law schools and worked in previous administrations, while I had gone to a public law school, and had little familiarity with the federal system. But when I left, I was told by many employees that I was the best person ever in my job because I cared about the people in the country and how the laws affected them. These comments gave me more confidence in the work that I continued to do.

## CHALLENGES

I was appointed by the Governor of California to be the Chair of the California Fair Political Practices Commission. Though I had worked in government ethics, I had never done campaign finance law. I approached the job as if it was essentially consumer protection to give transparency of political activity to the public. And that transparency is exactly what I fought for during my tenure. We brought the first case in the country to fight millions of dollars of *"dark money"* whose source was unknown when it was given in an election. We identified the people involved before the election so people could know who was trying to buy their vote.

Because of the notoriety of that case, I received a call from the White House asking me to be an Obama nominated Commissioner of the Federal Election Commission. I was unanimously confirmed for this position by the United States Senate, in 2013. I became well known - including for speaking out publicly on tv, in a documentary, and in the press, about the failure of the bipartisan Commission to do its job to regulate and require disclosure of money in politics, because of partisan stalemates.

In 2017, I returned to California to teach at UC Berkeley Law School, to work as a Mediator and Expert witness, and to work on Electoral issues throughout the world. The many experiences in my career have enabled me to continue to work in areas where I can make a difference in the world.

# Salvador

# H. Avila Cobo

CEO
*CONSERVELOPMENT INTERNATIONAL CORPORATION/*
*INTERNOVA INNOVACIÓN Y DESARROLLO, S.A. DE C.V.*

## On Becoming Me: My Personal Quest as a Multicultural Migrant Entrepreneur

### Entrepreneurship today

Being an entrepreneur is cool. Taking risks when venturing through uncharted waters on a business vessel is a statement of bravery, independence, and vision. However, not all entrepreneurs are created equal. Some are driven by external factors, such as the pandemic, the need to stay at home, the ever-changing marketplace, or a fluctuating job market, while others do so just because they feel like it or motivated by an obvious business opportunity. Some others become entrepreneurs because they feel compelled to respond to an inner call. In this last category are the truly altruistic, energized by transcendental values and ideals. The first category, however, includes many others who march to the rhythm of a more cynical motive: ambition. The aspiration for wealth is its powerful engine of creation, adaptation, and evolution.

Over time, technological change has provided huge entrepreneurial venues for creative spirits. The IT revolution opened the doors of entrepreneurship for many future entrepreneurs 50 years ago. More recently, Artificial Intelligence is empowering Information Technology to a degree never seen before, making it possible to use digital platforms to respond to markets in a better-informed way with incredible speed and accuracy, while allowing us to create previously non-existent niches.

However, regardless of how noble the individual motive may be, how complex the market or how sophisticated the business environment and tools at our disposal, it is still possible to identify in all the basic ingredients of entrepreneurship: an unmet need (a market niche), a way of satisfying it (with a product or service), and an individual (the entrepreneur), willing to take risks to make those two, need and solution, connect.

Becoming an entrepreneur also involves taking risks. Making that decision, rather than simply entering the market through more traditional work in an established organization, involves at least the risk of assuming the opportunity cost of the chosen path, among other more significant and obvious costs. The risk increases significantly when the decision to become an entrepreneur is made in a society that is not ours. Such is the plight of migrant entrepreneurs.

## How did I get here?

### A cultural heritage... with 3 different flavors

My family has roots in Mexico, Spain and now the United States. Since I was born in the city of Chihuahua, in the largest state in Mexico, very close to the border with the United States, I grew up quite bicultural. Frequent trips across the border, most often on vacation or to buy clothes, appliances or electronics and other specialized equipment for my father's electromechanical company, made sure my behavior resembled that of many young Americans. At the same time, my Spanish heritage, as the grandson of a Spanish merchant who followed the route of Mexico's mining towns in the first third of the 20th century, also provided me with a valuable contrast on how to do business in a foreign land, as my Spanish grandfather and his brother did in Mexico for more than 40 years.

## Multiculturalism as a business opportunity

The Cambridge Dictionary defines multiculturalism as *"including people who have different customs and beliefs relating to a society, organisation or city"*. Therefore, being an entrepreneur in a multicultural society means serving markets that are unfamiliar to us, often in societies that are not only foreign to us but are far from culturally homogeneous.

Consumption patterns are value-based, and since different cultures embrace and prioritize values in a different way, it is of utmost importance to become familiar with the culture and core values of the individuals in our target market, in order to maximize opportunities for success in serving them, particularly ethnic niches. A recent finding illustrates this point: Hispanics spend nearly 27% more time staring at a screen per day (cell phone, computer, tablet...) than the average U.S. population. Such behavior is attributed to the strong social and family ties they have. That provides valuable opportunities for advertisers. Additionally, it has been shown that Hispanics in LATAM have a much stronger loyalty towards brands that advertise in Spanish. At the same time, using a U.S.-based company that fully understands the cultures of the target countries often provides a competitive advantage over competitors, native or foreign.

## The challenges for an entrepreneurial migrant

### Migration

Contrary to popular belief, net migration from Mexico to the United States was close to zero during the past few decades. Only in recent years have more Mexicans stayed in the United States than returned home. According to data from the Pew Research Center (2022), the net total even declined in years as recently as 2019, when more Mexicans returned home than stayed in the United States. However, that has not been the case with the rest of the Latin American countries, particularly Central American, whose large influx of migrants to the United States is distorting life at the borders, while straining relations between the countries.

With notable exceptions, the United States has often reacted negatively to mass migrations to its territory. Over time, however, such migrations have contributed to enriching American society and culture. Hispanic migration to the United States is no different. A notable example of this cultural marriage of convenience is the predominant presence of Mexican cuisine throughout the United States (including the mixture of iconic rituals such as watching the Superbowl, accompanying it with a quintessential Mexican dish, guacamole, as the appetizer of choice).

## Market entry barriers for immigrants

### Language

The first barrier to market entry, even as a dayworker, and to society for new migrants is language. The deep-seated habit of migrants of taking refuge in ethnic pockets in their own neighborhoods does not help. That slows their ability to climb the social scaffolding toward more knowledge-intensive (and higher-paying) jobs. Very slowly, as they become more culturally familiarized, insecurity begins to subside and they integrate into society. The passage of time and the growth of the Hispanic market are helping. Today, 50% of American college students take Spanish as their second language in school, while 70% of middle and high school students do the same.

But the language barrier isn't limited to simply speaking the language of the adoptive country colloquially. Each sector and economic branch also has its own terminology and mastering it becomes a requirement to successfully participate in the business world. To further complicate matters, during my early years as a consultant outside my home country, I was often faced with the challenge of having to learn the lexicon of other disciplines, in order to succeed in advising companies and governments in different countries. For example, when working on Sustainable Development projects in the Circular Economy, to my surprise, the term Conservation often meant different things to Biologists and Economists, which forced me to learn the idioms and meanings of both disciplines, so that all my audiences got the same ideas.

Babel is ubiquitous in the business world and migrant entrepreneurs are permanently exposed to it in their adopted country and abroad, so it is better to meet the challenge head-on, becoming multicultural, multidisciplinary, and bi or multilingual, as quickly as possible.

### Education

The difference in educational attainment between first-generation migrants and the U.S. population at large is abysmal. According to a report released by the Federal Reserve Bank of St. Louis in 2020, while only 8.3% of the U.S. population lacked a high school diploma, 25.9% of foreign-born people in the United States did. This contributes to complicating access to the U.S. market and economic assimilation (even in regular jobs) of first-generation migrants.

On the other hand, understanding market dynamics takes practice. In that, education and experience play a critical role. For a newcomer to the United States, understanding the behavior of consumers and suppliers in such a complex market can take a lifetime. That's why most first-generation migrants are mostly limited to serving their own when they start their first venture, while their children, educated and raised in the United States, often go much further. Then, there's also the issue of skills. Many migrants end up deploying the skillset they learned in their home countries: manual labor, painting, gardening, pool maintenance, weaving and sewing, doing laundry, childcare, and other low-skilled (and low-paid) jobs.

### Cultural subtleties

Coming from a wealthy multiethnic background, my impression growing up in Mexico was that being bilingual would be enough to be able to thrive doing business in foreign markets. Spanish and English would do the trick for me, given that those two languages are spoken by about a quarter of the world's population, with many more people speaking English as a second language for business. However, when I moved to Stanford University, I realized that clearly wasn't the case. While speaking English helped me communicate with people from many different countries, language was not enough. There were many cultural factors that interfered with the successful communication of people from different cultural backgrounds. That became more evident when I started doing consulting work for the likes of Deloitte or The World Bank around the world. To succeed in conducting business with different nations, in addition to speaking the language, I had to master the cultural subtleties of each society. Cultural immersion was required. To my surprise, that was the case even with cultures that according to my then limited experience as a young professional were almost identical to my Mexican heritage: Guatemalans, Hondurans, Salvadorans, Costa Ricans, Argentinians, Chileans, and Mexicans speak Spanish, but we all have evolved our own ways of doing things, in life and in business. The same is true even in my native Chihuahua, where Indian nations survive, with their own rituals and way of transacting and doing business, based on their own cosmogony. Dealing with them in my youth would prove to be an invaluable asset later in life, allowing me to understand that people need to be approached in ways that are culturally appropriate for them.

## Markets

### Demystifying the market

Markets have layers. In the case of an economy as complex and sophisticated as the United States', there are markets within markets: the migrant market, the Hispanic market, the minorities market, the general American market. And then there are overseas markets. Each with its own level of complexity.

For some analysts, the U.S. market has been taken by surprise. The growing Latin American diaspora to the country has created many opportunities for established businesses as well as for newcomers. At first, the purchasing power of the Hispanic population was only marginal, but as the number of migrants increased, they became a market force, creating a Hispanic market and offering the market a significant amount of purchasing power (with a population of nearly 70 million people today). Hispanics in the United States have an estimated $2.5 trillion in purchasing power a year according to the Pew Research Center.)

This market evolved with the degree of sophistication and skills of the people in it, particularly consumers, in this case migrants and their descendants. At first, through stay-at-home activities, their commercial endeavors primarily served the nostalgic needs of first-generation migrants (food, clothing, souvenirs). They eventually began adding other services, more common in their adopted country, as households became more solvent and had more disposable income to invest. Over time, they created businesses that compete with those of other minorities (laundries, photocopiers, convenience stores). Finally, as their children have gone to school at institutions of higher learning and have been exposed to more knowledge-intensive jobs, Hispanics themselves ventured into more high-tech businesses, including some very successful venture-capital firms. An additional wave of more affluent Hispanic immigrant entrepreneurs over the past 10 years added yet another layer to the market, attracting foreign direct investment to the United States to create businesses capable of competing in the U.S. market and using the U.S. as a platform to serve markets abroad, particularly in their countries of origin.

## Some tools for each market

Fortunately, as in any market, in the battle to succeed as an entrepreneur in a foreign market there are some tools at our disposal, regardless of the nature of the market we serve.

- User-based design
  In the previous paragraphs I dissected the environment surrounding a migrant entrepreneur entering the U.S. market. As in all markets, knowing the customer in depth is essential. What are their needs? And their preferences? In what context will they use what we offer them? What are the most valuable features for them? How does our value proposition best serve its purpose in this market and for these customers? Is it culturally appropriate? Does it support and respect their values? Being thorough in answering these questions would allow us to design better products, services, and experiences.

- Innovation
  Being culturally sensitive can also provide opportunities to differentiate our business proposition. Ethnic niches are particularly valuable for that, given that customers in them are sensitive to very specific values. Once the questions mentioned above have been answered, the search for innovation can begin. What elements of differentiation can give us additional competitive advantages?

- Cross-Cultural Pollination as a source of creativity
  Observation and introspection are two valuable tools for immigrant entrepreneurs. They allow us to not only identify the cultural elements that are relevant to our future clients, but also the cultural subtleties that can and will make a difference for them. It is important to introspect and reflect on how these characteristics affect consumer behavior, to take them into account when designing products and services. We can also enrich our products and services to make them responsive and appropriate to the different cultures present in our current market.

## Establishing borders... in a distinct way

Being an entrepreneur in a foreign country is, paradoxically, also about building walls and establishing solid borders, albeit in a different way. Ours will define the reach of our products and services, helping us identify the scope of the market we serve.

## Developing a CLEAR sense of purpose

Returning to the beginning of this chapter, as we undertake entrepreneuring, we must be able to answer some fundamental questions: Why am I doing this? What do I want to achieve? Is it a question of financial benefitting? Is it too good a window of opportunity to let go? Is it to advance the state of the art in my field of interest? Am I trying to respond to an inner call? Is it clear to me what that call may be, what internal vocation moves me?

Our purpose and true motives will determine how we will conduct ourselves and our business, so we must be able to clearly identify them, and keep them in mind. The rewards will depend on it and on how we answer the fundamental questions listed above. If we resonate with our answers, we will extract joy from our journey as entrepreneurs, and magic will start to happen.

Once we've identified our transcendental motives to become entrepreneurs, it's important to go further and touch our potential customers: are we really creating value for them? Are we truly trying to serve them by providing easier and better solutions, closer to home, and more responsive to their culture and values? Do we want to serve them or just please them?

Everybody can attempt to be an entrepreneur. But becoming a successful one is a different matter, particularly for migrants. Such is the nature of our quest.

Kindly direct your suggestions and comments to shavico@gmail.com

# Litwak

### Chief Operating Officer, International
### *FEHER CONSULTING*

## Challenges: I think this part of my story could inspire others

I remember that day as if it was yesterday, and I doubt I will ever forget it. It was a cold Sunday morning in Maryland, where we lived at the time. Sunday December 12, 1999, to be precise. I was changing our first-born's diaper, and as I often did, I was blowing bubbles (raspberries) in his stomach to make him laugh. That day I felt something that I had not felt in his belly before, there was something hard in his stomach, something that just did not feel right. My wife and I had been told that babies can develop hernias and our first thought was he probably had one.

We had a great relationship with Oscar's pediatrician and my wife gave him a call to let him know that we would be stopping by during the week to see him. He said that it was probably nothing, but since he was going into the office to pick-up some things he needed, that we should swing by. It took him 3 minutes to examine Oscar and immediately asked us to take him to the hospital. We arrived at Children's National Medical Center in Washington, D.C.

Within the hour we had seen 3-4 doctors, Oscar had gone through a series of tests and scans, and when we were finally alone in the exam room catching our breath, the ER resident peaked in and said that the oncologist was on his way to see us. Having had a history of cancer in my family, I immediately understood what that meant. Oscar was diagnosed with bilateral Wilms' tumor, cancer of the kidneys. He was 4 months old.

What followed were 4 years of surgeries, chemotherapy treatments, trips to the hospital, emotional ups and downs, incredibly long days and nights caring for a child with cancer. Oscar passed-away on September 24, 2003, just a few weeks after his 4th birthday. Throughout these four years, as hard and painful as they were, I had no idea I was gaining incredible skills that I would use sometime later in my business life.

While I would emphatically and unequivocally make no comparisons in terms of the gravity and the stakes between taking care of a sick child and any business endeavor, in retrospect, I do find some similarities in how my thinking, attitude and behavior was/has been similar in both situations.

Soon after Oscar's treatments started, my wife and I quickly realized that there were many teams of doctors, nurses, specialist, etc. taking care of him. All incredibly smart, capable, compassionate, and caring, but also all incredibly busy and with different roles and responsibilities. We realized, either consciously or not, that we would have to be a funnel, to centralize information and be facilitators of that information for the doctors and medical teams, Then and there we knew we that, not only would we have to take an active role in our son's treatment, but also, we would have to lead it.

Leadership is often confused with rank, and these two concepts could not be more different one from the other. Rank is a position of authority, and while it certainly has a place and, in some situations and organizations (in the military, for example), is of vital importance, rank on its own is just that, a position within an structure. In contrast, and to quote one of my favorite authors, Simon Sinek, *"Leadership is not about being in charge. Leadership is about caring for those in your charge."*

Neither my wife nor I had any medical training, knowledge, or experience to deal with the disease, so we definitively didn't have the rank to influence, less direct the medical treatment Oscar would receive, but what we had more than anyone in the world, was the relentless drive, desire, and passion to see our son beat cancer, and without even thinking, our most important priority from that moment on became to ensure that every one of Oscar's needs, and every need of those taking care of him was quickly and adequately met.

Years later, I realized that these same principles were equally relevant and important in my professional life as they were when we took care of Oscar.

While there are several, I believe the first experience I transferred over into my professional life, was to understand that things happen. Not everything goes according to plan and situations, environments and circumstances can change in a moment's notice. Having the ability to quickly assess and understand a situation along with having the courage to adapt and pivot to meet the challenge in front of us, is critical. These changes will carry a certain level of risk and that risk will undoubtedly create uneasiness. Understanding that the feeling means that we are doing something proactive to address the issue and we are not letting things just happen will transform the uneasiness into reassurance.

I have been fortunate to have been given the opportunity not only to have an important rank within organizations I have worked with, but also, I was and have been entrusted to lead different teams within those organizations. As a leader, I immediately understood that to meet the desired outcomes my first and foremost responsibility, as it was with Oscar's treatment, was to make sure that the people who are ultimately doing the hard and important work, those *"in the trenches"* were in the best position to be successful. While this discovery was empirical in a way, as I continued my education and experiences in business I ran into the concept of Servant Leadership, a concept that was developed back in the 1970s by Robert K. Greenleaf which validated my approach to leadership.

Another important lesson we quickly learned during Oscar's treatment was that being a leader requires energy, and a lot of it. No matter how bad the day was, how lousy Oscar was feeling or how tired we were, if we did not keep (and often, force ourselves to keep) our levels of energy up, it would permeate and everyone around us would feel it. I remember one of the many trips to the emergency room, it was around 1:30 AM and we were received by the triage nurse, as it regularly happened. You could tell by looking at her face and body language that she was just done! We did not know anything about her, what she was feeling, what problems she may have at home, etc. but what we absolutely knew is that we needed her best that night and at that moment to provide the care Oscar needed. A quick positive conversation and maybe even a joke or two in the first few minutes of our interaction completely changed her demeanor. She perked-up and delivered the care we needed to help Oscar that night. If we had met her *"level of energy"* that night, while we are sure the outcome would have probably been very similar, after all, she was a professional, our level of energy made things easier and go smoother for everyone.

Being a leader in business is very similar. There is a popular saying that states that if you run, your team will walk, if you walk your team will crawl, and this is absolutely true. Having the ability to encourage and inspire your teams with positive energy, will lead to easier, if not better, results. This doesn't mean that you'll need to become a cheerleader within the organization, but it means that the way you conduct yourself, as a leader, sets the tone for everyone around you. It is not always easy to maintain high-levels energy, and it requires effort, but the effort will ultimately pay-off.

After Oscar's passing, my wife and I understood that his life had to mean more than the 4 incredible years we were able to have him with us. Having lived through and understanding some of the challenges and difficulties children going through medical treatment face, we decide to create The Oscar Litwak Foundation, a charitable organization that would dedicate its energy, time, and resources to *"lift the spirits of hospitalized children."* The foundation was created under the premise that while doctors and medical staff are amazing at treating the physical aspect of a child's disease, sometimes the emotional side is neglected. The Oscar Litwak Foundation provides Mobile Playrooms™ which are hospital-grade carts that filled with toys, games, books and arts & craft materials that are there to provide entertainment and a sense of normalcy to hospitalized children. At publication, The Oscar Litwak Foundation has donated more than 200 Mobile Playrooms ™ throughout the U.S. and international locations.

# Juan Carlos
## Lascurain

### CEO/Founder
*LASCURAIN-GROSVENOR AND GROSVENOR SQUARE CONSULTING GROUP*

## Challenges: I think this part of my story could inspire others.

We often find ourselves daydreaming about projects, projects that often could be deemed impossible. Even since I was young I was intrigued by the way sports organizations (especially football and motorsports) were run and would spend hours thinking about how I would get to run a sports organization. From then on, I have been daydreaming and obsessing over my goals. I always felt the need to change the things I thought were wrong and so my journey to change the way the sports industry works, started.

When I was in Highschool I started to get involved in the motorsport business.

I saw how F4, Rally and tourism races were organized and decided to make a project to attract foreign investment into the sport while involving college students in the teams, to also attract more viewers, live

**Grosvenor Square Consulting Group**

L

LASCURAIN-GROSVENOR

Sports Brokerage Firm

spectators and involvement within the community to boost sales. My ideas were rejected by several executives that organized races and some directors of the boards of many colleges, as they told me that I was very young and that my ideas would not work. Despite rejection, I continued pushing on, as this was my dream. From 2014 to 2017, I made approximately 20 pitches to different organizations for them to invest on a racing team that were rejected.

On December 2017 I started my own racing team, we were going to race in the most famous Rally in Latin America. I was a 20-year-old *"entrepreneur"* trying to run a racing team on my own. Back then I realized that in order to succeed in business you need to dedicate a sufficient amount of time to your projects for them to be complete and attractive to potential clients. I also confirmed that you need to be prepared to accept that there will face rejection, but have to continue pursuing your dream.

On February 2018 two of the most important companies in the world, one, a company that sold energy drinks, and the other an oil giant, decided to trust in me, however they had one condition, they would invest in my team only if both brands were involved, if by any chance one of them pulled back from the team, the other one would automatically withdraw their investment as well. I had everything ready, but I had an issue, that year Mexico (where my team was based) was holding presidential elections, and the front runner was an extremist who promised to back down from privatizing the oil industry and that foreign investment would not be welcomed as warmly as it had been welcomed by previous governments. This posed a big threat to our organization, as the oil company that would invest in our racing team was now the target of the candidate leading the polls, and him winning represented a setback for the oil giant and their operations in Mexico would stop, along with our investment deal.

That summer, our worst nightmares came true. The extremist candidate won, the oil company got in touch with us and let us know that they would not be investing in our team, as a result, the other company withdrew their investment as well and I was left with nothing.

I was all alone and with another project that had almost came to fruition, destroyed. That summer, after closing my racing team, I decided that I would not stop and would fulfill my dream to work in sports organizations while also preparing myself by getting several diplomas in sports business and basic economics. After graduating I started to look for opportunities with soccer player agencies and Sports Brokerage firms. I developed several systems that helped teams to make the right decisions when they were building their squads, match predictors, player transfer predictors, and a Moneyball type of system to find the best players for the best price possible, meanwhile I also developed several business models for those club. Many agencies contacted me and offered me to work for them thinking I was way older than I really was.

With them I developed expansion plans to reach markets in South America, the United States and Europe. I also learned how the sports industry in North America works. As my interest started to grow more and more, I started to study different courses on management while expanding my network.

Once the top executives of those agencies saw me in person, they grew worried about my youth and told me that my systems and business models wouldn't work, despite them using my systems to expand their businesses to South America and previously offering me to be a senior partner at their firms.

Again, a door was closed right in my face when I thought I was about to achieve a great feat. That didn't affect me, as the next day I started to better prepare myself and pursue other diplomas to further improve my knowledge in economy and finance.

Once I got my diplomas, and tired of the way the sports industry worked, I decided to start my own sports brokerage firm. Many people doubted I had the experience or the knowledge to start a business on my own, after all I was just 23 years old, but once again I didn't let those comments affect me.

I decided that in order to be successful as an entrepreneur I had to change my daily routine, as I believe that a daily routine that includes reading and constant exercise is essential to grow on a personal level no matter what career path you follow. Some books will help you grow as an entrepreneur as they will expand your vision on the way the business world works and show you the most important skill a successful leader has, and the exercise will make you more disciplined and healthier. Then you should change your mind set by identifying what your main goal is and what the secondary goals are. That main goal, will be for the long term, and the secondary goals must be goals aimed to be completed in a short time frame, that will help you get closer to achieving that main goal. The goals have to be backed by your talent and not just on your desire of having success. As you go on you will face rejection from potential clients, friends, family and employers but no matter what happens you have to keep going. If you do things with passion, dedication and knowledge, the opportunity will come to you, you just have to keep on going.

Once I had adopted this mindset and routine on a daily basis, I started developing a business plan for sports organizations to attract foreign investment. I decided to pitch this model to several companies, sports management firms, sports clubs, and even government officials, always looking to aim for the highest contact I could get. This led me to contact several important businessmen from all around the world, specially investors from the Middle East, Asia and the US who were very interested in this model and soon started to look for investment opportunities in the Caribbean, Central America and Mexico. After creating this network of investors, I contacted several governments in Africa and South East Asia to manage their bids to host the FIFA World Cup and several other sports events, and after that I started to help teams in Europe, Asia and North America with their sports models.

That's when I noticed how far I had gotten since I first started at 17, and that I was now doing the thing I loved most, just as I had planned all those years ago.

As I mentioned before, my first business idea was to have a Racing team. On 2015 I started to contact potential sponsors. It was until 2016 that I got in touch with the manufacturer of the racing cars and I got involved in the industry. And now 5 years later, after several failures, I realized that throughout the journey I had met a lot of wonderful people that showed me how the sports industry worked, how teams were managed and the interaction between politics and sports, I was able to establish my own firm and to finally address the problems with the industry in the region. I could never had gotten this far if it wasn't for not giving up. I never gave up despite the challenge.

Now, after a couple of years of building of running my own company, I have decided to start my own consulting firm, with the mission of helping entrepreneurs in their journeys and to aid them in their fight against self-doubt, lack of support and the many challenges they will face.

As I look back at my journey to get where I am today, I think that the most important things were to prepare myself, always aim for the top, have ambitious goals, have a plan and to always stick to it, despite of the challenges and the rejections.

If you are convinced of your plan, your goals and your dreams, you need to keep going no matter what.

As Winston Churchill once said *"Victory at all costs, victory in spite of all terror, victory however long and hard the road may be; for without victory, there is no survival."*

# Vaschetti

**Co-Founder**
*MAISON BENJAMIN*

## Chapter 1: From zero to three Michelin stars cooking

Earning the third Michelin stars in the restaurants industry is the upmost recognition that you can achieve as a chef, there is nothing above it- period! You are the summit of the mountain and can't climb higher.

The process to receive that award, is far from easy though and the path towards that success can be rough for the chef and his team. It requires an extreme work ethic, discipline, patience and commitment and it's something that is extremely stressful for the chef and restaurant's ownership. Because of the pressure from everything being perfect from the service quality, wine's taste, and obviously the food being cooked at perfection, chefs are constantly under the scrutiny of the Michelin inspectors, who can come and dine *"incognito"* at any time, therefore there is never a dull or relaxed moment in the kitchen....

As a cook employed in restaurant with no Michelin stars there is no pressure, if you work in a one Michelin star restaurant you can experience

# MAISON BENJAMIN

## CHALLENGES

some tension from the head chef but nothing extreme, if you work in a two stars restaurant, things start to get serious and you know there will be some tough times almost on daily basis.... Working in a Three Michelin stars you're In a for a bumpy ride as you know that everything single dish that you will cook and serve, the reputation of the head chef and the restaurant is on the line... Losing a star could be a colossal loss of revenue and reputation for the following years, hence the extreme rudeness, arrogance and nastiness and sometimes all at once from the chef...ultimately it makes your life pretty tough when you work in these type of restaurants.

Most of cooks are eager to learn and improve their cooking skills gradually to make their way by starting to train and work in a non-starred restaurants for a couple of years, then into a one Michelin star for two or three years, eventually in a two Michelin stars restaurant for another couple of years and finally after six, seven, eight years of hard work the door open to the crazy, scary, but exciting world of Michelin three stars... it's an achievement to obtain a position at the top of the game and keeping it, is probably harder as there is a waiting list of talented cooks that wants to work in these restaurants as its definitely a very good reference on their resume...

My story, is quite different...

After graduating from a culinary school in Avignon, France I obtained my first cook job in a restaurant in Paris where I learned the basics, and gained experience in a non-starred restaurant ...After about a year, at age of twenty one I wanted to go and learn English in a one Michelin restaurant in London, UK as it would have been a rather logical career path, from zero to one Michelin star.
I was ready and eager for the challenge .... Until the chef I worked-for in Paris told me *"Ben you are not going to London, but you are instead going to work at the famous Auberge de L'Ill restaurant in the Alsace region "*. I couldn't believe what was happening to me, it was a total chaos in my head!! I was surprised, excited, happy, sad (not to go to London) and stressed because it's not the usual path to go from zero to three Michelin star restaurant but somehow, my chef had believed in me and thought I'd do well there and in my career overall... he secretly arranged everything from me...

Fast forward, couple of months after, her am I, starting my new job in a top ranked Michelin tree stars restaurant, without any previous experience in a one or two starred restaurant ...! What a jump for something that I basically never asked or thought I was capable of...

Couldn't be more challenging than what I was experiencing at the age of twenty-two... the first sixth month were an absolute nightmare... I probably lost 10kg, as I was really stressed and wanted to quit that job almost every day, the working hours were a minimum of fourteen, fifteen hours a day and up to sixteen, seventeen on weekend and holidays...at some point I thought I was going go into depression... I knew I had to improve everything with my cooking, cutting and baking , being faster, more accurate with my knife skills, basically I felt like I was dumb in this three Michelin stars environment....it was almost thirty cooks working simultaneously in this kitchen, pressure was so intense that some of the cooks will get into a fight in a middle of a lunch service, luckily I never got in a fight but I once got kicked-in in my ankles by my superior for not being fast enough dressing the plate.... That's how though it is working in France in a top Michelin star establishment ... BUT after a year of resilience, not giving up, and overcome the struggle (and the struggle was real!) I was finally used to that daily challenge, and was progressively getting more confident, and all my skills improved fast forward, I was now almost at ease working in this environment and I ended up staying another year, in which I improved, learned even more, gained much more confidence and was actually (and as of today still are) grateful to these couple of years spent struggling, and this experience, has opened so many doors in my chef's career afterwards....Time to time, even twenty years later, I still think about my tough time working there and how I was able to overcome the challenge by not giving up...

**Chapter 2: Landing in the USA without speaking any words of English.**

Late January 2002, three weeks after finishing my job at Auberge de L'ill, here I am in the shuttle bus from JFK airport to Manhattan, jetlagged without knowing where I am...I don't understand when the driver announce the next stops, but somehow manage to get off at my midtown's stop on Madison and 51st street with my large suitcase. I remember, It was a cold Friday night with frozen bunks of snow on the sidewalk.

I arrived couple of days before starting my new role at Le Cirque 2000 (now closed) to adjust with jet lag and somehow trying to get a sense how NYC works before I dive into what is going to be another gigantic challenge for me...

That Monday, I showed up for day one of my *"new life"*, I had no idea what to expect, new job, new city, new country, new language, new everything!

**CHALLENGES**

I started working in a team of fifty+ cooks, because of my experience working in France, I had to somehow manage and lead the way...rather rough for someone who doesn't even know which is which between Tuesday & Thursday in English... Though time to be the new sous-chef that can't clearly express himself ...but eventually weeks after weeks with some patience and resilience I was finally able to hold an okay conversation ...Once my English improved, I started to gain respect from others cooks and was able to strive with my culinary skills and became one of the most valuable chef among this large team...

**Chapter 3: Opening a restaurant in NYC**

Fast forward almost 20 years, here I am in 2018, the eve of opening my own restaurant in NYC ... I always thought that owning a restaurant in the big apple, would be fun and smooth ride... but it turned out to be one of the most stressful and exhausting time of my career. You may have all the best ingredients to succeed, that city never gives you any break in all aspects... you are constantly dealing with pressure from food critics, never ending staff issues, food safety compliances etc... and New York City being know for the city that never sleeps, it also applied to me! Due to high cost of rents, you constantly must remain open to make ends meets, and as an owner that means no days off and after two to three months it's starts to affect your mental, and that's when you must remain calm and confident to last and succeed in this very though business....

After almost a year when I was finally able to take some time off as the team was now up to speed with most of standards and procedures of running a restaurant, you have the most unexpected event such as the Covid-19 pandemic that hits you hard in the face and therefore,  for the safety and wellbeing of  patrons and staff included, you have no choice than closing the doors and be sheltered at home...One of the hardest thing for a small business owner, not knowing when you'll be able pay everyone and when  to resume operations...

But after three months of non-activities, staff cuts, we eventually re-opened by doing take-out orders only... We were doing somehow okay business, but somehow not enough to sustain for many more weeks especially when in the summer most of our regular customers leave town for the Hamptons. In July 2020, after two and a half years of we took the tough decision to close the restaurant. This was a little hard to accept it, but it was probably the right move...

Few weeks later, in September 2020, after we handed back the keys to the landlord, my mind was already into another project and even though I could still not believe that a pandemic forced us to abort the mission, I was determined to never look back and only think positive and forward to my next venture...

**Chapter 4: Launching a brand-new business in 2020**

I always had that dream to launch a company that would focus on providing top notch concierge services and truly make the customer's satisfaction a top priority. With my years of experiences working in the most amazing households, luxurious hotels and mega yachts around the world, and despite 2020 wasn't' probably ideal, I had to seize the opportunity of the world being on the reset mode to go for it, and after a couple of months of preparation, Maison Benjamin launched in December...

The first few weeks of operations were very tricky as the world was slowly adapting to post-covid era with its new ways of doing business and living. During the first semester of 2021, we faced challenging times as we had to constantly follow and adapt to the new federal and state laws especially with catering events at reduced capacity, that we were providing...but like everyone else, we were able to comply and make our way through the obstacles with patience and resilience.

As of 2023, Maison Benjamin luxury Travel advisors & personal lifestyle concierge has expended its service globally and proudly affiliated to the Virtuoso network.

Whatever the circumstances have been, I have always been able to adapt to any situations the best I could and patiently overcome the challenges, by putting discipline into my work. This is still the case as of today. I keep believing in everything I do and that's what keep me going – Always.

# Swati
# Valbh-Patel

## Senior Vice President of Development and Design
### *PROSPERA HOTELS*

*I was a motel kid.*

While other seven-year-old girls were taking gymnastic lessons or learning to play soccer, I made beds and cleaned bathrooms at my family's 23-room motel in Orlando, Florida.

While other eleven-year-old girls were starting to babysit and have sleepovers, I refilled soda machines at the motel, wrapped coins, and took them to the bank for deposit.

While other fifteen-year-old girls were socializing with friends or sleeping in, I learned to run the motel's night shift, learned maintenance skills, and learned bookkeeping.

I was handsomely rewarded with a free soda at the end of the shift of cleaning, restocking or leading the night team. I did not receive pay or even an allowance, but I received immeasurable compensation.

For decades, my parents, grandparents, aunts and uncles ran night shifts to rent rooms on disrupted sleep. I watched, and I learned. While I understood my family's sacrifices to come to the United States, I also

PROSPERA
H O T E L S

knew bigger things were ahead for me. My dreams stood on the shoulders of that motel.

I have vivid memories of driving past high rises as a young girl, dreaming of how magical it would be to build such a magnificent structure. I wondered what that process would entail. What would it feel like to walk into a property that I designed, built, and owned? I imagined a euphoric feeling of pride and achievement. Did I have the courage and ability to take on such a challenge?

I had a strong work ethic. I had grit. And I knew from my experiences of working at my family's motel that I found exhilaration in taking on new challenges, learning new things, and accomplishing what others thought was not possible.

But above all, my curiosity and mindset have propelled me to levels beyond what I could have imagined. Curiosity flows through my veins, compelling me to continuously question, understand, apply, and challenge status quo. I learned from my father, a serial entrepreneur, whose ability to be nimble, adaptable, and innovative showed me that challenges and roadblocks often provided great opportunities. I adopted this mindset as my own.

Because of my curiosity and mindset, a series of life experiences and opportunities unfolded before me, teaching me universal lessons that enabled me to achieve my goals, planned and unplanned. By consistently pushing myself out of my comfort zone and believing in my ability to succeed, I reached my goal of designing, building, and owning those high rises that I dreamt about as a girl.

As a child, I had high expectations placed upon me. I shouldered many obligations at a young age. And I experienced successes early on, working at increasing levels of responsibility within my family's business. Getting a formal education was the next step for me to level up from the motel. It was unspoken that education was my ticket to increased opportunity, and I also needed the street cred that comes with the degrees. I was charting my own path, not yet defined and without limit.

I used my education to gain a seat at a different table - providing me with access to a higher bar of conversation, exposure, and networks. The education I received in the classroom opened many doors to me that would have otherwise remained closed.

That said, it my curiosity and mindset - about myself and the world around me - have been the most fundamental ingredients in my success. Digging deep into who I am, what I wished to become, and what would fulfill me has informed my path. I knew that creativity, community, and purpose were requisites in my work.

I learned through introspection that I was the only one who stood in my own way. While coming from an immigrant family, being a woman, and being a South Asian has not always made life easy, I found that my beliefs and attitudes about myself were the sole things that could hold me back. When I got out of my own way, I flourished.

Additionally, I uncovered my inner power and strength - and I felt a true sense of acceptance, purpose, and fulfillment. By understanding what I was capable of, I turned a dream into a reality. Working with my husband, we built the Hyatt Place Anaheim Resort near Disneyland. It was the third hotel in our portfolio, but the first one in which we served in the three roles as developer, general contractor, and operator. My limits were tested by this herculean project - intellectually, mentally, physically, and emotionally. I drew upon my skills from childhood and brought in the lessons I had learned along the way to seamlessly move between the three roles we had taken on and to manage my mindset through setbacks and long, arduous days.

Self-awareness, born of deep curiosity, helped me identify the inflection points in my life. These points came in unusual and unexpected ways, and by knowing myself, I was able to recognize them and make decisions that changed the trajectory of my path.

This self-awareness allows me to be a transformational force for our business and our team. Making a sequence of deliberate choices into my leadership and philanthropic roles with Prospera Hotels, I found work that challenges and fulfills me. And in living my purpose, I am able to move beyond my own needs to engage with what my team members and my communities need. I strive to bring my curiosity and mindset of unlimited possibilities into my work every day to better understand what makes each person on my team tick and thrive, what aspects of the business can be improved, and how I and Prospera can better serve the communities in which our properties reside. My journey of self-discovery has ultimately led to the creation of a powerful corporate culture that is the foundational pillar of our company's growth and success.

## CHALLENGES

Believing in my ability to transform possibility into reality developed my problem-solving abilities. When I hit a roadblock, I take a breath and adjust my view to seeking for the opportunity in the challenge. While sometimes easier said than done, I have found that changing my attitude towards one of opportunity engages my imagination, creativity, and resourcefulness. I feel empowered, and I am energized to push through the next roadblock.

Whatever path you are on, I encourage you to bring a sense of curiosity and a mindset of possibility to your personal and professional lives. The personal development work I have done (and continue to do as I evolve) fueled by the curiosity to deeply understand myself has given me with a sense of clarity in the way I live, work, and in my relationships. Knowing myself was the first step of positive forward movement in determining what I wanted to accomplish - and then doing it. It has also been the key to becoming a leader who is able to help others grow and thrive in their professional lives.

I encourage you to be curious - about other people, opportunities you wouldn't normally consider, and paths that weren't part of your plan. Prototype a new career path. Try something new on for size. Know that, even if the challenge that you take on doesn't work out, you will learn much from the experience.

I urge you to explore with a mindset of possibility. You can learn something from every person you meet. With an open mind, you may walk into unexpected opportunities that thrill you. You may find that your initial plan could use an adjustment. And you may discover that there is so much opportunity ahead that you will have the opportunity to make deliberate decisions about which will be the path of your choosing.

Swati Valbh-Patel is the Senior Vice President of Development and Design for Prospera Hotels, LLC

She oversees the development, design, and architectural aspects of the firm's hotels and lead the development, design, and construction teams. She also leads the pre-opening process for each hotel, serves as the brand liaison with each hotel brand, and is the company's link to the local community, integrating aspects of the community's culture into every project.

Swati oversees Prospera´s charitable work and contributions to organizations including the Ronald McDonald House, Illumination Fundation, MUZEO, Akshay Patra, Sahara, Orangewood Fundation, Project Lighthouse, CASA and Pratham.

She holds a Bachelor's of Science degrees in Business Finance and Criminology from the University of Florida, and her Juris Doctor from the University of Miami.

# Liliana
## Remus

### Founder and General Director
*REMUS & ASSOCIATES CONSULTANTS*

## Fulfillment... is it possible?

Having a fulfilled professional life, leaving a good impact, besides being a full commitment parent and spouse, and a spiritual person should be something achievable for everyone. I have seen too many people sacrifice a part of themselves thinking is impossible to have it all. There is a moment when we think we have to decide one or another, especially being a woman. I faced that moment some years ago...

I was raised in a family that taught me to work hard and take all the opportunities to build my future. I was encouraged to study as much, and as many useful skills as possible. Following that path, I have studied all my life and worked hard since I was 16 years old. I have enjoyed all the different aspects of life. It has been challenging, but it has been possible.

I studied psychologist dreaming of working in a charity foundation, giving therapy, teaching, and doing social research. When I finished college, I look for a job in many associations, but no one hired me. Instead of that, I had a job offer in a company. I accepted thinking it was going to be a short time, but I ended working there for 13 years. Even when my plans were so different, I found that everywhere there are many opportunities to contribute to the world. I worked in the Training and Total Quality

REMUS &
ASSOCIATES
CONSULTANTS

## CHALLENGES

department, so I could organize scholarships, many different kinds of development programs, integrations events, continual improvement processes, recognition programs, and many other interesting things.

I loved my job, so I absorbed myself in it. I became an executive when I was very young. It was exciting, very challenging, and full of learning. There were a lot of great experiences, and also some very difficult ones. I faced a strong mobbing situation, which was hard and painful, but with the time, I became stronger. For several years, I was completely focused on developing and learning, and I deeply enjoyed it. In 2004 I suffered an accident that led me to be in bed for a few months. During those months in bed, I continued working. That time made me realize that working from home was an excellent option and could allow me to fill several roles at the same time.

When I became 35 years old, I was traveling for business around 50% of my time, and if I wanted to keep growing professionally, I had to change my residence. I had a few years married, and I wanted to become a mother. Besides, my father had passed away, so my mom was alone and depressed. My career was very important for me, but also being a present mother, supporting my husband´s career, and taking care of my mother. Keep traveling at that rate and changing my residence did not seem to fit. I looked at many options, but I did not find what I needed, so I decided to create it. I ceased working in a multinational company and started my consultant firm. Stopping having my monthly salary, benefits and the support of a big company was scary, but the vision of the future, and my husband´s support, gave me the strength to do it.

The decision of what type of company to create was clear. An experience that had marked my life in my youth was during camping trips, invited by University Pastoral. The breeze at my face, the music, the sunsets, the challenges, the creativity, and lateral thinking... learning through experience, was my passion. Since I was 17, I became a teacher to small children. From that on, facilitating learning and development had always been part of my life: I gave group therapy and workshops to elderly ladies, I have taught at high school, college, master's degree, and Ph.D. Also with abandoned kids, in remote towns as a missionary, and many others scenarios. All my professional life has been about education and development, and I truly believe that is the best way I can contribute to the world. So, starting a company of experiential learning, boosting the well-being, the effectiveness, and the success of people and organizations, was the thing to do.

So finally, in December 2006, Remus & Associates Consultants was born since the beginning, very important companies had trusted in us, as Continental Corporation, HP, Intel, Siemens, etc. As I had already discovered before, I was successful working from home whenever I was not in front of a group. In the beginning, I was executing a big percentage of the processes, so I kept traveling as before. Eventually, my dream of becoming a mother came true. So I decided I wanted to be most of the time with my baby. I kept working very hard, designing, creating, organizing, but I decreased the programs I delivered personally, by inviting consultants that I have already worked with before. Going backstage to conduct the orchestra was an excellent decision; it not only allowed me to be a fully present mother and enjoy all the development of my baby, but it was also great for my company. That year, it grew in a very interesting way. I kept that path, and in few years, we were already 50 consultants, working with more than 300 companies, in all of Mexico and other countries. I was always there for my daughter. It was not easy, but home office allowed me to do it. My daughter always has seen me in virtual meetings, working on my laptop, in conferences, but always there for her. Frequently I was working outside of the ballet classes, or in a corner of a children's party, or an excursion.

My husband and I have shared different responsibilities; his active paternity, his presence in our daughter´s life, and the help of my mother have been key ingredients to running a successful company. It has been very demanding, it has required all my physical and mental focus, and often a lot of effort, but it has allowed me not to give up any of the most important areas of my life. Now, besides my husband and mother, the help of my daughter is important. I have learned so much from her. Instead of or a burden, they are a great support.

**How has my company grown?**

I have never kept the knowledge to myself. I have shared all that I know with my team. I have invited very talented people whom I respect very much, and together we have created a group of continuous growth and learning. We are always truly and deeply interested in helping our customers to be better, more effective, and more successful.

We have already 15 years of learning, growing, and success. There has been a lot of great times, and of course, some very difficult ones. Many things had worked very well and others I would have liked to do differently. But at the end, I have had the opportunity to do what I dreamed of: teaching, therapy processes, research (I am author and co-author of some books) and collaborating in different ways with different not profit institutions.

In summary, 9 ingredients has been key to our growth:
- **TALENT AND PASSION:** Doing what we love, what we believe in, and what we are good at.
- **EFFORT:** Trying to give our best; not being afraid of commitment. There is always something in our control and it is important to find it and use that power.
- **LEARNING:** Keep learning always, from every person, every situation, and every mistake. We are never fully done.
- **SELF AWARENESS:** Recognize our strengths, weaknesses, emotions, motivations, fears, and mistakes.
- **ENJOY:** Focus on enjoying every step of the way. Observe all the good things and celebrate even little achievements.
- **TRUST:** In our self, in others, and in life.
- **KINDNESS:** Trying to be good with ourselves, with others, and with the environment.
- **CREATE:** If it does not exist, we create it. We had made things happen, by using our lateral thinking and remembering where there is a will, there is a way. Never giving up... even when it has been hard.
- **RESILIENCE:** Becoming stronger while facing difficulties and challenges.

And at the center of everything, there is synergy ... the help of God, my family, my team, and my friends, all of it has been fundamental. Without them, I don't think none of this would have happened.

So, having a fulfilled professional life, besides being a full commitment parent and spouse, and a spiritual person, requires a big effort but is possible, and for sure, it is worth it. If we don't find the opportunities, let's create them, for us and for others!.

# Espree
## Devora

**"The Girl who Gets it Done"**
*WEARELATECH/ WOMEN IN TECH PODCAST*

## "I think this part of my story could inspire others"

My community work isn't successful by luck, it's by design. Hi   my name is Espree Devora aka *'the girl who gets it done'*.

You may recognize me from being the face of the Clubhouse app, on stage at South by Southwest or listening to my podcasts.

This is the story about why I created WeAreLATech which helped fuel Los Angeles to become the 3rd largest tech community in the world. To have an idea about how much the LA startup community has grown -  in 2009 the LA Tech community all fit in 1 photo, now in 2023 people are moving to Los Angeles to build their startup and chatting about tech in local coffee shops is more common than Hollywood script chatter.

WeAreLATech, which I founded in 2012 (just had my 10 year anniversary) was created for people working in tech to feel safe being vulnerable and to collaborate with one another. The biggest compliment

## CHALLENGES

I received about my community was from a founder in a fancy top tier accelerator saying he got more value out of WeAreLATech than from the accelerator. I was surprised since he had access to the top venture capitalists and tech executives so I asked why... and he shared that in that accelerator he could never ask for the help he needed because he had to always appear like everything was going great. This stunned me, he had all the access to the most inaccessible people and still it was my organization that propelled him.

In 2015 I launched the Women in Tech podcast (produced by WeAreLATech) because I kept hearing how impossible everything was for women in tech. I wanted to share stories of possibility to expand what listeners believed they could achieve. The mission of the Women in Tech Podcast is *"If She Can Do It, So Can I."* I had already built the first action sport social network, I had already raised money, I had already moved onto my next company... I had no idea that I wasn't supposed to be able to achieve most things. My Mom always says every *'No'* is one step closer to a *'Yes'* so I just stay focused on finding the Yes. I wanted to create something where the community felt empowered to also find their moment of Yes.

I consider myself to be an *"artist of human connection"*. I'm proud to say my connective community work has brought thousands of business people together both digitally and in person to form long lasting high quality relationships. These relationships have turned into fruitful business partnerships, employment opportunities and even meaningful friendships and marriages. My focus has been building technology, events and content to unify community by focusing on 7 senses. Every last element from smell, sound, sight, taste, touch, mood and mind all come into play when I am 'painting' either a digital or offline experience.

Anything is possible, no matter how big I dream. I do my best to create without limitations in mind, holding onto confidence that I will figure it out. This perseverance comes from reading the book *"The Alchemist"* by Paulo Coelho, where I I learned that no matter how big a dream is, if a sincere heart is behind it, the whole world will conspire to make dreams a reality.

My journey becoming an entrepreneur all started playing in my father's home office clicking away on the computer making friends in the AOL chat rooms. I started dreaming about how I could bring people with similar interests together through an online community and ended up building the first action sports social network back when it was MySpace vs Facebook. Pulling from the pains of my personal founder's journey building my sports tech social network is what inspired me to create WeAreLATech. I wanted to create a place to safely lean on one another, a place to be vulnerable and ask for the help we need.

My organization's sole unbiased purpose is to propel individuals in the Los Angeles tech startup community so they don't have to experience the pain I had growing my startup. The evolution of WeAreLATech turned into an additional endeavor, my Women in Tech podcast. All I kept hearing was that it wasn't possible for women to win in tech. This confused me, when I had already achieved so much. As I mentioned above I set out to empower the global women in tech community in addition to my Los Angeles tech work by sharing stories from women in over 100 countries.

Entrepreneurship has been simultaneously the most difficult gut wrenching experience and rewarding experience all at once. I invent my life, I have freedom in how I spend my time, everything is a source of creativity from my coffee mug, to a flower I see, to overhearing words from a passerby. My path has no boundaries other than my own self limiting beliefs. Being a creative (aka founder, aka writer, aka community builder) is like playing a video game with an infinite amount of levels. You have to jump the frogs, capture the stars and save the princess each and every day.

Each leader has their own super power. I've overcome a lot in my personal life which I think hard wired me to become a deeply empathetic person. This empathy is a superpower for community building. I need to be careful not to give so much of myself away that there's nothing left of me energetically to serve. When creating I assess my own energy levels. If I am not operating from energetic overflow then I'm not able to serve to my highest ability.  So it's essential I do all the things; eating clean, sleep, fitness, breathing. It's ironic that what makes a great leader is how we show up and what is encouraged in tech is to diminish our health in order to succeed. The two don't go together.

That deep desire to *"succeed"* has led me down both bright and dark paths. The word success continues to evolve and change. When I was a new founder success meant being on the cover of a prominent business magazine like Kevin Rose featured on Inc., then it meant IPOing and being as big as Google and of course at times it meant who stacks the most revenue. It was in the past few years when I truly started to reflect on my own happiness. I questioned if success had anything to do with business growth at all. Afterall, would you rather be poor and full of joy or the wealthiest and feel empty inside... Of course we'd all like both abundance in the bank and a happy heart so how do we get there...

Often I make the joke that I found purpose before plentiful profit and I am waiting for profit to catch up. Purpose is definitely a key ingredient in my recipe to be a respected leader and build a credible referrable company. There's that annoying saying, 'it's about the journey, not the destination' and the more years that go by the more I find that to be so very true. A lot of business people who have gained financial success end up fearing apathy, nothing excites them anymore, after having achieved all their pursuits. They feel lost with nothing left to strive for. So with that reflection I am grateful I've had the tougher, slower road. The win will drip out in bits and pieces so my ride can last longer. In the tech world we get so caught up to create a major company by 20 and if we don't we feel we're done for. It seems the opposite is true. The longer our drive is, the more curiosity and adventure there is to be explored . It's not emotionally fulfilling playing the comparison game on social media thinking we're behind. What if in the full scope of our entire life, the journey in its entirety, the longevity of our ride does indeed end up making complete sense.

I want my life to stand for something. That thing that really matters to me is showing leaders aren't perfect. We're all flawed. I'm a vulnerable leader always afraid to show my vulnerability. Despite my fear, I do it often and it never gets easier. Showing up with open candidness regularly feels right so I bypass my fear that sponsors and customers may not trust my lack of perfection - when in reality no one is perfect, some people just pretend to be. The beauty in genuine relationships is having the opportunity to get to know one another's flaws and strengths and elevating each other in the process.

The job of an entrepreneur is a professional problem solver. It's all about being resourceful. I always say *"Your Intuition Is Your Oracle"*. The job of a leader is to help others achieve their dreams too. Everything I work on is about being compassionate, pushing myself to grow and creating an ecosystem for community to believe in themselves and be supported in the impossible. If we suspend disbelief even for a moment, our minds find solutions and possibilities. We're stronger by collaborating than we are by competing.

# Jennifer

## "Jaki" Johnson

### Founder and Chief Executive Officer

*WELLMISS*

I never saw myself starting a digital care clinic. I never saw myself working on trauma care for women. None of this was on my radar, yet the unexpected led me on this path.

April 22nd, 2019, was a day I will never forget. It was on that day that my 15-year-old son Christian passed tragically unexpectedly. It was the first time I felt pain, grief, and loss so profoundly. My life would change in so many ways, and because of that, I would later build a startup focused on helping women heal from trauma. The road there is where the journey begins.

It was the beginning of my healing grief journey, where my experience with the mind and body connection happened. Immediately after my son's passing, people told me to get a therapist, get into a support group and lean into a faith-based community. Those were good recommendations, but they came with their own set of challenges. Finding a therapist to help me with my grief was hard, and not every support group was interested in healing. I initially went to a previous therapist that had helped me when I was experiencing hormonal anxiety while pregnant with my younger son to see if she could help me. But she wan-

ted me to write a goodbye letter to my son on our first visit, and I had yet to process what had just happened. So, that started the journey of me looking for a new therapist. The first therapist I met with shared no emotions as I cried and told her about my last moments with my son, and she did not give me a piece of tissue. The second therapist could not remember if she had ever worked with a parent who had lost a child and had to think about that. The last therapist I met with was an older therapist who showed compassion and leaned in as I told my story and shared a few tears of her own as I shared with her what had happened to me. She told me she was a grandmother and mother and had never lost a child, but she helped women who had lost a child and that we would take this one step at a time. This was a lightbulb moment for me because I finally felt like I had found my person, the perfect therapist, after repeatedly telling my story to different therapists in hopes of finding someone who could help me with what I had been through. That was the beginning of my therapy journey.

The heart knows, and the body speaks. It was six months after my son passed when I noticed I was having alot of heart pain and felt like my heart was hurting. I scheduled an appointment with a cardiologist, and he ran some tests. I shared with him what happened to my son. He later told me that I had Broken Heart Syndrome, that it was an actual diagnosis, and that it was fatal and could be treated with medication. He also told me that my heart was leaking and that I had high blood pressure in my heart. I had already felt like I needed more than just mental health care for my healing grief journey because my heart and body felt like they were also grieving. My cardiologist said that I had to work on my healing and that until I worked on my healing, my body would continue to break itself down. That's when I searched for care that nurtured me as a whole person, heart, mind, body, and spirit. I went to the Omega Institute in Rhinebeck, New York, and spent a week there for a retreat called, Life Rentry After Loss with Christina Rasmussen. It was at that retreat I learned about my silent losses, my thriver self, and the different layers of how grief and loss affect different parts of ourselves that no therapist or clinician had shared with me. I also took yoga, tai-chi, and meditation classes. I grounded in nature, walked nature trails, and ate farm-to-table plant-based meals. It felt truly refreshing and

centered me from all the stress I was feeling from my grief. When I arrived back in Atlanta, I was determined to put together a care team that could bring those elements into my healing grief journey. I searched for a trauma-informed yoga therapist. I started seeing a chiropractor who talked about how grief can sit in the body and wrote up a treatment plan that included massage therapy to help with the somatic embodiment of my grief. I took up journaling for a grief course and incorporated breathwork, mindfulness, and meditation into my daily routine. I also consulted with a naturopathic provider who I met when pregnant with my younger son when I had hormonal anxiety on what natural products I could use with my grief since it was causing anxiety and panic attacks. I found alot of these various modalities to be very helpful on my healing journey, but it also came with a price. My health insurance only covered some of the care I was receiving. I also did not see alot of women of color in the spaces I was in, both as a receiver of these care services or a giver of these care services. The words trauma or traumatic experiences was never used by anyone I saw in describing what I was going through and what had happened to me. The unexpected loss of my son was a traumatic experience, and its impact on my heart, mind, body, and spirit were all signs of trauma. I also learned that other women had experienced traumatic experiences and were looking for holistic ways to heal their trauma. The disparities I saw in holistic care were that it was not easily accessible, it was not culturally competent, and it lacked a trauma-informed approach. This ultimately led to me creating WellMiss.

WellMiss was born out of a need for both myself and other women. I knew that bringing the worlds of conventional medicine and holistic and complementary evidence-based care to provide whole-person trauma care was needed. Here I was a year after experiencing such a difficult traumatic experience; I was using my lived experience to create a solution for a gap in our fragmented healthcare system that only saw trauma as a mental issue when data shows that trauma affects both the mind and body. How would I do this? Who am I to build this? How would I get it covered by insurance and make it accessible, culturally component, and trauma-informed? This was the next part of my journey, where I learned about integrative medicine and the Osher Collaborative of Integrative Medicine. Defined by the Cleveland Clinic, I learned integrative medicine uses an evidence-based approach to treat the whole person — mind, body, and soul. Your physical, emotional, mental, and spiritual needs are all involved, so integrative medicine uses a combination of therapies. It *"integrates"* conventional approaches and complementary therapies to achieve optimal health and healing. I learned about how integrative practices and clinics were billing and getting services covered by insurance. Healing in community was also another element of care and healing that I had sought out but learned many support groups were not focused on healing but rather on staying in a bad place. So, I eventually discovered shared medical group appointments and learned about that.

## CHALLENGES

I think this is the part of my story that can inspire others and that this is where my life took a full circle turn. My past experience working in a group practice and at a hospital in every role, from front desk check-in to claims reimbursement, medical records, patient appointment scheduling, and insurance verification/pre-authorizations, now had a new purpose in my life. I would be able to tap back into these skills that I learned while pregnant and raising my son, who passed was now being used. Here I was on a mission to build the first trauma-informed digital care clinic specializing in providing holistic and integrative trauma care to women. Research shows us that one in two women will experience at least one traumatic experience in their lifetime, affecting their health and well-being. The UCSF Center to Advance Trauma-Informed Health Care research shows us that unaddressed trauma is the hidden cause of most preventable illnesses and is associated with eight of the 10 leading causes of death, including heart, lung, and kidney disease, cancer, stroke, diabetes, suicide, and accidental overdose.

When we fail to address the trauma that underlies these diseases, prevention and treatment are far less effective and, in some cases, not effective at all. WellMiss was needed, and I was charged to create the solution.

I never thought I would be focusing on trauma and working on trauma care for women. On average, each of our WellMiss has experienced at least five different traumatic experiences and has been experiencing depression, anxiety, emotional eating, sleep issues, cardiovascular challenges, and traumatic grief. Now, they can come to WellMiss where they receive trauma-informed holistic and integrative whole-person care that is delivered through personalized care teams, shared group medical appointments, and community support.

**Daniela**
González
*THE HAPPY SELF PROJECT*

**Jack**
Laskowitz
*PAYIT DIGITAL GOVERNMENT*

**ANDREW**
Pollard
*NIDO*

**Cristina**
Riveroll
*NUBE HOSPITALITY*

**Jeremy**
Hochman
*MEGAPIXEL VR*

**Maria I.**
Zepeda
**Mario E.**
Moreno
*MORZEP COLLEGE COACHING*

# 4.A letter

**Ana Laura**
Arias Reza
*AIM GROUP*

**Nicolas**
Hauff
*FILLGAP BUSINESS GROUP*

**Ian Christopher**
Figueroa Schmehl
*STATE FARM*

**George**
Montgomery

**Natalise**
Kalea Robinson
*PARALLEL HEALTH*

# A few words or advice...

**Gustav Juul**
Founder & CEO
*AIM GROUP / XO LEADERS*

We are so different, and yet we are the same person. I have now lived twice as many years as you, so if nothing else, you know that you have survived until the age of almost 50.

I have been wanting to write this letter to you for quite some time, but there always seem to be happening things in my life that change what I would like to say to you so I put it off a while longer. I have also had a hard time deciding if I should try to save you from a specially painful situation or if I should let you experience all of it, the good, the bad, and the ugly. Our life, has not always been easy. I have been tested many times, and although God has not let me hit rock bottom, he has given me quite a ride and let me come close a couple of times. What I will tell you, is what has allowed me to get back up. As the saying goes: *"What defines you is not how hard or how many times you fall; it is if you get up again".*

I'll start with an extract from an interview I saw the other day with Tom Hanks and a few other actors. I reaffirmed what I have believed for many years; that no one has it all figured out. He said the following:

*"I wish I had known the saying"*, *"This too shall pass"*. You feel bad right now, you feel pissed off, you feel angry... *"This too shall pass"*. You feel great, you feel like you have all the answers, you feel like everybody finally gets you... *"This too shall pass"*... *"Time is your ally, just wait it out"*

My next piece of advice to you is one my father told me hundreds of times: *"Don't live above your means, pay cash for everything".* I have never taken a loan and neither should you. He would go on to say: *"Don't borrow money or you will end up working for others. Save up as much as you can, so that when hard times come along, and I promise you they will, you don't need to run to someone to ask for money. Lenders are in it for the money, and if you let them put a chain around your ankle, it is going to be your fault, not theirs."*

## Non-conformist

Life rarely turns out the way we expect it to, ours, yours, and mine,

**231**

surely hasn't. Right now, you are so busy that it seems absurd to even think about slowing down. Don't worry so much about what you think your parents or your friends expect you to be. Be reverent of people with more experience than you, but never turn into their puppet, be non-conformist. Try to burn fewer bridges than I did, or maybe burn more, I don't really know, but whatever you choose, have fun doing it. What you end up regretting the most is usually what you didn't do. Allow yourself to be a bit more silly and frivolous; just try to stay a bit further away from the dangerous adrenalin rush more than I did. Know that it is the unexpected that will bring out a smile on your face when you think back.

This brings me to my next point. Never be scared of failing. Being scared of failing will just lead you to experience less and live less. *You don't become happier, for being alive more but by being more alive.*

Like Mark Twain said: *"20 years from now, you will be more disappointed by the things that you didn't do than by the ones you did do. So throw off the bowlines. Sail away from the safe harbor. Catch the trade winds in your sails. Explore. Dream. Discover."*

I have, at times, given priority to other people's opinions more than my own and have lived less because of it.

At your age, I worried so much about what others thought I should and should not do, that I started creating a version of myself that was different from who I really wanted to be. It took me some time to figure out that I can't be someone I are not and still expect to be happy. You have to figure out who you are. It is your life. You have to reach for your dreams, not theirs, or you'll never reach a place that truly fulfills you.

I think that I have always known what I wanted; it was just that I had to go through a few hard lessons God had in store for me since I didn't get it. It took a good many years for me to realize that it is my journey and no one else's.

In that process, I learn to differentiate between things that matter and things that don't. I can tell you this much, Peter, Paul and Mary's opinions don't matter. They will be somewhere else in a very few years in pursuit of their own dreams and new people will come into your life. Are you also going to try to follow what they think you should do? And even if Peter, Paul, and Mary haven't followed their own dreams either and stayed behind, do you really want to be around them?
When you are able to identify what really matters to you, you will

see a new world appear. Your levels of energy and ability to focus will reach new unimaginable heights. You'll be happier. You'll start to breathe. You'll realize that you, until then, were been living in a fog. As the fog lists you'll see that the sky really is bright, blue, big, and beautiful.

Watch out for when the fog starts to descend again. The good thing is that you should know your way to finding blue skies.

The voices of all the people that think that what they can imagine for you is better than what you can dream for yourself, will be quieter each time. Don't let their words rob you of your getting the most out of your life.

Chances are you're going to ignore all of this and do whatever the hell you want to do anyway. Even if you're sitting there nodding your head in agreement, let's face it, five minutes from now you'll probably have forgotten 90% of what I said. I don't blame you. I've been there. In fact, I'm probably still there. After all, I'm the one who ignored every piece of good advice I received for the first thirty years of my life. So I'm not about to sit here and point the finger at you.

So if nothing else, be the reason someone smiles today. Build others up around you, and inspire them to be the best they can be.

When you have a dream that you can't let go of, trust your instincts and pursue it. But remember that fulfilling dreams requires work and an incredible amount of patience. I know you don't have a problem with working hard, but you have to work on your patience. Fulfilling dreams sometimes require you to dig down deep, very deep. The good news as you will see in a few years is that dreams do come true.

Have Passion with a capital *"P"* in your life. If it's not a HELL YES, it's not Passion. Don't be afraid to jump on an opportunity if you are passionate about it, even if it might bite you in the ass. Life is too short to live without passion.

Gustav, everything will make sense someday. So, for now, laugh at your mistakes. Keep going. And keep reminding yourself that *"this too shall pass"* and that everything happens for a reason.

# Ana Laura

## Arias Reza

**CoFounder**
*AIM GROUP*

My dear Ana Laura,

I am "you," albeit in a few years. I'm nervous about writing to you, but I am doing it because part of me feels that it might be therapeutic for me now, and another part hopes that my children will read it. There is just something permanent about the written word, compared to speech, that disappears in the wind. I want to share with them what I wish I had known. I hope it will be a wonderful and inspiring letter too. I hope they will like it more than the other "letters to myself" as their mom wrote it. I hope it will touch their spirit as it is written from my heart. There are so many more things I hope this letter will be, and yet I don't know where to start... I am scared that I will disappoint, especially them, but I will not know if I don't try.

Stop arguing so much with Mama. Time will show you that she was right in so many things. Although you don't see it now, later in life, you will realize what an incredible pillar she was in your childhood and appreciate the sacrifices she made for you and your siblings. She is a wise woman. She is a woman that has been through a lot. Remember what you know about her childhood. Observe how she struggles every day for you. Try to step into her shoes and understand why she makes such an effort in, for lack of a better word, educate you. Don't try to change her. Don't think you know more than her. Let yourself be guided more, and you'll have a much easier time.

You feel calmer with Papa. That is perfectly all right. He is lighthearted, talkative, and jovial. Value and treasure those traits more. Learn from him too. Just like Mama, he has been through a lot too, and he was always there for you when Mama was being too harsh. Be more affectionate with him (and with others). As you start showing him that you love him, you will discover a whole new side of him. Just because he is easygoing doesn't mean that he doesn't care. He needs you more than you know. Listen to him more; he has a different kind of wisdom than Mama, but just as valuable.

Although your parents have gone through economically scarce times, it is not something that you can control.

What you can do is learn from it. You can become resilient. Every time you help your parents overcome the challenges posed by their fragile economy, you will realize how many things you are capable of. Make the obstacles your allies because they will help shape you into becoming the woman you one day will be. You still can only see some of your potential, but believe me, it's a lot. So start believing in yourself and keep your head held high.

I know you don't want your high school to end. You've had fun, laughed, and found good friends, but you can't stay in high school forever. Stop wasting time hoarding memories when you have so much to live for. No, you're not going to die at 25. This is not the best time of your life. Believe me when I tell you that I'm better at 45 than I ever was... in every way.

Before I get into the recommendations I want to share with you for your adult life, I will tell you the following; it may seem tedious but study more, much more. Focus on your studies, not just to get a passing grade. Spend more time learning another language. If you do not do it now, you will have to do it later in your life. You will have to do it anyway; if you wait, it will just cost you more time. Learn English. There will also be doors that won't open for you. Or why not Danish? On second thought, that door will probably be open for you anyway, even if you don't know a word of Danish. Read more, stand up straighter, be punctual, listen more, and talk less; these habits will make a difference in your life.

I am grateful for the difficult things that have happened to me. Thanks to them, I have discovered who I am and what I am capable of. I feel confident giving you the following advice:

- **Get noticed**

Learn to have confidence in yourself for you to be able to show others what you are capable of. This ability is something you should master because you should not expect others to notice you because of what you do. The trick is to learn how to communicate what you do well.

You will meet a person that notices everything you achieve, and he will also give you this advice. Take note of that conversation! Learn it quickly, and don't forget it. If you don't, one of two things will happen to you, either you go unnoticed, or someone else will show off your achievements; then you are back to square one, going unnoticed.

- **Don't doubt yourself**

People are going to doubt you. Don't worry about them; it speaks more about them than you. Never doubt yourself. When someone tells you that you can't, it says more about their capacities than yours.

This is very important. If there is something you would like to achieve, just start looking for the way. Where there is a will, there is a way. When you meet someone you want to learn from, don't be shy about looking them up.

- **Friends and acquaintances**

Mom is right, be careful of whom you befriend. Some people are friends; most are acquaintances. If you walk with the smart ones in class, it has a way of rubbing off on you and vice versa.

You must select what people you want to be part of your life. From time to time, you will have to leave those who don't add anything positive and become closer to the ones who do. Those who remain will, in the end, be your true friends, where time or distance will have little effect on how much joy they bring. Hint: Traveling with these friends will be some of the best experiences in your life!

- **Patience**

If you feel that someone is advancing more quickly than you, don't despair. It is not all about "advancing"; moreover, life has a way of rewarding resistance much more often than speed. Everyone has their path and times, and you do too. Don't compare yourself to others. Remember Desiderata's poem and why it made sense when you heard it. Until this day, you will treasure it.

- **Always have goals**

Success is achieved by people who have goals. Make sure you don't lose your way because what you aimed for was left by the wayside. You will need two skills for this, discipline and will. If you have that, you will achieve anything you set yourself to.

- **Learn to communicate**
-

This might seem similar to "getting noticed," but it is different. You need to develop your communication skills because when you speak, you are able to show the world who you are. You may think you already are good at communicating, but you still have much to learn. Don't doubt yourself, and get to it!

- **Be rational**

Although your heart is essential, it is just as important to be rational about the decisions you must make in your life. It would be best if you found a balance. If you are ever in honest doubt, you should do two things; first, you should find that quiet place within yourself where you are able to manage your emotions, then listen to what your inner voice tells you to do. When you've done that, you have very rarely gone wrong.

Finally, I will share with you a few phrases that have helped us at certain times:

- If you don't have anything kind to say, don't say anything.
- The important thing is not to have what you want but to want what you have.
- The important thing is not what happens to you but how you react to what happens to you.
- You are not what you achieve; you are what you overcome.
- Gratitude is an expensive gift; do not expect it from cheap people.
- 10% of conflicts are due to a difference of opinion the other 90% are due to the wrong tone of voice. (It's not that you call me a bitch, it's the bitchy way you say it)

- Everything passes, both the good and the bad; nothing is eternal.
- Dare to take away your fears!!!

I hope these lines are useful to whoever reads it and although I only mention the desiderata poem it will be a great contribution to whoever reads it

# Nicolas Hauff

### Founder/CEO
### *FILLGAP BUSINESS GROUP*

## FROM BUSINESS OPERATOR TO STRATEGY-BASED LEADER

*Many times, what makes you successful in something is not necessarily what you think it was.*

In the fall of 2015, after two years of work I published a book titled The Three Challenges: How to Become the Strategy-Based Leader that the Modern Business World Demands.

I had been very successful in an information technology business for years until I encountered a severe setback between 2007 and 2008. As I stood in that difficult situation, I realized that I wasn't aware of what had made me successful and why my success was suddenly slipping away. After I started to assimilate my loss, I began a time of self-discovery to uncover both, the roots of my success and the obstacles that stood in the way.

My discovery process led me to conclude that I personally had not fully undertaken whatever was necessary to grow as a leader and meet

the new demands of my growing business. I had not maintained a unified vision for the company as it grew. And I had not consistently made things happen. I realized where I had fallen short on each challenge.

From that process, it also became clear to me that I was not the only business owner trying to grow his company day to day without direction, that most of them lacked a sense of personal purpose, and that most leadership teams of small and mid-sized companies were missing alignment around a shared vision and a well thought out strategy to get there.

As a completely unexpected benefit of this discovery process, I was introduced to a new but fascinating opportunity for me: The world of commercial personal and business growth programs, for which I quickly developed a big passion and became actively involved with; partnering with some of the leading international content and program providers and, this way, helping other entrepreneurs expand their awareness, grow as individuals and leaders, and grow their businesses.

There are so many programs and sources of knowledge to address specific business and leadership issues that when people would ask me whether they should go for A, B or C, I would answer, *"You will most likely benefit from all, but in the right context of your life and business and in the right sequence."*

Based on my intention to help others find the common denominators of all that wisdom, is that The Three Challenges model came to life; first as a presentation for my speeches, later as a book, and today as a model to blend the different methodologies into one roadmap.

I created The Three Challenges as a model for personal growth for entrepreneurial leaders. The book, however, was far more than just a retelling of other people's ideas. I blended in what I had lived through countless experiences that had given me a unique perspective. I had seen success, experienced troubled times in my life and career, and reassessed myself.

As I was about to finish this work, I realized that I was addressing a large part of it to my past self. I had been telling that younger man what he needed to understand about life as an entrepreneur and business owner. I had been sharing the things that I wish I had known then, while I was also telling my present self what I needed to remember for my own future.

Based on the above, I would like to go over three of the most important lessons hoping that they serve you in your own entrepreneurial leadership journey.

## 1. BECOME AWARE OF YOUR LIFE PURPOSE AND YOUR NATURAL GIFTS

Each of us has a purpose. I believe that everybody and everything in the universe has a reason for being, and early in life we should develop an awareness of it. Don't wait until you are middle-aged to discover your own purpose.

Start by identifying your talents and gifts. The book StrengthsFinder published by Gallup is a great resource for becoming aware of what you do best and how to build upon it. It will step you through how to identify your top five strengths. The book suggests that building on those strengths will bring you a greater return on investment than trying to fix your weaknesses. The online assessment included with the book revealed my five strengths: I turned out to be a strategic, a futurist, a positive, an input, and an adaptable person. Now I know how where I personally can add the best value to my business and what kind of people should surround myself with.

After finding out your talents and gifts, learn to live from love. I have learned that all emotions can be reduced to two basic ones: love and fear. Everything we think and do is based either on love or on fear. We can come closer to understanding our life purpose by becoming aware of the things that we do from love, as we experience fulfillment and flow. Last, but not least, find ways to make these gifts and talents available to others.

From this thought process I concluded that my life purpose is to connect others with new possibilities. I feel flow when I introduce two persons to each other and when I help people learn and realize new things. And based on that, I have structured my business and my life.

## 2. LEARN TO THINK AND ACT IN TIMEFRAMES

There is a before and an after for me from the day I understood the One Page Strategic Plan developed by Verne Harnish in his book Scaling Up and learned how to apply it in my own business and many other businesses.

Before getting acquainted with this invaluable tool, I always struggled to define a direction for my company, and therefore, I never established one and was never able to align my team around a vision and a strategy. It was always day-to-day operations without a clear path forward.

The main thing it taught me was to think and act in the following five timeframes:

1. **Long term:** What is the big bold vision for your business in ten or more years? What do you want to have accomplished by then?
2. **Mid-term:** What do you need to accomplish in the next three to five years to get closer to your big bold vision? What capabilities to you need to build?
3. **Short term:** What are you going to do this year to get you closer to your mid-term targets?
4. **Immediate term:** What are your priorities for this quarter? What is important to get your company moving in the right direction?
5. **Today:** Are the things you are doing today aligned with the direction you defined for your business?

Besides of the timeframes, I also learned that your company must have a strong cultural foundation based on core values and core purpose.

Everything you decide and do must be aligned with your cultural foundation and your strategic plan. This will keep you focused and avoid distractions.

### 3. ALWAYS BE AWARE THAT NOTHING LASTS FOREVER

One of the most difficult things that I have learned to recognize is that nothing lasts forever. And I am not alone here; when things go well, it's very easy to remain in your comfort zone, thinking that nothing is going to change.

The only constant in business and life is change. I once read a quote saying, *"when you think that you are going to live forever, you do a lot of stupid things."* That happened to me when I was at the peak of my career in my technology business; I unconsciously chose not to see that changes were underway.

But in truth, everything wears off, goes out of style, dies, or changes over time, and it is in the period of transition that crises arise. In those periods of transition, there is indeed great risk. But it is also in those periods when there are the most opportunities – when we are leaving the old behind as we enter a new stage.

Always stay attentive of the trends in your industry, in other industries, in politics, in the economy, in society, in technology, in the environment, and in the legislation.

## HOW DO YOU BECOME A STRATEGY-BASED LEADER?

A true entrepreneurial leader brings ideas to life, aligning the right people and resources and makes sure the idea stays alive. As a leader, you need to be humble enough to either step aside when your business has outgrown your skills or proactively invest in your professional and personal growth and, this way, stay current with the growing demands of your company. You may also need to bring in people with different skill sets. It's all quite challenging.

From my own experience in business, from my ongoing interactions with many other business owners from different countries around the world, and from what I have learned in the business training and coaching profession, I have identified three core challenges that, as a business leader, you must master to reach greater heights:

1.  You must become and remain fully aware of yourself; understanding who you are as individual, why you do what we do, how you add value to others, and where you want to go.
2.  You must build and maintain a common vision of the direction your company is going.
3.  You must take consistent action to get great performance.

If you are growing a business, now is the time to buckle down and build your leadership skills before your company becomes too large for you to manage.

I wish you the best of luck in your entrepreneurial leadership journey!

# George
## Montgomery

## Some things that I have learned that may help you

I am writing this letter to a younger George who has just graduated from University and will soon start his working career.

### Success

You achieved success in the academic world and now it's time to think about success in the working world as well as life in general. Until now you have been too focused on short-term success, you need to set some lifelong goals and principles. Yours will be based on career, family, friends, financial stability and adherence to the Golden Rule. Dream big as you will someday become a CEO; you need to prepare yourself for the challenges you will face. Envision your future and work hard to achieve it, life is not a dress rehearsal so get the most out of it and don't waste time.

There is not much use in settling for mediocre goals, you don't get much career satisfaction from them. Challenge yourself. Once you have established goals, then establish specific steps to get you there. This is the action plan that you will focus on most of the time – daily, weekly or monthly activities. Keep accomplishing these specific steps

and you will eventually achieve your goals. Don't be afraid to change these action plans, remember they are only steps in the process and not an end in themselves.

Keep your mind focused, your motivation high and your goals in sight. Hope is not a strategy, set a goal and a plan to achieve it. Don't get distracted by day to day activities, keep an eye on the long game.

## Your first job

Don't just think about finding your first job, think about starting a career. Look for a growing sector; it is much easier to have success in a growing market. Every business has a life cycle so try to join a company in the early stages of growth, not in the mature or shrinking phase. You will have to work hard whatever you do; you will get much more back from a growing business.

Every job is a training ground; your first job is only the first step in a long career ladder. It is more important to get on the right ladder than to worry about starting on a low step on the ladder.

If you like what you do on a daily basis, if you like the people you work with and if you feel good about your accomplishments then you have a great job. Life is too short to work for assholes. You will never be successful working in an unhappy environment.

## Lifelong learning

Never stop learning, the technology of today is not the technology of tomorrow. Stay on top of technology trends and continually refine your expertise. Use your company's performance review process to identify opportunities for personal improvement and commit to continuous improvement. Their perceptions of your performance are more important than your perceptions. A company will use customer surveys and employee surveys to keep a finger on the pulse of the market. You need to develop your own feedback loops so that you understand where you stand with a company. Are you in line for a promotion?  Are you in a dead-end?

You will have a tendency to stay with one company for too long, enjoying the experience and relationships. You will have to challenge yourself and switch jobs whenever you stop learning.

Most people will change jobs about every five years but there is no magic timeline. Change if you are bored, stop learning or if you don't have an opportunity to advance. Just don't get caught in a cycle of looking for a bigger, better deal by changing jobs too frequently. You need some time to prove yourself in a company and sometimes you have to wait for the right position to open. A company will usually want to know they can count on you before they promote you. But changing jobs can be the best way to get ahead.

## Innovate

Find new ways to do your job. This is critical to improvement and critical to success. If you always do the same thing in the same way, don't expect improvement. Think through cause and effect, it will help you find ways to innovate. Identify opportunities and chase after them.

You will enjoy part of your career in new product development, this is all about creativity. Try new things and take risks, there is a fine line between a breakthrough *"a-hah"* moment and a *"ha-ha"* moment. You have a very creative mind, use it.

## Collaborate

No one person is as smart as a group. No one person can accomplish as much as a group. We all have something to contribute, find out how other people can help you. Find a mentor, someone who can spend time and give you specific advice. Build a good network of friends who can help you. You have a tendency to keep problems to yourself, you need to open up and listen to advice from your trusted friends.

Surround yourself with talented people and establish a process to foster communication and collaboration. When I joined Taylor Made Golf, there were a lot of talented people but no process for new product development. As a consequence, new product launches were not always successful. We reengineered the process, established formal roadmaps and immediately started launching market leading products.

## Make good choices

Use data as much as possible to make informed decisions but remember that behind every number is a story, so make sure you know the story. When I was young and green, I made a decision to fire a sales representative who was not performing (real data). As I got older, I now know that I should have spent more time understating the causes of this underperformance. He may have been responsible or there may have been circumstances out of his control. Don't make this same mistake.

Use a balanced scorecard to review the outcomes of every decision; very seldom is a decision all good or all bad. Understand the tradeoffs so that you can make nuanced decisions.

Once you make a decision, have the courage of your convictions. In your time Thomas Jefferson was revered as one of the Founding fathers, he will later become reviled for owning slaves. I saw a hand written draft of the Declaration of Independence by Thomas Jefferson that called for the abolition of slavery in the US. Jefferson was eventually overruled and this clause was stricken from the final version. Imagine how different the world would be if Jefferson had stuck with his convictions.

Don't let other people get to you: you are neither as smart or as dumb as some people will call you. Have a sense of humor and remember the golden rule; then people will like working with you.

## Compensation

You don't want to be in a position to always get paid by the hour. You want to eventually get paid for your contribution, not just your time. This can come from a bonus or sales commissions or hopefully from equity. Equity in a growing company will almost always give you much more wealth than any paycheck. This is not always a guarantee, as I did not make any money on stock options in two companies but I made good money with stock options in other companies.

## Work hard

Everyone will fail at some time but not everyone will succeed. Why? Sometimes it's as simple as keep trying. *"Failure is never fatal and success is never final, giving up is what makes it permanent."* Hard work is almost always required; it will not come easily but it will come.

## Personal finances

Be careful and wise with your money. Save and invest some money in growth stocks every year, you will be surprised how it adds up over time.

Buy a home as soon as you can and don't be afraid of mortgage debt. House prices will increase dramatically in the next 40 years, start now. Keep trading up to better homes when you can afford it, take advantage of the tax code to shield capital gains on your primary residence. Learn to maintain and fix things in your house and know when to call in experts.

## Attitude

I learned that *"Attitudes are Contagious, make sure that yours is worth catching"*, please remember this and keep composed and positive in your professional life. Always believe in yourself, this can-do attitude is the first step towards success.

Call it karma, the golden rule, or whatever you want; it is imperative not to have a habit of judging others or it will simply bring that negativity back to yourself. Negativity will only sabotage you as you strive to achieve your goals.

We all blame others to a degree. Blame is tied to success in reverse proportions. The lower your degree of blame-the higher degree of success you'll achieve. Take responsibility for your actions and decisions. Successful people take responsibility for everything they do and everything that happens to them.

## Opportunity

The world is constantly changing and change creates opportunity. Opportunity often appears as adversity, sometimes the biggest challenges give you the biggest opportunities to move ahead. First, recognize it. Second, act on it. Opportunity is elusive. This means taking risks because you are seeing opportunity before other people see it. No risk, no reward is the biggest understatement in the business world. It should be stated as: no risk, no nothing.

You will have a successful and happy life, but you will also make mistakes on the way. Learn from them. Keep pushing to make the world a better place and having a positive influence on your friends.

# Jeremy
# Hochman

**Founder**
*MEGAPIXEL VR*

## Transformation & Trusting Your Gut

Sitting down to write this letter to my past self, I had a moment's hesitation wondering what I could possibly say that would feel relatable to the next generation of leaders coming up amidst today's unprecedented times of an ever-in-flux pandemic and all the uncertainties that come with it. But, then it dawned on me that a similar time of upheaval and personal health crisis actually shaped who I am as an inventor and CEO far more than I often give it credit for: I was diagnosed with a brain tumor at age five.

For what seemed like a never-ending summer, I vividly remember being stuck in a hospital room that felt nothing short of a prison cell for the active kid I was back then. What's more, after a successful surgery, I immediately found myself in what felt like a different person's body facing bio-chemical changes I'd need to learn to live with for the rest of my life — suddenly the beanstalk-thin kid who was always outside playing sports had transformed into a chubby kid on bed rest who had to slow down and heal.

# MEGAPIXEL
VISUAL REALITY

# A LETTER

Laid up in that hospital bed, I quickly started developing new interests to save myself from boredom — namely, the sports that were now off-limits gave way to Legos, puzzles, and other games that involved analytical thinking. Then, pretty soon, I was applying my competitive nature and newfound love of problem solving to starting a series of small businesses and spending my weekends begging my parents to drive me to patent lawyers' offices and machine shops.

At the time, I viewed my shifting hobbies as something temporary I was doing out of necessity to make the best of my situation, but looking back I see how this time of struggle was shaping me and my path in a lasting way.

Furthermore, on a much bigger scale I now see this transition time not only shaped my interests and helped me redirect my competitive focus from physical to cerebral endeavors, but it taught me the broader life lesson of becoming a highly adaptable person who knows how to pivot.

This ability to pivot — a skill I hadn't even been aware I was developing — eventually proved vital when I founded a furniture company fresh out of college and then (mere months later) ended up making the decision to turn it into a tech company. This kind of shift sounds nuts, right? It certainly did to most people I knew back then, but at the time I had noticed a trend I couldn't ignore: one of our table designs had LED lighting inside of it, and when the light-up top started selling like gangbusters to music video and concert designers, I knew it was time to take advantage. Years later, I realize this pivot gave birth to a whole industry that hadn't existed before — the industry of creative LED in which there are now hundreds of companies and tens of thousands of jobs as a result of this one inflection point.

Honestly, I'm not sure if I would have been able to see this out-of-left field opportunity to pivot my first company if my childhood illness hadn't prompted me to reimagine my life so drastically at a young age. One thing I do know for sure is I definitely couldn't see the whole scope of what my health experiences were teaching me about adaptability when I was five. Let's be honest, back then I was mainly bummed I couldn't play baseball anymore, but I think there's great inspiration and hope to be found in how life's lessons sometimes cumulate and pay off when we least expect it. Put another way, sometimes the deal we don't close today ends up serving as the exact set of training wheels we needed for a much bigger deal 10 years down the line.

Lately as I face the era of the COVID-19 pandemic along with the rest of the world, the lessons I'm learning and the ways I'm transforming look a lot different than they did decades ago. In part, I know this is because my vantage point is different. After all, I'm now in year five of running my third startup, which is a far cry from the early days of scraping to get my first company off the ground, and yet now more than ever I find myself feeling acutely aware of how I am still constantly learning.

This brings me to the second key lesson I most want to share with the next generation of leaders and creative thinkers: the lesson that no matter how senior someone else is, you can rest assured they're still learning, too.

Just because someone has a lot of experience doesn't mean they have all the answers, and as a leader you owe it to yourself and your company to rely not on experts but on your own gut for every big decision you make.

Does this mean you shouldn't seek the counsel of others or surround yourself with experienced mentors and colleagues? Absolutely not. Whenever a seasoned professional is willing to share their institutional knowledge with you this is a valuable resource, but it is never more valuable than your own inner resources — aka, the voice in your head saying either *"yes, I agree, this is the way to go"* or *"no, I just have a feeling I need to go my own way on this."*

I really cannot overstate the importance of always pausing to listen to your own instincts and trusting your gut. In fact, remembering back to my first startup, I realize it's staggering the way all my worst decisions correlated with moments when I wasn't following my gut.

Back then, I trusted my co-founders and board members because they were older and more experienced, but sometimes my gut said that by following their advice I wasn't doing the right thing for the company or for myself as a leader. Sometimes my gut wanted me to suggest different strategies or business partnerships. But, the fact that these people around me were also smart and capable made me feel my concerns weren't real or weren't worth rocking the boat. More often than not, these instances where I ignored my gut and neglected to speak up snowballed into a pattern where I wouldn't let myself voice concerns or divergent ideas the next day because I'd said I agreed with everyone else the day before.

Sounds like a dangerous cycle, right? I'm also guessing it sounds familiar to a lot of young leaders out there. So, my advice on avoiding this cycle is: if something doesn't feel right, stop, self reflect, and speak up — do whatever is necessary in order to make sure you are proceeding in a thoughtful manner and not simply moving forward because that's what you did yesterday. Much the same way you don't always need to follow the advice of experts, it's not always necessary to follow your past self.

To help me listen to my gut when it comes to the most creative and forward-thinking elements of my work, I've adopted a simple rule of thumb: always create behind a closed door and then edit with an open door. I first heard this from my wife (a writer who literally creates and edits every day) and she says she learned it from Stephen King. Regardless of who first coined this wisdom, I can vouch it's always the way to go.

Give your big ideas time to germinate behind a closed door before inviting anyone else into your thought process to offer advice. Make this a habit if not a rule whenever possible and it will pay off in dividends. If nothing else, this practice will help you avoid groupthink, and I can tell you from experience groupthink is far too easy a way to stagnate and fail to push companies and industries forward.

In closing, I will leave you with a piece of advice I still give myself often. During times of crisis or big change, I center myself by simply remembering to take a few seconds to reflect on the deeper reasons of why I do what I do. Everyone's *"why"* is different, but for me my *"why"* is that I love creating boundary-pushing technologies that surprise and delight people with something they've never seen before... I love weaving together art, entertainment, architecture, and technology in unexpected ways that just might brighten someone's day with a sense of wonder. And, I love imagining that one of these people might be a scared five-year-old kid stuck in a hospital room who suddenly finds himself feeling a little less scared and a little more inspired when he glances at my work on a TV screen and simply says *"wow."*

I look forward to seeing all the ways you and the next generation of leaders surprise me and wow the world.

# Mario E. Moreno

# Maria I. Zepeda

**CEO/Co-founder and President**
*MORZEP COLLEGE COACHING*

## QUIXOTES VS. WINDMILLS

**Education, Advocacy, Bias to Action, and Systemic Change**

This spring, sitting comfortably at the State Farm Arena at the University of Illinois at Urbana-Champaign, impatiently listening to the names of nearly 800 students receiving their Engineering degrees, I was distracted while waiting to hear the name of our youngest daughter, who was occupying one of the chairs among the graduates.

My mind wandered to various topics until it stopped at a philosophical one, dense, difficult-to-handle, and even inappropriate thought for that moment because reason told me that it had to be all about her. For

months, we had gone through deep introspection to define the WHY of our company. During the exercise, we discovered many things that clarified the reason for the existence of Morzep College Coaching - our company which we founded in Chicago in mid-2008 - where our life as individuals, as a family, and as a company was defined.

By this spring, my wife and I had already gone through several graduations of our own and those of our older children. Amid our little girl's graduation, logic told me that I should focus on living in the moment and savoring the results of her efforts. Still, my mind resisted simplifying the moment because of my old habit of being unreasonable. So, inevitably, I plunged into my thoughts, trying to visit my past quickly. But why here? Why us? Why at this moment? WHY? WHY? WHY?

Without knowing it, since my early years, my life revolved around EDUCATION. It was never conscious; it was more like *"it had to be this way."* It was an inherited obligation that ran in our family to get educated, excel, and grow. With that thought, early in my life, I began to define a vision of *"constant improvement"* that I did not fully understand. I tried to conquer unattainable goals for myself and my condition. Whenever I encountered a challenge, I rebelled, became unreasonable, and my hunger to overcome grew. I asked myself: Why were my goals impossible? Why would I not be able to do it? It was my dream, and I wanted to achieve it. I didn't see why it was impossible. My immature mind resisted understanding my situation, not knowing what my desire implied.

I didn't have a definite goal; I just wanted to replicate and surpass my parents' inherited aspiration to achieve something *"more"* without knowing what *"more"* meant. With that mentality, I tried to study at the schools considered *"the best."* Later, I realized that this notion of *"the best"* had more social overtones than factual ones. Nevertheless, I didn't get into any of them. Still, I wanted to make my parents proud of my academic achievements, so I studied as hard as I could all through high school. I had no help beyond a pat on the back and a *"Yes, you can do it!"* but as I heard those words, my insides desperately screamed: *"But I don't know how to do it!"*

My constant search for *"the best"* paid off when, in my second year of college, I got into what was considered one of the best universities in Mexico, which even my parents classified as financially unattainable. That's how I saw it too, but something profound inside me refused to accept it as unreachable. Having a dream and then framing it as unachievable didn't make sense. On the contrary, this impossibility made me want it even more and caused me to be irreverent, rebellious, and UNREASONABLE by most people's standards.

My dream, although it seemed unreal, was cemented in my mind as something possible but without a defined path. Fortunately, my girlfriend at the time, who would later become my wife, seemed to share and resonate with many of the same dreams I had. She encouraged me to fight for my goals, and we visualized paths that seemed impossible. Her irrepressible drive and vivacity to see roads where there appeared to be none was the perfect fuel to keep the flame of hope very much alive. She inspired me and forced me to visualize the possibilities of achievement. But she didn't know much either and had few resources to fall back on beyond believing in a shared dream. We soon became a team that overcame obstacles and broke down barriers. We also ran into insurmountable walls and impossible obstacles, but with each fall and each achievement, there was learning, many bumps and bruises, and much growth and maturation. The advantage of having someone to ADVOCATE for you, providing the needed support, became evident.

As a couple, we had a BIAS TO ACTION. *"Let's do it!"* We constantly challenged each other, and when she said it was impossible, I refused to believe it, and vice versa. Action became our mantra, and without assessing risks or consequences, we sought new adventures. We didn't settle for an opinion or a statistic. We constantly went to the source to verify whether the information we received was accurate. Regardless of the answer, we never used the information as an excuse to justify the impossibility of achieving what we wanted. Instead, we showed a fearless desire, although I must admit that on many occasions, we knew that our chances of attaining the goal were slim, but even then, we were inspired by the adventure and the satisfaction of having tried.

We learned to respect systems, but we were never intimidated by them. On the contrary, bureaucratic and inefficient systems inspired us to seek changes and alternative paths. We understood that, in many cases, the systems were more intimidating than practical. Unfortunately, the administrators of such systems quickly lost their compass and focused on keeping their rules safe instead of serving the interests of their users. For us, that was unacceptable. So, from the get-go, we decided not to be intimidated by the systems and the bureaucrats who administered them. More often than not, we felt like Quixotes fighting old windmills that remained undaunted by our onslaught. So we broke down walls, surmounted obstacles, and challenged the status quo by fighting for constant SYSTEMIC CHANGE.

Based on our past and history, and through a slow, tortuous, and sometimes painful process, we landed at the four pillars of Morzep College Coaching's WHY: EDUCATION, ADVOCACY, BIAS TO ACTION, and SYSTEMIC CHANGE, which had been evident driving forces in our past, but that we, until now, hadn't had the opportunity to describe it in words.

---- oOOOo ----

My daughter's name on the PA system dispelled my thoughts. I jumped up and yelled at the top of my lungs for her accomplishments and then took multiple pictures of our beautiful little girl as she was getting her Engineering diploma. In my outburst, I was externalizing our history and life as we saw her epitomizing our WHY. A tear accompanied my euphoria as I sat down, blissful, savoring that experience and trying in vain to put words to my feelings.

This letter to us, although unorthodox, would make little sense to have started any other way. We had to trace the path we had walked of daily experience and daily actions from our beginning to make sense of it all. Our past, dreams, and passion had spoken loudly to us, but we refused to listen, obnubilated by the deafening social cacophony that often pointed out why we should not aim to achieve our dreams. The temptation to follow the masses like sheep, sacrificing our aspirations and playing along to fit in with a society that cares little for anyone, was huge. In a deliberate act of rebellion, we decided not to conform, thus triggering many plans and projects far from the norm.

Regarding the business aspect of our lives, we believe that we should have started our own company at least twenty years before we did it. But, of course, there will be those who say we started too late and those who think we did it just at the right time. Today, what other people think is irrelevant. What is very relevant is the learning we got out of our experiences. Would we go back in time if we could? Probably yes, but not at the cost of relearning all the lessons we learned through the years. So, a more appropriate answer is: No! We would not go back in time; after all, our experience and growth through painful lessons were well worth it, and all those experiences helped us to clarify our purpose in life.

Fortunately, we learned how to learn a long time ago. Earlier, we wanted so many things, but we failed to work in a focused way toward those desires. We learned many topics and skills, but we never put them into practice. The most unfortunate thing was that we didn't share our knowledge with others. We learned that what is presented as *"good for you"* might not be that *"good for you."* So, we learned to WORK for our desires, to PRACTICE our skills, and to SHARE our knowledge; with that, we became happier than ever.

In our early days, and even as adults, we got used to the education system and society prescribing what they thought we needed, and it felt great to conform and travel the well-traveled path that involved opening our mouths and feeding on pre-existing knowledge and behavior, under the precept that everything *"was for our good."* Yet, even that experience enhanced our lives and helped us clarify our reason for being here today.

Through the four pillars that define Morzep College Coaching's WHY, extracted from our origins, we can see the past and understand how we evolve into the present as we react toward an unsure future. During our unique journeys, we obtained invaluable life lessons that we wanted to share with you in the hope that they will help you in your future endeavors. This is the MORZEP's WHY decalogue:

1. Don't ignore who you are, what makes you tick, or what activity makes you lose track of time because therein lies the key to your success.
2. Identify how you learn, and please, take advantage of it.
3. Find those activities, teachers, professors, mentors, and friends that encourage your creativity.
4. Desire to achieve your dreams and conquer your goals, however impossible they may seem, but go beyond the desire; work for it.
5. Consistently implement the skills and knowledge learned; practice them so they do not become inert knowledge.
6. Whatever you know, share it; there is no better way to learn something than by teaching it.
7. Don't wait. Start early. If you fail, you will have time to try again many times.
8. Continually educate yourself, constantly seek support, take action, and break the status quo through systemic change; the results will be evident and tangible.
9. Please, always be unreasonable! We do not believe that there is a truly successful entrepreneur who hasn't been unreasonable, and
10. Be happy!

**MUCH SUCCESS IN YOUR SEARCH FOR HAPPINESS.**

# Andrew Pollard

## Founder
*NIDO*

Fresh off my 40th birthday, I was making almost a million dollars a year, I had access to anyone you can imagine in Manhattan's social scene, I was being featured in the press and I was in a thrilling affair with a famous actress. This was it- I had made it.

I had worked so hard to say these three words I MADE IT. I found myself needing to repeat it to myself to try and believe it. The lingering truth was, no matter how much the outside world recognized my success, I had a gut-wrenching feeling that something was still missing. The money, the parties, the headlines and yes, the women—nothing was filling the void. Somehow what was supposed to feel like the conclusion to my journey in *"making it"*, felt nothing more than a dark hole.

The voice inside my head had never been louder. Except it was a voice that didn't seem to understand the darkness I was experiencing. It was pushing me for more—maybe I just haven't made enough? Do I continue or do I navigate the darkness?

Today, I think back to that Andrew and wish I could say this to him...

# A LETTER

Dear Andrew,

I have some advice that may help you feel better about your life. Are you open to listening?

Let me be direct; you are an addict. You have built your entire decision-making process around scoring the next hit. The high, in your case, is a dopamine rush from endorsement. Any action that generates the approval of others has become the subconscious intent of your decisions. I know you can see this pattern, and I am sure it's pretty profound and possibly something you may not want to look at, but denying it won't cause you to unknow it.

Over time life will become easier, more purposeful, and even joyful, if you start by;

- Understanding your flawed decision-making process.
- Limiting your addictiveness to the approval and acceptance of others.
- Focusing more attention introspectively.

The dark hole you often find yourself in is a lack of self-confidence. You learned from a young age to seek the approval and validation of others, which turns out to be a masterful skill you have. To better understand how you make decisions, let's unpack the emotional narrative that goes on inside your head after you get the approval of someone;

- I am successful — because someone else who is successful praises me.
- I'm excited – I feel validated and experiencing a euphoric rush.
- But wait — I still have an anxiety-filled heart.
- It must mean I haven't achieved enough — I just need more; then I will feel better.
- But wait – I have been here before, and it only feels better for a fleeting moment.
- My life is meaningless — I am nothing.

All you need to do is insert a few additional lines into the script, and you will see changes in no time.

- I know the intention driving my decisions – to be liked, loved, and accepted.

- It will feel better once I develop some self-worth - me approving of myself.
- I recognize I have built some excellent skills - now direct them toward a noble purpose.

You are successful (in the traditional sense) partly because you grew up in the outback of Australia and developed a high level of self-reliance at a young age. Also, partly because you had a decent education, you're a 6'4" white male with above-average intelligence, handsome, and charismatic. You were born privileged compared to 95% of the population and have only recently realized this fact (another story for some other time).

- Your father taught you the value of hard work.
- Your late uncle taught you the importance of drive.
- Your mother the value of morality.

You set off at a young age to see and experience the world, full of excitement and with plenty of naivety. In your twenties, you were fearless and just wanted to feel good. You didn't care much about success or building a career. You wanted enough money to see the world, go to incredible places, be around fun and influential people, be stylish and meet lots of women.

In your thirties, things drastically changed! You lived in New York and were grossly affected by becoming someone and making something of your life — whatever that means. I think that's where you got a little lost.

You didn't have an apparent reason for working your butt off, no real vision for the future, only a desire to achieve greatness and be popular.

It felt good to work hard. Be promoted quickly. Increase your salary from $35,000 to $350,000 by the age of thirty-five. You had plenty of skills, a novel foreign accent, and an influential network to get high off the NYC lifestyle.

Things started to change in your late thirties; an eight-year relationship ended, and your life savings went into a tech start-up that failed spectacularly with the crash of 2008. Your father attempted suicide (thankfully, he failed). You found yourself sleeping on a dusty couch in your office, feeling foolish, alone, and very frightened about the future. Could you be heading toward a similar fate as your dad?
Regards,
Your future self.

I listened to my advice; but it took two decades to sink in. Now back to the moment when I realized I was successful. In the weeks and months after this, I softened the voice telling me to get more and amplifying the one encouraging me to focus on building purpose for my life.

Purpose requires a deeper understanding of emotional patterns, beliefs, and values. Unpacking these was the most challenging thing I have ever faced because I experienced a level of emotional pain that was utterly foreign to me. Now in my forties, this was the decade of my mid-life crisis.

I was full of rage and anger, fear and anxiety, humiliation and loneliness, which forced me to surrender myself completely.

I wasn't open to feedback or criticism, and I wanted someone to tell me I was good enough, whether what I did had good or bad effects. This addiction to a very myopic view of success kept me small. It got me many things: jobs, opportunities, access, notoriety, women, etc. But it didn't give me what I wanted, which was self-confidence.

I wanted to wake up every day without a dark hole in my heart, without the voice inside saying I wasn't good enough, and without me looking in the mirror saying you are a fraud. The only way forward was to give less oxygen to the idea of success and failure and more attention to finding joy through purpose.

To be clear, a purpose to me isn't a goal to get something.

It's a blueprint of how I want to live; how to make decisions, treat others, deal with adversity and relate to myself. It's a plan I intentionally construct to bring the type of internal feeling I want to experience daily.

I can say I have lived a happy life. But these feelings of happiness were related to what I got in the world, physical assets, or personal affirmations. Looking back now, I lived with a constant fear that I wasn't enough, and it was, and still is, exhausting!

These principles didn't magically seep in after I wrote them down; they required testing repeatedly. In most cases, it required a shift in mindset, a rewiring, if you will.

The hardest part of this process was uncovering the very difficult-to-find narrative that runs my entire life. The hurdles to this process are the insecurities that never want to be found and the ego that never wants to acknowledge them. So overthrowing them required much work, which is code for many failures.

The turning point for me was, hitting rock bottom again in my early forties, realizing that the people I cared about didn't leave or abandon me. The irony is that the further I fell, the more people rallied around me. I experienced so much generosity in financial help, accommodation, job offers, and emotional support; it was difficult to accept and comforting to experience.

I recently turned 50; I became a husband and father and decided to change my career, all decisions with much responsibility, risk, and reward. It feels like I am getting a second shot; this time, I have the prudence to be more discerning about my decisions.

As I transition into part II of my life, I have developed a different mindset from the one I had thirty years ago. I have now defined my purpose in life, and part of that was to identify my values.

My core values are; family, wellness, personal growth, and humanity. My purpose in life is to build and nurture lasting relationships. Whether these are family, friends, or colleagues, they are all with other humans. They allow me to solve problems, reveal insecurities, build empathy and expose my emotional patterns.

The major shift here is that my purpose has evolved from a destination to a way of being.

I still have preferences, things I love doing like; starting businesses, seeing the world, physical activities, and being a husband and father. These all need interpersonal relationships to be successful. The better I communicate with understanding, empathy, and compassion, the better I become at these pursuits. The more transparent and honest I am with my intentions, to myself and others, the better the outcome, even if it's often harder to do in the beginning.

I often daydream about having this kind of wisdom when I was twenty years old and how different my life would have been.

I don't suffer a lot about what could have been but rather use it as fuel to motivate myself daily to stay the course. It reminds me to connect with what's essential and disregard what is noise.

I realize there isn't much I can control in life; the only things are my thoughts, emotions, and reactions to things. Most of the time, it doesn't feel this way. Still, with practice, I have started to experience the power of controlling my reactions to everything.

Finding that small window of space — between being emotionally triggered and the moment I react — and sitting in the certainty that this is all I control. The more I find truth in reality, I have no control over what happens in the world, and total control over how I react to it, the more joy I experience.

I am dedicating more time to solving big problems in the world, working with people I care and respect deeply, being present to experiences with friends and family, and finding time to reflect on living my most joyful life.

When life becomes difficult, I hold my son tight, look into his innocence, see him as my NorthStar, and ask myself, how will my decision right now impact him and his generation's experience of life?

# Cristina
## Riveroll

### Founder & CEO
*NUBE HOSPITALITY*

S uch a broad yet brief sentence, times do fly and I would say many things to myself that I have lived and learned along the way. However, had I known them then; I would not be the person I am now.

My professional journey started as a teacher in my hometown, Mexico City. I loved being a preschool teacher and always strived to be the best as I was forming and touching many lives. It was a very rewarding profession as Children and elderly folks have always had a very special place in my heart.

I would say to myself, to enjoy and deeply cherish every single minute of that journey; which I did, up until the time I moved to the United States and fate pulled me away from education and invited me into Hospitality.

This transition was tough. I was not able to teach then due to not having a teaching credential in the States, and hospitality at the moment was quite my only option, due to many personal circumstances and my need to join the labor force back then. I remember having dreams which I called *"nightmares"* where, as I was opening hotel rooms there was an empty classroom behind each door. A subtle mental transition. It was the beginning of my Hospitality career and little by little the opening of those doors led to guest rooms.

## A LETTER

I would say to myself to follow every step I did, but to stomp firmer and with more confidence, as these steps have led me to the right path. My passion and talent for Hospitality was unfolding during this journey.

The Hospitality industry is a very noble yet demanding one. Its doors never close and the demands that come with that nature of it, never stop as it is an industry that operates 24/7. I wore many, many hats to climb the ladder in this industry, and yes, I climbed it one step at a time. Always with dedication, focus and eagerness to do better; despite the many odds against me, such as learning a new language and the discrimination that comes with it, and more. I would say to myself to keep doing what I was doing without any fear and not to worry about the odds, as they one day, may be in your favor.

I have cleaned rooms, done laundry, checked guests in and out, made reservations, carried bags, picked-up and drop-off guests from and to their destination, served and bussed tables, taken guest compliments and complaints regarding their stay, and many more line duties that often go unappreciated by most.

I would say to myself that one day I will be very proud of what I have accomplished up until then, and acknowledge how these duties laid a very strong foundation for the next ladder steps I was yet to stomp up on. I would also say thank you!

The next phase of my career was more on the strategic side as I played many roles within the managerial team of the hotels I worked at. I would say to myself with no doubt, to loosen up a little and slow down to smell the roses.

I was at a given time, responsible for overall hotel performance, sales, leading teams, employees, management company, hotel owners, guest satisfaction, rate strategy, planning, hiring, firing, budgets, profit and loss, community relations, union relations, etcetera.

My first role in management within a hotel was in the Sales Department and my last role before I moved on to the corporate ladder was a General Manager. I would say thank you for grounding a very strong foundation to get me ready for what was coming next!

*"Success is not measured by what you accomplish, but the opposition you have encountered, and the courage with which you have maintained that struggle against overwhelming odds."* ~Orison Swett Marden

I was recruited for a recognized Hotel operating company in Southern California as a Regional Director of Operations. It was a lengthy but worthwhile process to get hired. I was hired to oversee the development and operations of a portfolio of many hotels owned by a very important and prestigious group of family hotel developers in the United States. After a few years of having opened and operated many branded and independent hotels within this portfolio, I was promoted to a VP of Operations role where I was responsible for the oversight of all the openings of the company. It encompassed many brands, sizes, types of hotels, and ownership groups. I led hundreds of team members at once and enjoyed every minute of it. I was still touching lives in many different ways. I would say to myself that I have come a long way. Although it was not easy to get where I was, I am proud of it and would not change a thing. Emphasizing that this message is not coming from the ego stand point where we can easily believe that we could have or should have done something better or different, or that we have done everything right, but from the heart; knowing that I poured it into everything I did at all times.

At the beginning of the Pandemic, all of my projects were put on hold szwindefinitely.

Little did I know what was coming next. Had I known, would I have done something different when it came to managing up? Perhaps, but doing things differently may have led me to not following my dream of independence.

Being in development always allows you to learn more about upcoming trends and not necessarily what's in now. I have mentally encouraged myself, prior to this event to start my own Glamping brand. I had gained the knowledge of brand development and this upcoming niche was very intriguing for me, so I applied myself to doing so full time. I could not have sat around while the pandemic passed, I am hyperactive and proactive. If I had done it successfully for others, why would not I do it for me?

Amidst the pandemic, I had developed a comprehensive Glamping brand that was ready to be promoted, NUBE. A brand that encompassed my bicultural background, love for the outdoors and hospitality. I knocked on many doors and although the pandemic came to accelerate the knowledge of glamping in the market, the lenders were not ready to embrace it as something that was here to stay. One of many doors I knocked on, led me to what was my next step on the ladder within the hospitality industry.

I accepted the role of Sr. VP of Operations for a leading glamping brand in the US and did it under a verbal agreement that my brand could eventually become a part of this portfolio.

The pandemic was coming to its second wave.

I agreed to put my dream on a *"shelf"*, and rolled up my sleeves again. I did what I know best, and put all my knowledge in leading teams, development of brand and standards, pre-opening, operating assets etc, into practice. During that time, the fire within to pursue my dream was a daily burning sensation that kept whispering in my ear to go back to it, so I did. I resigned from my role after having done it for almost a year. Would I now have said to myself not to do it? No, it was a great learning and growing experience for me. I would give myself kudos for going against all odds and follow my gut feeling, when I felt the timing was right despite this great opportunity.

*"I am not a product of my circumstances. I am a product of my decisions."*
~Stephen Covey

Four years have passed since the inception of NUBE. I have traveled hundreds of miles, met hundreds of people, knocked on many, many doors in the United States, Mexico, Spain, and the Dominican Republic. Despite the numerous complexities and challenges, my joy for NUBE allowed me to persevere through the journey, although from time to time I felt like giving up.

I am super excited to share that I have found the funding for my first NUBE resort (which will be the first of many), and will be located in Los Cabos, Mexico. I would say thank you to myself again for having the determination to not give up and keep going against the odds. The professional and personal growth and setbacks have made me who I am, and I am proud of the woman I have become. I would say thank you, again! Keep going Cristina, the best is yet to come.

# Natalise
# Kalea Robinson

**CoFounder & CEO**
*PARALLEL HEALTH*

Dear Natalise,

To celebrate your 16th birthday , I wanted to write from the future and provide some insight to support you on your journey ahead.

### As the wind blows, let stress go

This year, you will be accepted into Stanford (I know, I'm spoiling the surprise. I'll do that a lot in this letter, sorry – but it's for your benefit, I promise). I'm telling you about Stanford because I don't want the anxiety of college acceptance to overwhelm and distract you from being present. You've worked hard, so take some time to breathe and enjoy the small moments with friends and family. Your high school friends are absolute gems and will be with you for many years to come, but life will never be the same after graduation. Time will be more fleeting and hard to come by in the future, so relish the time that you have now with those you love.

### Recognize that life is in the moments

While you're in college, you'll have a rare and special opportunity to graduate early and pursue your dream of music. And what an amazing

# parallel™

discover your true parallel

adventure it will be – you'll get to hear yourself on commercial radio, see your music videos on TV, be featured on a few television shows yourself, and even walk a few red carpets! Not all moments will be glamorous, in fact, most will be filled with hard work, late nights, and some days a bit lonely if I'm being honest. But this chapter will be a period of unquestionable growth for you. During this time, because you are so future driven, it will be easy to focus on the end goal, but try to enjoy the process of creating and the journey itself. Achievements are recorded on paper, but what is etched in your memory are the moments. It's the seconds and minutes when you are living your truth – in the studio, on stage, during quiet moments while traveling, in the writing room with other songwriters, at home with your dog, or being enveloped in nature – that will matter to you in the end.

## Just be you

You have always been self-conscious about how you appear to the world, especially given the way you grew up. But the big secret is that no one actually cares. So, spend more time practicing living comfortably in your own skin. Accepting yourself for who you are – everything that is awesome and everything that is still evolving – will serve you well not only in your personal life, but also your professional life.

To that end, don't worry about fitting in, either. You are wholly, wonderfully you. But not everyone will see that. There will be people who misjudge you, misplace you, underestimate you – that's on them. One day, there will be a guy at a big record label who will tell you that he can't sign you because you're Asian-American – and *"America just isn't ready for an Asian recording artist."* Yes, those words will actually be said, and yes, you'll feel pretty shitty. You might ponder how you might be able to make choices that make you *"less Asian."* But that would just be a futile exercise in insecurity. Don't let others take away your power. The more the world pushes you to change, the more you should lean into living and speaking your truth. Realize that all the traits that make you unique are your superpower. These traits allow you to bring something different to the table, to think and color outside the lines, and to pave your own path.

## Don't be afraid of imperfection and failure

You are a born entrepreneur. What can I say, you got it from your mama; it's in your genes and your bones. But entrepreneurship for you will come with emotional struggle, not just because it's hard, but because you are a perfectionist. You know how you've gotten straight A's since you got that B- in history in 5th grade on your *"quarterly"* report card check-in, which, by the way, wasn't even real? (It was a check-in, but I digress). Well, let me shatter your expectations; it's easier to control your grades (which is actually really hard) than your entire life. So you're going to have to deal with being imperfect. Perfection assumes that you can control all the pieces on the board. But entrepreneurship, which you're going to choose over and over again, is actually a commitment to uncertainty. There will be challenges, uncertainties, and risks. And you will be imperfect; you will fail sometimes. You will go through a series of starts and stops, along with a host of disappointments. But realize that the imperfections and failures make life (and you) more interesting. So when you feel that fear tensing in your throat, lean into it. Experiencing fear is being confronted with the choice to live an authentic life. Choose what's real, not what's perfect.

**Money is a means to an end**

Money stresses you out. Look, money is nice to have. More than anything, it can afford you experiences that you can relish and, if you have enough of it, a life where you have one less thing to worry about. That being said, there will be times in the future when your financial picture is, let's call it... dicey, shall we say. ;) But as a musician, as an entrepreneur, as an adventurer, you are, in essence, choosing autonomy of creation over stability. But even when things are financially scarier than your parents (or you) would prefer, you will make due. You'll even commit to going to two new countries you've never been to every year (and you will actually keep it up until something called COVID happens in 2020). And you will realize that you don't actually need that much money to create worthwhile memories. You'll find that actually, the most worthwhile memories have nothing to do with money at all. Most importantly, don't ever let your idea of success, your self-worth, or your identity hinge on how much money you make. And here's a pitfall to avoid: because you will be lucky enough to meet some incredibly pedigreed, extraordinary, and, candidly, rich people, you might fall into the trap of comparison and feel like you really haven't done anything of significance. Don't fall for it. Everyone's path is unique and different. To achieve true wealth, focus on impact, creating value, and improving lives. Success is about building something you're passionate about and cultivating a more beautiful, more positive world.

## When you're hurt, the answer is empathy

Remember that everyone goes through their own emotional journey in this life. People will hurt you, disappoint you, take advantage of you, and (prior to a movement called *"Me Too"*) even hold your career hostage - this will happen a few times, unfortunately. All of these experiences will make you stronger. And over time, you'll reflect back on these experiences with empathy for these individuals. That doesn't mean you need to maintain contact or deal with their toxicity, but it does mean you can forgive and move on with your life – and be better for it.

## Authentically connect with other cool humans

Make meaningful connections. As an introvert, connecting with others, especially in groups, will be difficult for you to be enthusiastic about. But reframe the way you think about it. When you meet really interesting, cool people, get to know them on a human level, and you will find that you will not only access valuable insights, opportunities, and support, but also friendship, personal impact, and growth. And that's a two-way street.

Your life partner is the most important career decision you will make.

While you are incredibly driven and your career ambitions will lead your priority list for most of your life, deep down, you are a creative, romantic at heart. And after some tremendous heartbreaks and major duds, be patient. You will end up finding someone who's pretty great. At first, it won't be super obvious to you that he's *"the one"* because you will perceive that he is so different. But actually, he's quite complementary. He will be equally career-driven, intellectual, and on a quest in this life to grow and evolve. He also won't be too bad to look at. But importantly, together, you will support and champion each other in your careers; you will challenge each other's assumptions about the world, which force self-evolution and growth, and you will respect and encourage each other to be your best selves.

## Treat yourself well

This one is from Sylvia (your mother). Sylvia would be happy to rattle off all of her health reminders to you: don't consume so much sugar, sit straight, walk straight, wear a jacket more often, drink warm water, eat blueberries and walnuts, smile more, etc. But her most poignant rule for you is this: treat yourself well. *"You can have everything in the world, but if you don't have your health, none of it matters,"* she says. And you have to admit, your stress, anxiety, and self-induced pressure is, indeed, out of this world. You constantly press play. It's ok to press pause sometimes to take a breath. You'll find that some of the most beautiful moments in a song are the rests between the notes.

**You got this**

Lastly, no matter what happens, you got this. I believe in you. I love you. The universe is big and you are more than you ever imagined.

Happy 16th Birthday. Catch you on the other side.

Love,
Me from 2023

# Laskowitz

**Vice President**
*PAYIT DIGITAL GOVERNMENT*

Dear Jack,
You're hosed.  That's it.  Good luck.  Wish I had a better story to tell you.

Kidding!  You know that.  It's going to be great.  Clearly, every minute won't be great, but if it was, would it really be great?
   As your grandma used to tell you, you're constantly making memories.  Here are a few pointers to think about as you travel along this journey so the memories you make are the best ones, and there will be some awesome ones.

   Finally, before you read all these nuggets of wisdom, know that you won't be perfect. Far from it.  You'll struggle with spending too much energy seeking approval and acceptance from other people and from avoiding conflict.  That means you'll try to provide diplomatic answers too often.  If you stop reading now (well, in a moment. Bear with me!), know this: be yourself.  Trust your judgement.  Speak plainly, clearly, and stand behind your convictions.  Just do so with an openness to be wrong and give yourself the grace to evolve your thoughts and opinions.

   Okay, on with the show:

## Time – do something with it.

Some people will have all the recommendations on the best shows and movies to watch or the best video games to play. It may suck in the moment to not be that guy. Don't worry. You know what that means? You're not spending HOURS of your life behind a screen doing very little. Worst case, just look up some rec's on Reddit as a gap filler.

We've all heard that time is your most precious resource. Think about how you spend it as an investment of your time. Are you investing that time in yourself? Your health? Your family? Your career? These investments should pay dividends, and that's not always just financial.

Consider spending some of your time where you have a passion or a purpose greater than yourself. You likely won't paid for it (that's what we like to call a job), but guess what? Some of these experiences will be the most valuable of your life. Sometimes just minutes or hours of your time will improve the entire trajectory of the lives of other people. Along the way, you'll generate lasting friendships from networks you'd otherwise never touch. Will it be easy and tons of fun the entire time? Heck no. It will be something better: fulfilling. You're going to find that people like to set the camera lens on themselves more and more. Don't get sucked into that. Find your focus outward. I promise you the inward benefit is immense.

You're probably asking, *"why is he mentioning all this 'hard work, not fun' malarky?"* Here's the best analogy I can give you. You know when you've done an hard workout or intense run? It was awful and/or painful while you were doing it. Your muscles literally stopped working after a while. Why did you do it? Because you know that it made you better. That extends beyond physical fitness. There's bad stress (*"you're terrible! Do a better job!"*), and then there's good stress (*"this is hard, but it's so worth it!"*). The good stress is the same as a hard workout. You'll be better in the long run!

## Leave the Joneses to themselves.

There are going to be more instances than I can count where you're going to compare yourself to others. It's going to be a struggle. You're going to fall victim to this. A lot. It's easy to do! You want to be successful. You look at others that you consider successful. It can lead to unhealthy thoughts. Should you be competitive? In the words of Hulk Hogan, *"hell yeah, brother!"*. BUT... should you feel like a failure because someone else has done something better than you?  No, silly.  Someone somewhere is always going to be better than you.  Appreciate them for the talents God has given them, appreciate (and use) what He has given you, and seek to find the behaviors that helps these people be successful.  Then move on and get to work!

Find ways to measure your success in different ways.  Do you feel as if you're giving your best?  Are you investing your time the best ways you can?  Are you bringing joy and belonging to others?  These will be much better barometers.

Oh, and you won't nail it every time.  As one of your mentors will say, *"nobody bats 1.000"*.  He'll also tell you that it's inevitable you (and he) will screw up.  It's how we respond to those moments that counts the most.

**Conclusion: we're all gonna die.**

Unless there's something about science I haven't heard about, we're all mortal.  There's a time when our parents are going to die, when our friends die, and when we die.  We don't know the time nor the order.  At some point, there's a date where no tomorrow comes for each of us.  Don't allow that to get you down, but let it motivate you to take advantage of every moment we have.  Allow those moments to become memories, living on well beyond our time.  Frankly, even those memories fade, and we're left with the ripple effect of our efforts to leave this world a little better than when we entered it.  If you love someone, tell them.  Romantic, friendly, or caring love – share it.

Bonus: If your kids love a game where you say *"glow"* and not *"go"* when they want to race up the stairs to go to bed, for the love of Pete, just spend the 2 minutes doing that.  They'll get more out of that than ten vacations.  This ain't rocket surgery.

It's going to be a lot of fun.  Enjoy it.

Jack

# Ian Christopher
# Figueroa Schmehl

### Operations VicePresident
*STATE FARM*

Dear Ian,

Y ou're about to embark upon an amazing journey, and this is just the beginning of your story. Think of it this way – your life is a movie, and you're the main character. Let's just refer to you as the hero because, let's be honest, every story has one. There'll be days you won't feel like the hero, but trust me, your loved ones will always think you are. Sometimes long movies have intermissions that let you get up, move around and grab more snacks. Well, young Ian, this is your intermission. Let's take a short break from being the hero and reflect a bit. Grab a popcorn (extra butter, please), your Diet Coke and get comfortable in your seat. I'm going to share how your story develops over the years, all the plot twists and turns, and what you need to keep in mind as the reels roll on. I want you to take everything you've learned in life so far, hold onto it and be grateful. The final credits have not scrolled across your screen. The best is yet to come.

### Marathon not a Sprint

Long days, short years – I've heard that saying. It's certainly true for your professional life. You began your career in the leadership program of a respected Fortune 10 company (different from my current

employer). You're part of the largest leadership class in the history of that company (90 members strong). I want you to know, you'll do just fine. You'll gain so much from every role you have within the company, including life-long friends. You can be proud that two decades after your first day in leadership, there'll be scant few remaining at the company from your class. Don't worry when your classmate is promoted to director during his second year, and you aren't until your seventh year. You'll relocate eight times with this company, including one international assignment, and you'll have 15 different roles along the way. You'll work in operations, business development, sales, product development, and human resources. The opportunity to move around so often and have many different roles is rare in today's labor market. Enjoy every assignment, every learning, and every team you'll work with along the way.

### Give Yourself a Break

I need you to know you're not perfect. Every hero has his flaws. It's fine to have high standards, but it's also good to take a breath. You will make mistakes, just learn from them and move on. And please listen to Melissa (your amazing wife), when she shares you should give yourself a break if you make a mistake. Her advice is spot on (as it usually is). Learn to trust your instincts and reach out to your closest advisors when needed.

### You make sacrifices and choices

Sometimes being the hero means making sacrifices and choices. And you can't be the hero when you aren't healthy. Remember your health is precious. Don't squander it. Eat well (at least most of the time...sometimes you just need pizza). Make exercise a part of your routine and understand you're a corporate athlete. You can't deliver results if you're not healthy. And when you're being wheeled from the operating room after the kidney stone procedure, please remember you don't *"need to send an email"* while in recovery.

When your beautiful daughters are born, don't miss those events. Unlike watching a movie, those moments in your story can't be rewound and re-played. Realize now that there will always be a meeting, an email, or a call. Family is the most important thing in your life. Don't cause regret – create memories instead.

## Time is the most precious resource

You'll hear your mentor say, *"Time is the most precious resource,"* after a decade plus into your professional career. I share this now because it's one of the most valuable lessons you'll learn. Manage your day, manage your energy and most of all be intentional. Everyone is busy. The reason time is the most precious resource is because none of us knows how much of it we'll have.

Respect other people's time. Take the time you need but understand its intrinsic value. Act with a sense of urgency and operate with precision.

Understand that family is the most important piece of your life. Cherish your time with your wife, daughters, parents, siblings, and extended family. You'll never regret investing your time in them.

## Patience and Humility

Continue practicing what your parents taught you. Patience and humility are the two most valuable traits a hero can have when interacting with people. This goes for both work and non-work situations. Have a high standard and expect the best from yourself at work but know you'll make mistakes every day. Give yourself and others grace. Push yourself and welcome other members of the team. Remember that before you can ever be a leader you must be an excellent team member. Always realize you have no idea what others are going through. As you lead teams over the course of two decades, know that people work with you – not for you.

## Networking vs. Connecting

Yes, you need to learn to network, but be true to yourself. The relationships, the friendships you forge – those are real. Don't worry about being seen. The hero ultimately gets what he goes after. Deliver results, be a voice in the room when it matters and pay it forward. That's how you make real connections. You'll have so many opportunities through the years to help others. Keep doing it. Everything happens for a reason, and it's usually for the best.

## A LETTER

I hope you've taken away a few things from our little intermission. Never forget that your faith, family and loved ones have given you a strong foundation to rely upon. Heroes always have a great cast of characters, and yours are the best. As your movie rolls on through the years, lean on that foundation your family has given you. When times are tough know that you're equipped with everything you need. Young Ian, I'm extremely proud of what you've done so far and what I know you'll do before your final credits roll. If critics Siskel and Ebert were watching, I believe they'd give you two thumbs up.

# Daniela

# González

**Founder**
*THE HAPPY SELF PROJECT*

To my younger self,

Dany, I´ll start with a spoiler alert, we have an amazing daughter, we named her Andrea, you know, after our favorite doll. She´s your same age: 16 years old, and much like yourself, she´s dealing with her own battles, but you don't have to worry about her, that's my job, and you know what? she is actually doing great.

In 6 more years, you´ll get to meet her; I know, that´s soon, right? But don't panic, becoming a parent is something that pushed us ahead. You will be surprised and proud of what a pretty good job we are doing parenting. Last week she was asked to write about the best relationship she had with someone, and guess what? She chose ours. I assume it's because no matter how imperfect we can be, Andy knows we will always be there for her.

I know that right now you´re going through a lot, you´re wondering if it´s possible to feel completely happy, and I won't lie, life may not get easier, and sometimes you may not feel like it, but you are strong and resilient enough to face anything that comes your way. Trust me, things

are not always what they seem, and everything in life is temporary. So, enjoy the good moments, and when bad times come (because they will), know that they won't last forever.

I know I still owe you many of the objectives and goals you have, but some of them have changed, and others are still in progress. As we grew, we learned how to prioritize our goals and we have paid attention to what's most important. As I told you before, we are a good mom, and guess what? we are a psychologist with a master's degree in Human Development. We love learning and doing research, specially by listening to others and reading lots of papers and books based on science.

Nowadays, we are doing such a good work that we even started sharing our knowledge and experience with others; we´ve been creating workshops and live sessions, inviting people to do profound introspections about their own selves, and we encourage them to find their own path to happiness.

Since you are me and I am you, I'm going to cheat a little and help you out in these years to come. I'm going to share with you some of the key tools we will use in the following years to find our own path:

**Be present**, stay curious and savor the moment, that´s the best way to enjoy life. Don´t rush yourself or the processes. Allow yourself to pay attention and enjoy the here and now. By being present, you can be in better shape to take care of yourself and others. Practice mindfulness, which means to be intentionally fully present, without judging. Accept the pleasant and unpleasant experiences with openness and deliberately use all your senses. Keep aware of yourself by observing your thoughts, feelings, sensations, and actions. Develop self-awareness, your body has lots of information to share with you. And most important: BREATHE!!

**Be purposeful**, use your strengths and talents in different contexts. Find your life's purpose; try thinking about your best self, your skills, and things you love since you were little. Purpose lies in your essence, it´s the most authentic self. Purpose can also be your life compass, and a great tool to establish, prioritize and achieve your goals. Let me tell you that real magic happens when you clarify your life purpose and put it into others´ needs service. So, find your uniqueness by thinking about what will be missed if you´re gone. You´ll see that without doing great changes, you can unlock your greatness just by leaving wherever place you are, a little better than it was.

**Be a listener**, toward yourself and others. While listening, show empathy and acceptance. Don´t be anxious about what to say or what to advice, just listen. People want to be heard not to be lectured. That doesn't mean you have to agree but be respectful and open-minded to learn from others´ experiences and wisdom. Listen to your body, with your physical sensations you can learn more about your emotions. Avoid the need to classify them as good or bad; emotions just are. Each of them is useful, so don´t try to change them, instead, you can change the way you relate to them. And don´t forget to validate emotions, mostly yours. Validation is the best way to show that you´re truly listening, and it will strengthen your relationship with yourself and others. I´m pretty sure that listening to Andy and validating her, is our most powerful parenting tool.

**Be a doer**, don't let laziness nor procrastination get in your way. Instead, let yourself fail in order to succeed. Maslow stated that *"in any given moment you´ll have 2 options: to step forward into growth or to step back into safety"*. You will regret more the things you didn´t do than the ones you at least tried. Therefore, be brave. Not by pretending that you don´t have fears, but by getting to know yourself better. Try to understand yourself, your fears, your core values, your perfectionism, your wounds, your worries, your triggers and behavioral patterns. It will help you not only for prioritizing goals and for time management, but also to develop self-confidence. Remember that we are all humans, we all have fears, so you´re not alone.

**Be compassionate to others**, but specially to you. Be your best friend. Treat yourself and others kindly. Keep on mind that kindness will never be a waste. According to recent research, self-compassion will allow you to be healthier and happier. Compassion will help you reduce stress and avoid harsh criticism. It can also lead you to strengthen your belief that you can improve and get back on track with your goals as many times as you need. It´s a great antidote against perfectionism. Compassion can get you to a place of forgiveness. And forgiveness is a powerful boost. Some studies link it to a reduction of anxiety, depression, physical symptoms, and even mortality. Think about what you need to forgive, and just let it go. Remember to offer yourself understanding and kindness when you fail or make a mistake. Don't be a harsh judge, life´s hard enough.

**Be grateful**, appreciate goodness in your life. Gratitude will help you focus on what you have instead of what you lack. Because of hedonic adaptation that we all share as humans, we tend to adapt fast to everything. Consequently, it´s easy to take good things and people for granted. But gratitude can lead you to become more attuned to the good things in life, improving your well-being. Research suggests that it can also help you cope with hard times, be healthier, keep optimistic, and build stronger relationships. To achieve this, I recommend you start writing about what you are grateful for. You´ll see that soon it will become a habit.

**Be you**, get to know more about your strengths and weaknesses as a way of showing and accepting yourself. Avoid being so harsh on your expectations, and most important: embrace your ordinariness. Let yourself be imperfect, we all are, even nature is imperfect. So, stop looking up for perfection. Don't let your inner critic voice rule your life, it is the voice that grows from fear of disapproval from others. Just imagine how wonderful life would be without worrying so much about how well you're doing and what others think of you, instead of simply enjoying life.

**Be happy**, as simple as it sounds, you´ll learn that happiness is not a goal, is a way of being. And learning to be happy is like trying to get fit. It requires discipline and practice and eventually can become a habit. Deciding to be happy, is a lifelong project and it is the best commitment you can do for yourself. Start by thinking about what makes you happy. Research has shown that happiness is not about money or success, and I truly believe it. Happiness is more about genuinely connecting to others. And it is the quality of your relationships what matters. I can tell you that we have a family where we feel heard, seen, safe and loved. So yes, we´re happy after all, and John Lennon was right: *"all you need is love"*.

You are probably wondering right now if we have already mastered those habits. The answer is no, or at least not all of them, yet we´re still working on it. As I said, we are all humans, we are all a work in progress. However, the difference between now and 22 years ago, is that we know more about us, we´re more patient, careful, compassionate, grateful, and kind to ourselves. I guess part of the problem was that we misunderstood what makes us happy, now we know more about it. Dany, as I said before, I can´t promise you that life will be easy, but I can assure you that we are a person full of kindness, resilience and we are very good at listening. I actually think that's what we do best.

I imagine I possibly chose to write you this letter because in the book Chatter by Ethan Kross, he explains how effective it is to talk to yourself in third person. But perhaps the real reason I´m writing to you, is because I know that in some point, I lost you. Fortunately, I didn´t lose your enthusiasm, joy for life and constant thrust for moving ahead.

Anyway, I'd like to tell you that I´m ready for you, ready to help you heal your wounds, ready to listen you, to give you the validation you needed, to let you be imperfect, to believe in you, to welcome you into your happy ordinary life. Meanwhile, as we figure out how to bring you back into my life, I promise to stay on track and keep moving forward and help ourselves by helping others to have their own Happy Self Project, the one that saved us.

Dany, please come back home, your future daughter and future self, need you.

With love,
Your older self.

**Edvard**
Philipson
*PHILIPSON BUSINESS CONSULTING*

**Sandra Lilia**
Velasquez
*NOPALERA*

**Juan J**
Gallardo
*COLLIERS*

**Eduardo**
Rosales
*SOCIALINKS*

**Frank**
Kasnick
*INDEPENDENT WELDING DISTRIBUTORS COOPERATIVE*

# 5. Change

**Paula**
Haza
*HAZA GLOBAL PARTNERS*

**Javier**
Lattanzio
*TIME EQUITIES INC*

**Jennifer**
Lahoda
*PACIFIC RESOURCE RECOVERY*

**Erik**
Huberman
*HAWKE MEDIA*

# No excuses

**Gustav Juul**
Founder & CEO
*AIM GROUP / XO LEADERS*

I have left the companies I've worked for, for one of two reasons. I will only mention the first briefly so as not to leave you wondering what it was about. It was a conflict of values. I realized that the owner of the company was profoundly racist, to the point where he probably to this day doesn't even realize that he is. It was a situation of "the earth is flat" kind of thing.

The second, was because the companies I worked for didn't want to change. This has happened to me more than once. The most painful separation is, without a doubt, realizing that I had to leave my uncle's business group, which I was being groomed to inherit.

Change is, in my opinion, something as inevitable as the rising of the sun and the changing of the season. One can't avoid change; we can only decide whether to deal with it or not. Dealing with change can be hard, and it definitely requires effort, but it is fated. When we decide not to pursue the opportunities that change offers, we ultimately will disappear. So in my experience, regardless of how "hard" and challenging changing might be, not dealing with it will set us up for failure. Putting it in real business terms, the success rate of not dealing with change, in the long run, is 0%.

Nevertheless, our human instinct is to avoid changing and, as we grow older, the feeling usually intensifies. Our fear of failure is so wired into our brains that we prefer to fall backward than forward. I too have those fears, but I have taught myself to believe that, if you fall forward failing to reach your objective you will at least have moved forward. If you fall back, you will not even be able to see where you are falling.

In a recently published series of studies done by researchers Ed O'Brien and Nadav Klein of the University of Chicago, they found that most people assume that failure is a more likely outcome than success, and, as a result, on the one hand, we wrongly treat successful outcomes as flukes and on the other, we accredit bad results as irrefutable proof that change is difficult.

When the participants in one of their studies were presented with a season's worth of statistics for a star athlete who had logged worse numbers than usual, the participants concluded that the player's career had begun an (irreversible) downward spiral. When they were presented with the stats of players who had extraordinary results during their season, the same people concluded that the player's boost in performance was transitory and nothing but a stroke of luck.

The researchers found the same negatively-biased evaluations in all sorts of situations; when an average student tries to become an excellent student, when pessimistic people try to become more positive, when an overweight person tries to get in shape, when angry bosses try to cut back their outbursts and when business analysts discuss whether the economy is ripe for a recession, their perception of the outcome is usually bleak.

It is, therefore, not surprising that even organizations that pay me good money to help them transform into a healthier company, are affected by these biases when we start working with them. We are very aware of that, and we know that if we are not able to change that, it could become a self-fulfilling prophecy. We have created a whole methodology around it which we call "Energy for change." It is one of the cornerstones of what we do. Depending on how fundamental the changes we need to make in the company are, i.e., the depth of the Organizational Transformation, we know where the resistance will be, and we are able to account for it in the design of the program. The level of energy will change throughout the program, and we know how to handle it when it is low and how to make the best use of the spikes in motivation. It has taken us 50 years to perfect our methodology.

## My journey

Nowadays "Experts" seems are a dime a dozen. Most have taken a few online courses and they are on their way...

In my case it has been a very winding and bumpy road full of highs and lows, It has been an incredible journey to get to where I am today. By the time this book is printed I will have written 8 books, started 5 companies of which 2 failed from the very beginning (not a horrible ratio to be honest). I give lectures at universities and to organizations. What I enjoy the most, though is being an "Organizational Doctor". I know it is a novel term, but it is somewhat like being a Mentor, although focused on teaching the tools that are required for organizations to reach their full potential. We are a rather small but very senior team of "Organizational Doctors". We are fortunate to have a bit of a waiting list for companies that want to work with us, and we have a committee that vets companies based on the owner's/CEO's mindset prior to initiating any project. Still we would love to hear about your journey and figure out what the best way is to support you. This vetting process is much like getting a thorough diagnosis done as a patient by a medical Doctor before he/she is able to prescribe you something. For the treatment to be right, the cure needs to be the right one.

When I started out on my journey, I felt like I was blessed with extraordinary intuition, but my first failure in building a business taught me otherwise. I think it was my mother who said to me: "The devil knows more through being old than through being a devil," and it has made a lot of sense to me since. Experience and guidance are invaluable, which is why I feel this book is such a great resource. I actually read at least one article every day. It is a gift that keeps on giving.

### Bumps and scratched

Any type of initiative will invariably hit bumps in the road; the cost might be slightly higher than expected, it may fall a bit behind schedule, or need further adaptation than initially planned. When this happens, and the organization (owners and/or team members) believes that change is unlikely to be successful, they will regard these situations as a momentary setback and do nothing about it. This "We know better, so full speed ahead" attitude is something that most companies that ultimately fail, find great comfort in. The thing is this; You Will Fail!

### Do change initiatives really fail?

The myth that change initiatives usually fail is disturbingly widespread. It is really not uncommon to read "experts" state that over 70% of change efforts fail. I guess it depends on the perspective of the beholder.

Let me give you an example: April 20th, 2023 - Elon Musk congratulates SpaceX team after "Starship" rocket exploded over the Gulf of Mexico minutes after launch, failing to reach orbit. He says: "Congratulations to the entire SpaceX team on an exciting first integrated flight test of Starship!" "With a test like this, success comes from what we learn, and today's test will help us improve Starship's reliability as SpaceX seeks to make life multi-planetary." What do you think critics were thinking? Was this part of the 30% failure or the 70% success?

At AIM Group, we state that 80% of the possible improvement points are solved or significantly reduced by the end of the first year of implementation of our methodology. I guess that we are pretty good at what we do.

Anyway, regardless of the rate of success or failure that anyone might have, the researcher Mark Hughes from the University of Brighton published his study in 2011 in the Journal of Change Management, demonstrated that there is no empirical evidence to support that an organizational change effort is more likely to fail than it is to succeed.

Mark Hughes traces the mythical "70%" failure rate back to Michael Hammer and James Champy's book "Reengineering the Corporation," in which they state: "...our unscientific estimate is that as many as 50 percent to 70 percent of the organizations that undertake a reengineering effort do not achieve the dramatic results they intended." From that point on, the "unscientific estimate" took on a life of its own, and in peer-reviewed journals, the "50 percent to 70 percent" was abbreviated to just: "Rate of failure of change = 70 percent."

It is funny that Hammer, in a later book, "The Reengineering Revolution," actually tried to set the record straight, stating that the previous simple descriptive observation had been widely misrepresented into a normative statement and that "There is no inherent success or failure rate for reengineering.". Despite Hammer's clarification, it is still continued to be cited as fact.

I wonder if all of these nay-sayers ever might wonder if Darwin's laws also might apply to organizations.

## So what does this all mean?

Anyone that has read a few of my articles knows that I like to make references to sports. Everyone, and I mean everyone, can run a marathon, if we are willing to change. But change is hard; it requires significant effort and sacrifice. The fact that it requires effort, doesn't negate the fact that most people who commit to running a marathon or to a change initiative, and try hard enough, will eventually succeed. We become healthier and better for it, both as people and in the organizational setting.

However hard changing and evolving might be, it is necessary. Remember Darwin? Who survives, and who ends up disappearing?

## Look at the bright side

Change may stir up a host of emotions, including sadness, fear, and anger. Almost every change brings a sense of loss and a wistful desire to return to the way things were. What should we do? Mourn, if you need to, then move on.

When we do move on, make a perfect effort, but don't expect perfect results.

This reminds me of a time I was working with a company close to Sioux Falls, Nebraska. The son of the owner came to me and said that he was scared of telling his father that he had just discovered he had made a mistake that would cost the company a little over $100,000 and that he would get demoted or even fired for it. I told him there was no way around being honest about it. He was surprised to hear his father say: "Why would I fire you? I just invested $100,000 in your education!"

## How to start changing

I have learned that sudden and overwhelming change, although exciting to one of the 4 personality types, will trigger a fundamental survival instinct in the 3 others. Since we have all types of people working in our organization, we need to make it manageable.

The trick to making change manageable is the same way you would move a mountain; one stone at a time. It is the same in business; my recommendation is to break big changes into very small chunks.

The methodology that I apply with my clients recognizes this. We do move quickly but we help everyone in the organization find a sense of balance and equilibrium within change.
… so what happened to my uncle's company

Going back to the beginning of my story. After finishing my MBA and failing my first business venture, I got my dream job in my uncle's organization. We were headquartered on an island in the Mediterranean Sea. I worked with cruise ships and huge yachts. We were selected to participate in a bid for a huge 10-year contract with US Navy and won it! The future seemed bright, but despite all the opportunities a contract like this represents, the company was not able to change. We were barely able to do what we had to do to honor our commitment, but did nothing more. We were offered a series of other opportunities, which my uncle did not even consider going for. As a result, after almost 10 years of hard work and leaving a big part of myself in the process, I decided to leave. Now ask me where to company is now...

Since then, I have done a lot of things, amongst other things, written more than a few books, and I learned and perfected the organizational transformation methodology. I have become an Organizational Doctor. I now help companies understand where their opportunities lie, how to detect problems that are natural and which are not, how to work together to take advantage of the opportunities, how to solve their problems in the right sequence (the sequence is surprisingly important and largely misunderstood), and implement a methodology that makes people cooperate, choosing a path consciously. I love the fact that we are able to make the implementation of whatever decision is taken, successful.

This is not a sales pitch! I share this with you because I honestly believe that if I had known what I know now, I would have been able to find a way to better understand my uncle. I would also have been able to make him understand what I was looking for, and maybe, just maybe, we would have been able to keep his life's work from disappearing only a few short months after his death.

If you'd like to talk about your company's situation and what you'd like to achieve, look me up...

# Gallardo

## Executive Vice President, Client Solutions
### *COLLIERS*

## My Migrant Story

I finally got my Residence card in 2021. It took me 23 years since I first came to work in the USA. Up until then, I had been a Non-immigrant Alien which, other than confusing (sounded like I was an extraterrestrial), meant I could not get a long-term driver's license, my wife could not work, my payments to Social Security and Medicare were going to waste, and my children were condemned to a non-existent path. I had not realized that, until I read the Welcome Letter that came along with the Residence Card listing its benefits. I then went to renew my driver's license and the officer that reviewed my documents said: Welcome to the USA. You are not going to need all those immigration documents ever again!

It has been a wild interesting ride. I originally came to the US in 1998 on a temporary basis. Mexico was coming out of an ugly crisis (one of those recurrent tragedies where the currency collapses, inflation goes through the roof and everybody loses hope), when I got a visit from an old friend. He called out of the blue, saying he was going to be in

town. We met 24 years earlier, at his home in Paradise, California (yes, the town that burned to the ground a few years ago). I went there as an exchange student and had the time of my life. It was a little town in Northern California, with less than 3 thousand happy and friendly people at the time. I was 12 then, about the age of Kevin Arnold, the main character of "The Wonder Years" TV series. It was the early 70´s and Vietnam was still ongoing. My friend´s older sister played Cat Steven´s music all day long. Her friends were terrified with the possibility of being sent to war. I went water skiing, ate sweet beans, and attended church services and baseball games with the family as a temporarily adopted son. That was my first real glimpse at the American society. I learned their language, heard them laugh and cry, listened to their fears and dreams, experienced their structure and discipline, and realized they were also human beings - and not TV characters - that I learned to appreciate.

I was a curiosity for them. Darker and taller than most children my age, I caught the girls' attention. Their conception of Mexicans was based in the farm workers that crossed the border illegally, to work the fields. Kids asked me if I had seen a TV ever before, or if my parents knew what a car was. I don't think they were ill intentioned, but it was cruel and offensive. Still, I decided not to react defensively, and soon it became a nonissue. Later in life I realized there were many versions of my country, with our own racism problems, and education and gigantic economic disparities, but at the time I believed that Mexico was me, and all Mexicans were in my same position. A year later, my friend came to visit us in Mexico. My parents took us to the country house, and we went Iguana hunting. Decades later we were still laughing when recalling my friend's reaction as he spotted the first one. My father told us to stay low and quiet, but he yelled "Iguana papa, Iguana", and the reptile took off. The years went by, and I had the opportunity to spend time in other places, including Buffalo, Toronto, Montreal, Paris, and Heidelberg, but of all my trips as a young man, none compared with that first one.

Life went on and I began my law degree. Right when I was studying the Mexican Constitution, the President in turn decided to violate it flagrantly, nationalizing all the banks. Mexico's currency went from 24 to 48 pesos per dollar in one night, and eventually reached 2,890 pesos per one dollar by the end of the next administration. Inflation went rampant, workers lost their acquisition power, and most people lost their savings. I was in my third year of law school and thought to myself that the Rule of Law did not rule in my country. By then, I had already worked as an intern for a law firm, but my first assignment had been to take a brief-case full of cash to an authority, as a bribe to get a mining concession. I quit in disgust, and went to another firm, only to realize the lawyer was bribing a judge to free a gang of car thieves. I tried evicting a tenant of a property my father owned, but the tenant pulled a knife and threatened my life. I realized I did not have what it takes to be a lawyer under those conditions. Besides, the lawyer was paying me 4 thousand pesos a month, and I was spending 6K between gas and parking. Not a good business.

So, I called an uncle that worked for a multinational corporation. My uncle seemed to be an honest and hardworking man. Maybe I could emulate him. He sent me to a headhunting firm his company worked with. They received me out of courtesy, but said they only dealt with professionals with master's and a solid background. I was still a student and had no real experience. Still, while we were talking, the executive looked at me and suddenly thought he might have something for me. A friend of his, a former banker from before the Nationalization, had to leave the private sector and went to work for the government at the Ministry of Tourism. He was looking for an Executive Assistant, and I could potentially fit the profile, because he wanted someone with no prior experience in government, young and malleable, with no "old habits" to brake. I was certainly young and came from a similar background than he did. You may fit! he said.

I went to visit his friend and had an easy and pleasant conversation. He said he felt he did not fit in the new environment and did not trust his direct reports. He was looking for loyal eyes and ears, to properly navigate the challenge. I said I was ready for the challenge, but he replied he did not have an office for the position. I said I would sit outside his office on a chair. He then said he had no idea how much the position was going to pay, but I told him I would take whatever it ended up being. To my surprise, he hired me on the spot. I started working for him immediately, and when I got my first paycheck, I realized my salary was 22 times higher than what the lawyer was paying me. I was rich! I bought a nice car, and had plenty of spare money to throw around, but the real excitement was just about to come. A former President had just died, and my boss was part of the team that took over an organism that had been created to keep him busy. It managed 33 offices around the world, marketing Mexico as a tourism destination. We were suddenly playing in a different league, with access to global marketing firms that produced costly campaigns and had representatives all over the world. That is when I fell in love with international business.

## CHANGE

Eighteen months later, my boss left the Ministry to follow a friend that had been designated to head another large organism. He asked me to come along, but I wanted to finalize my thesis and get my law degree, to start my own practice. He promised to assign me a secretary to type my thesis and give me enough lee way to successfully conclude my studies. I reluctantly accepted, and as we settled into the new job, Mexico City endured a terrible earthquake on September 19th, 1985. I headed a group of workers to try to unearth people from a collapsed building. A horrible experience, but one to think about, regarding the frailty of life. I decided it was time to stop fooling around and get serious. I went to look for my former girlfriend and asked her to marry me, leaving her an engagement ring, but she came back a couple of weeks later, giving me the ring back, and saying I was not ready. And she was right.

I expedited getting my degree to open my law firm, leaving a well-paid job, only to realize I now had to pay a rent, electricity, secretary, phone, expenses, taxes, insurance, etc. It was an educational year. That year I made very little money, until a widow I solved an inheritance for, asked for help to sell the house she had inherited. I sold it and made more money with that, than as a lawyer the whole year. A young architect I met had gone through a similar situation, when he sold a house that a couple asked him to build and then cancelled the wedding. We traded stories over cocktails and decided to partner. He was 23 and I was 25. We formed a company and ran it for a decade, growing it across the country. We were young and fearless, and although we lacked experience and exposure, our perseverance paid off.

Success allowed me to finally marry the girl. We had two gorgeous daughters and were doing fine, until the next crisis hit: 1995, my best year in sales. I had to sell my cars, my piano, my wife's jewelry, my stereo, my gold chain. We went broke! We were behind rent payments for months. Inflation was over 11% a month, and my credit cards were topped. My income had gone down 85% and my credit was destroyed. The End of the World, I thought, but even that would pass, and eventually I was able to come back. I finally sold a large property, and with the fee I got, I was able to renegotiate my debts and paid them out. We had just moved to another apartment when my American friend showed up. He called saying he was going to be in town and wanted to stop by. He wanted to become a Catholic priest and was on his way to a seminar. I reluctantly agreed. When he came, we carried the conversation in English, as he had forgotten his Spanish. I had not used the language for a long time but remembered enough to blame Americans for all the economic struggles Mexico had gone through since the 70s. I explained that when we met in 1973, you needed 12 pesos to buy a dollar, but that by 1996, you needed 9,000 pesos. I blamed them for the oil crises of the 70's and the stock market crash of the 80's, arguing that the North American Free Trade Agreement had been a secret arrangement between politicians on both sides of the border, to secure cheap labor for the US. My friend just sat there, patiently staring at me. He knew nothing about politics and was all about God's love. We had not seen each other since we were 15, and 20 years later we hardly recognized each other. But he allowed me to let off steam. By the time I was finished, I realized I had spoken nonstop for two straight hours, blaming all my problems on others. As the days went by, I had to accept that not everything was to be faulted on politicians or other countries. I was to blame for my own imprudence, excessive risk-taking appetite, poor preparation, little process, too much drinking and partying, and naivety. On the other hand, I had been speaking in English for two hours, and although I was rusty, the language was still there, somewhere in my "hard drive". I concluded that neither my friend nor the Americans were to blame for my own doings. I had been the maker of my disgrace, and it was up to me to come out of it. But how? A few months later, Lady D had died in a crash. We were the same age, and I had had a crush for her since she started her public life. But the beautiful princess did not have a happy ending, and if death had come to such a lovely person, it could come to me any time. I needed to wake up and do something radical to change my life.

Four years earlier, I had taken postgraduate studies in International Business. The lesson I remembered the most was the first few words the professor said: "Multinational Corporations are the new Feudal Lords of the world. They are more powerful than countries, not being bound by frontiers. They have a ton of money and a flexibility no country will ever have. They will consolidate into fewer and fewer players, until there are 3 or 4 of every trade". At the time I thought he was crazy. He had never worked for a multinational corporation, and was just a "library rat", but having witnessed what happened in Mexico after NAFTA was signed, convinced me he was right. Medium and small firms like mine were disappearing. The Big Boys had come into the market, and because I could not fight them, I realized I needed to join them. I knocked the door of an international firm in my trade, and told them I had expertise in their trade, and certain language skills. They did not even test me and three days later I was working for them. I did not know the team that was taking care of their international business had just walked out the door to form their own firm a few days earlier, and I had knocked the door at the right time.

## CHANGE

I tried talking my partner into shutting down our firm and joining me at the new one, but he had a different financial position, and preferred to buy my shares and continue as an independent. It was not an amicable split, and he resented me for many years, for having jumped ship. He still owns the firm I sold him, but it never took off. My professor's prediction kept coming true, and just a few weeks after my incorporation to the new firm, it merged with another one in Europe, becoming the largest in the world. They needed someone to be based in Miami, and I offered to cover the post. That is how my migrant adventure began.

Deciding to leave the country was bittersweet, but my wife and I were in our mid-30s, and our parents were in their sixties, so we thought we could get away for some time, without risking losing them. We planned to stay in the US four years, just enough for the girls to pick up the language, coming back to our country right before they became teenagers, to avoid drug and sex problems we believed to be prevalent in the USA. That is why we did not even think about getting a Green Card back then. Besides, it was the year Bill Clinton was being impeached. My guess was that the whole project was going to collapse soon, so we should enjoy the ride while it lasted.

But Clinton got away, and the show went on. We moved to Miami, where we rented a lovely house in the suburbs. I started doing business across the Americas, with some scattered trips to Europe. I was delighted, as I could never have dreamt of this with my little firm. I learned to appreciate the American way of doing business: Straight and to the point. No waste of time dancing around for hours before you start talking business. Work started and ended early. Lunches were short and without alcohol, allowing to go back afterwards, and still be productive.

Miami was a weird place. The Melting Pot of the South, they called it. My boss was European, number two from Venezuela, and the rest from Haiti, Bahamas, Spain, and the UK. There was only one American in the team, and we made her feel an alien in her own country. I was surprised at how little we needed to speak English in Miami. Spanish was spoken everywhere. There were even signs outside businesses, clarifying that they did speak English. My wife could spend weeks without needing to pronounce a word in English. Although more than 90% of students and teachers at our children's school were Latins, the school ratings were very high, as most children were coming from private catholic schools from their respective countries. They spoke English at school, and Spanish or Portuguese at home, and were not socially ostracized because of that.

Our boy was born about a year later. Between pregnancy and our daughter's school, my wife had very little – if any - contact with Americans. Even though she had no maids, like we used to have in Mexico, or her mother to support her, she managed to deal with everything, and was not ashamed pf doing things herself, because her friends were doing the same. I was constantly travelling because back in the late 90s, electronic connectivity was very limited across Latin America, and long-distance calls were prohibitively expensive. Besides, back then you needed to be there to get things done.

We believed life was great, but there were clouds in the air. In January 1999, the Brazilian economy collapsed, creating the Samba effect, followed by the burst of the dot-com bubble in the US, and the Argentinean Great Depression of 2001. The September 11 attacks were the final drop. Our Latin America division generated a very small percentage of the company's global revenues, and the new owners decided to consolidate it with North America, shutting down the Latin American headquarters. The company kept ownership of the Mexico and Brazil operations, giving away the rest of the offices, no longer paying salaries and expenses. I was offered to stay in the US on a commission basis, but my visa was tied to my job description and a steady income, so I had to leave. I took a temporary job with another firm, to stay long enough for my children to finish school, but by September 2002, we were back in Mexico. This first trip lasted precisely the 4 years we had originally planned for, but our return had not been neither planned nor voluntary. We lost a small fortune between getting rid of vehicles, cancelling leases, and moving costs. The only gain we had made was an additional family member and a puppy. I thought we were never going back to the States, but 7 years later, we came back. Now my daughters got their master's and have great jobs. They live close by and come often to visit. My son is doing a PhD in Saint Louis Missouri, and my wife and I moved to the financial district, to be closed to the office. The USA has been very generous with us. We made our lives here, so when the time came to decide, it was easy: we stayed.

# Erik
# Huberman

**Founder & CEO**
*HAWKE MEDIA*

## How I Dealt with Change Throughout My Career

There's no shortage of quotes and cliches regarding change. Albert Einstein said, "The measure of intelligence is the ability to change." Winston Churchill said, *"To improve is to change; to be perfect is to change often."* Some random fortune cookie I had said, *"Change is the only constant."*

These are all accurate. Who am I to argue with the likes of Einstein, Churchill, or fortune-cookie wisdom? But over the course of my career, I've started to shape my own definition of change.

I've dealt with change in every stage of my career. The most memorable moments of transition are tidal waves, and throughout my career, I've gone from getting sucked under to learning how to ride them.

### When Change Happens to You

I started my career in real estate, which is a great industry where I could leverage several of my strengths. The only problem was I happe-

ned to kick off my career around 2008... Not exactly the best time to start to dabble.

As soon as I started work, the landscape changed in unprecedented ways. My saving grace in this wave of change was that I hadn't been in the field long enough to have preconceptions about the "norms" of the industry. Sure, I was educated to prepare for a traditional marketplace, but entering the field without a true sense of the status quo forced me to recalibrate constantly and buckle up for the ride.

As most people do when they first start their professional journeys, I was struggling. When I look back, I'm not sure how I made ends meet. I was fully in survival mode, but my clients and customers didn't know that. They saw a young professional who stayed optimistic and kept his head above water no matter the turmoil happening around him.

There aren't a ton of reasons to look back at that era in my career with a lot of fondness, but it taught me I was adaptable. I didn't realize it at the time because it was all happening so fast, but I was rolling with every punch for years. That was an unrivaled period of change for the whole country, but it taught me that change doesn't have to drown me.

Learning I was adaptable to change was important early on, but I still had a long way to go in my relationship with change.

## When You Are Part of the Change

In my subsequent professional pursuit, I wouldn't be pushed around by a changing industry. Instead, I was going to be the change to shake up an industry. Think of it as the entrepreneur's version of Ghandi's "be the change you want to see in the world."

I launched a clothing subscription service called Swag of the Month. As a real estate professional, I'd established my own name as a sort of brand, but this was my first time building a brand from scratch. I landed on this service because it was something I thought I could use. I've never wanted to put a lot of energy into my wardrobe, and a subscription-based service to keep my clothes fresh seemed like a hole in the market that I could fill. I didn't have a background in the fashion industry, or even the ecommerce industry, at the time. But I had a unique perspective that could change those models.

The brand was successful for years – successful enough that the more prominent players the in fashion field got wise. After the success of Swag of the Month, more and more subscription-based clothing brands began to pop up, and established brands like Nordstrom were starting their own competitors to my product.

I'd been successful in changing the industry, but once again, change was happening fast around me. I knew I was adaptable, so I looked into ways my brand could evolve to keep pace, but the truth was, my heart wasn't in it anymore. I'd accomplished what I set out to accomplish.

Of course, I was hesitant to sell off a brand that I had worked hard to build, but when the opportunity arose, I had to admit to myself that I needed the change personally and professionally.

My company was successful in changing the industry, but rather than trying to keep up with the continuing evolution that I'd help set in motion, I decided to take the capital from selling my company and start my next endeavor.

The lesson about change from this part of my career was the realization that change didn't have to be something I always had to keep up with, but I didn't have to drown from it either. If I leveraged it right, I could use change to my own benefit, whether professionally or personally. In this case... it was both.

## When You Lead the Change

For my next endeavor, I swapped out D2C for B2B. I launched Hawke Media, a marketing brand with the goal of making great marketing accessible to all brands.

During my time in ecommerce, I noticed two things about most ad agencies. First, they only wanted to work with the biggest name brands they could find. They were concerned about building their own portfolio, not actually building my brand. Second, most of them were full of shit anyway. They pitched lofty ideas, not tangible results.

Hawke Media was created to be an answer to that frustration. We referred to ourselves as "Your Outsourced CMO" because we care about the success of our clients the way an internal hire would... but with lower costs and more flexibility.

## CHANGE

By the time I was establishing the Hawke Media brand, I'd gotten a lot better at looking ahead and being prepared for change. I was even asked for an interview in the early days of Hawke about what I considered to be the biggest threat to the digital marketing model I was building. The interviewer proposed freelancers as a threat to the agency status quo. In my experience, freelancers were not nearly as reliable as the agency model. Companies wanted to hire marketing help that they could count on the way they could depend on their own employees. Freelancers would never match agencies in that regard, even if the freelancer structure evolved for the better.

I answered that artificial intelligence was the most significant potential threat to the current business model. AI is and was a certainty that would eventually impact every job, and marketing was no exception.

This was around 2015, so talking about AI replacing marketers still seemed far off, but check out industry news in 2023. The future is here.

The good news is that by forecasting that trend at the foundation of the company, I was able to not only prepare Hawke Media for the shift, but position us to lead the way. Shortly after that interview, we began development on AI technology that could advise on marketing strategy. Down the road, we collaborated with another company that created AI dashboards that would benchmark data industry-wide.

The blend of hard work, resources, and good luck led us to launch HawkeAI in 2022. This has completely changed how we measure and report analytics to our clients at Hawke Media. It's also positioned us well as new AI technologies seem to roll out every day. AI is embedded in the workflows of every team member at Hawke Media, and its influence will only continue to grow.

Of all the "tidal waves" of changes that have taken place in my career, I'd argue none have been as impactful as artificial intelligence will be in the next several years. I view this as the ultimate example of something that is inevitable and will either propel businesses to the next level or sink them entirely.

### Triumph Over Change

I am fortunate for the ways I got to learn from change through the early stages of my career. I learned that I was adaptable to change –

that it didn't have to crush me. Then I learned I could actually leverage it to propel myself to my goals. And now I've learned that if you're lucky enough to see change on the horizon, don't stick your head in the sand. The better you can prepare yourself for change, the more likely you'll be to pioneer innovation.

Bracing for change will ensure you don't just survive in changing tides; you'll thrive.

At this point in my career, I'm finally starting to develop my own perception of change. I agree with everything Einstein, Churchill, and all the other great minds have come up with, but it's good to have my own definition.

Sometimes you can prepare for change, and sometimes it comes out of nowhere, but you can always utilize it to your benefit.

You're more adaptable than you think you are. If you can roll with the punches of change, you can set yourself up for personal success and for professional domination against the competition.

# *Paula*

# Haza

**Managing Partner**
*HAZA GLOBAL PARTNERS*

I experienced the first big change in my life when I was 7 years old and lost my father to a disease called Syndrome of Guillain-Barre which quickly progressed and in 2 weeks' time took his life. Even though I was very young, to this day I still have few flashes of memories from that time. One day early this year it downed on me that I was the same age as my daughter is today when I lost the most important person in my life. As I reflected on that life changing event 38 years later, it was the first time that I felt compassion for my 7-year-old self, triggered by watching my daughter interact with her father…. the loving and close relationship they have and how big his presence is in her life and how much she needs and adores him. I realized right there that the love and security that a father figure represents to a 7-year-old girl was taken away from me at such an early age and forced me to build resilience and courage as a young girl - which now I realized how it has influenced my actions and behaviors throughout my entire life.

I was born and grew up in southern Brazil with my mom and 2 brothers, my mom was only 36 years old when my father died at 40 years old, so her life focus was to raise her 3 kids in a financial unstable situa-

tion although very supported by extended family. My mom is my biggest reference of strength, resilience, and courage and her biggest gift to her children was always making my father's presence felt by reminding us what he wanted the most for his children.... focus on getting proper education. I remember in my early teens going thru a big change and adjustment as we needed to move for few years from my "big city" hometown to a very small town in the countryside of Brazil. Despite the change, I was always very focused on my dreams and the things I imaged wanting for myself. I always carried inside of me an energy that kept my dreams alive .... I would spend hours looking at fashion magazines and I was always very inspired by women in magazines, beautiful, independent, travelling the world.... And wanted to be just like these women!! ... Fast forward to college years back in my hometown I was going to my last year in college when I met my American husband Chris while he was there in his first international job assignment after college. Noting that I had jobs throughout my 5 years in college and saved my entire salary to one day travel to the USA to further my education. When I met Chris I was going to my last year in college and was getting my savings ready to invest into a business graduate program. A big life change experience for me moving from my hometown of Curitiba to the USA 22 years ago!

After business school (I ended up getting an MBA from UNCG in North Carolina) I moved to Washington DC metro/northern Virginia area where I worked in commercial banking for 3 years. Noting that in my last few years in college, I interned in a commercial bank therefore at the time it made sense to continue pursuing a career in banking in the USA. During my time in Washington DC I was still spending most of my free time reading fashion magazines and watching fashion shows on TV (just like I used to do during my teenage years!). So, when the opportunity came for my husband to move to NYC to pursue a new career opportunity, he encouraged me to change industries and look for an opportunity in the fashion industry. That was my first big career change from commercial banking in suburban northern Virginia to the fashion industry in NYC!

I was very excited to pursue a career in an industry that was my passion.... However, I quickly realized that I would need to take a step back and start from the beginning by taking more of an entry level position since I was new to the industry. I was so excited when I was offered a position as an International Licensing coordinator at a hot young fashion brand at the time. That was a dream opportunity working in an office right on Fashion Avenue in NYC! Unfortunately (or fortunately as everything happens for a reason), that dream job lasted only 3 months as the company was acquired by another company and my position eliminated. That was a big disappointment losing the job so quickly. However, at the time we do not realize that things happen for a reason.... and we just need to focus on doing what feels right at the moment and let the universe guide us. After a few months, I got a second job in the industry, which was not exactly what I wanted but still valid to build experience in the industry. Most time as we go through life and change, we don't realize that certain decisions we make will lead us to get what we want in the future. I was in the job for 6 months when I got my next big opportunity working in international expansion for a bigger and more recognized American brand. I ended up building my career at that company, where I stayed for 10 years, working in International Licensing for the Nautica brand which at the time was owned by VF Corporation. I could not have asked for a better opportunity to build my career in the industry doing what I loved the most which is building relationship with businesses and people around the world. That was an amazing experience where I learned so much about the business, travelled the world and made professional and personal connections and friendships that I cherish to this day.

After 10 years with Nautica, I felt the need to change in order to continue advancing on my career. I left Nautica which was a difficult decision to make as I loved the people I worked with for the last 10 years and felt so comfortable with my job. However, I felt that I needed to experience something different within my area of expertise and changing companies was a necessary step for me. I went to work for Gap Inc, overseeing the company's franchise business in Latin America. It was a new and exciting opportunity, working for one of the biggest apparel retailers in the world and with brands that are known by so many people around the world. Change is good and necessary for career progression, and I was very enthusiast and happy with my new career opportunity, however, after 10 years used to a certain way of working, it took some adjustment to Gap's larger teams and new ways of working.

As I was approaching my 5 years with Gap Inc. I started to become very un-settled.... It was time to change; the job was not fulfilling me anymore... but what would I do next? Go to work for another American brand? Wouldn't that be more of the same? After much thinking I came to the realization that I would love to leverage my experience and network built in the last 15 years working for the most well-regarded American brands to help Brazilian brands grow distribution internationally. That would bring me more of a sense of purpose. With that in mind I started doing some due diligence in identifying and connecting with Sr. Management of the companies that I was targeting and learned that most likely the easiest way for me to be hired by these companies would be if I offered my service as a consultant. That meant leaving behind the security of a full-time job and the identify that I built in the last multiple years working in corporate, a very difficult decision to make and the biggest changes in my career so far. In the last few months with Gap Inc., a change in management accelerated my decision and was the push I needed to make the decision, coupled with a great session with a life coach which helped me to go back to my 7-year-old self, and see how brave she was then and how brave she is now.

I'm in such a special moment of my life and career... as now I understand the importance of listening to myself and following my intuition, and that has given me strength and allowed me to take ownership of my next career chapter. I'm very happy with my transition into consulting and already helping my targeted clients to build and execute on their global expansion strategies.

Paula Haza BIO:
Paula Haza, based in NYC, has recently launched her own global consultancy "Haza Global Partners" with the main goal of helping Brazilian/ Latin brands to expand and grow their presence globally. Prior to pivoting into consulting Paula spent more than 15 years helping global apparel/ retail brands expand their international presence. Paula worked at VF Corporation for 10 years, as Director of International Licensing for the Nautica brand, where she established a vast network of retail operators across multiple geographies. For the last 5 years, Paula was the Director of Americas for Gap Inc.'s Global Franchise, Strategic Alliances, and Licensing division, where she led the expansion of Gap, Banana Republic, Old Navy and Athleta brands throughout the Americas. Paula is originally from Brazil, moved to the US 22 years ago and has been in NYC for the last 17 years where she lives with her husband and 7-year-old daughter. Paula is also a volunteer at Trekking for Kids, a nonprofit organization offering purpose driven treks to iconic destinations around the world benefiting orphaned children living in those areas.

# Kasnick

### President & CEO

*INDEPENDENT WELDING DISTRIBUTORS*
*COOPERATIVE*

One day while growing up in Ashland, Kentucky, my father came home from work and gathered our family around our kitchen table to make an announcement. "Kids, I have decided to change jobs and we will be moving to Iran." Knowing my brother, sister and I would have no idea where that was my mom grabbed our globe, spun in around and pointed it out for us. The adventure was on!

By the age of twelve, we had moved from El Paso, Texas, after my father was discharged from the US Army to Pennsylvania to Kentucky then on to Ahwaz, Iran. After living several years in Iran, my siblings and I were sent back to the U.S. to boarding school for a year around the time of the 1979 Iranian revolution. Thankfully, our parents evacuated safely and rejoined us stateside. We then moved to a new town and new school for our junior year of high school, making it the third school in three years that we had to acclimate to.

I reflect on these formative years to seek answers to why change comes so easy for me. I think my experience is analogous to children who grow up in an environment where multiple languages are spoken.

Independent. Cooperative.

For the rest of their lives, they possess a strong language aptitude, effortlessly learning their next language. In my case instead of language, I developed the ability to read and connect with people. Frequently adapting to new communities, schools, friends, sports teams, climates, cultures and geographies honed my social and networking skills.

After graduating college earning a chemical engineering degree, I went overseas into the oil sector working for the Flopetrol division of Schlumberger, a multinational oilfield services provider. In 1985 they hired an international class of engineers, two of us from the U.S. and then the balance in Europe, Africa, and Middle East. We worked on wildcat drilling rigs and were trained to open new reservoirs to measure oil and natural gas potential. In my first year out of school I was working primarily in the North Sea stationed in England, Holland and then France. I was sent out on two-to-three-week assignments, a new place every time ranging from a pasture in England to the largest semi-submersible drilling platform in the world at that time off the shore of Scotland. Needless to say, I think this first career role leaned heavily on my nomadic upraising.

Then, big career change number one hit. As you know, the oil industry is cyclical and in 1986 it crashed. Our entire class was sent back to their home countries, many of us laid off. I was due to report back to a unit in Houston, Texas, and as I was waiting for that to materialize, I started searching for my next job. **So, lesson one: take action, do not wait for something to happen.** That Houston opportunity never panned out as exploration rigs are the first to stack up during downturns. I would have never pivoted to my next opportunity if I had sat around waiting. **Lesson two: use all resources you can when faced with a challenge.** In this case, I went back to my alma mater, Pennsylvania State University and took advantage of their alumni career resource center. That led me to the chemicals industry where a majority of my career has been focused.

I joined Union Carbide as a technical sales representative based in New Jersey and ended up working with them for a decade. It was by far the most formative part of my career in terms of learning about business, leadership and receiving mentoring. I came on board shortly after their tragic chemical leak in Bhopal, India, resulted in over 2,000 deaths. Union Carbide never recovered and was acquired by Dow Chemical in 2001. As I think about that part of my career emerges **lesson three: change management is a process.** In this case, it was all about company survival, but the five principles apply just the same:

1. Prepare for organization change (Union Carbide shifted its focus to its core basic chemicals business and sold its leading consumer products brands: Eveready® batteries, Glad® bags, Prestone® antifreeze)
2. Craft a vision and plan for change (Union Carbide led an industry changing "Responsible Care" initiative)
3. Implement changes (Union Carbide made divestments as noted in 1, and then made investments in large scale chemical complexes like EQUATE in the Middle East and OPTIMAL in Malaysia)
4. Imbed them in culture (through townhall conversations and employee review processes)
5. Review and analyze results (by conducting internal and external benchmarking)

During this stage of my career, I learned **lesson four: you are in charge of your career, the company you work for is not.** I decided to pursue a company sponsored MBA and after earning that degree I reached out to a mentor and expressed interest in marketing & business management. Up until that point of my career I had been a field engineer and sales professional. Recently married, my wife Martie and I relocated to Connecticut where I worked at Union Carbide's corporate headquarters in Danbury. This move was a career springboard to a progression of commercial leadership positions.

Wanting a change from basic commodity chemicals we left Connecticut with two small children for a commercial development role at Castrol Industrial, an entrepreneurial metalworking fluids company headquartered in Downers Grove, Illinois. For the first few years, Castrol was an autonomous North American unit of Burmah Castrol but eventually it was gobbled up by British Petroleum (BP) driven primarily by BP's interest in Castrol's consumer motor oil brand. BP was an interesting company and taught me **lesson five: when pursuing change management, do not take your eye off core business fundamentals.** BP was very progressive and aspirational as evidenced by their early stance on equality and inclusion and their focus on renewable energy. BP rebranded their logo to the now iconic sunflower called the Helios, who was the Greek god of the Sun. Then came their oil spill disaster in the Gulf of Mexico where basic maintenance and operational excellence were rightfully called into question. It should never be an "either or", rather it should be an "and".

During my time at Castrol / BP I had a mentor who eventually reported to me prior to his retirement. He taught me **lesson six: step away** from the day to day, go somewhere, hole up and think deeply about your career, life, family and goals. He called that a personal retreat. My personal retreat camping trip led me to my current industry - the industrial gas & welding business.

From the retreat I concluded I wanted to try out a privately owned enterprise. Our family uprooted with three young kids and relocated to South Bend, Indiana, headquarter of a growing, dynamic large regional independent distributor, Mittler Supply Company. As an outsider to this specialized industry, I was drinking through a fire hose at first. Luckily, we had many team members who knew the facets of the business which allowed me to focus on helping the company formalize their structure and go to market growth strategies.

This led to creating the "Mittler Way" which defined our culture and operating procedures and the "Mittler Difference" which sharpened and articulated our value propositions. Unbeknownst to me at the time, emerged **lesson seven: show up, stay in the present and give every project or task your professional best.** While at Mittler Supply I was asked to serve on a committee charted by a cooperative we were a member of. I became chair of that committee and must have made a good impression because that led to an opportunity five years later which I will come back to. My privately owned business stint was a brief few years as Mittler Supply ended up selling to Praxair, a large multinational corporation.

At Praxair our family had to move again, back to greater Chicagoland, where I was based out of their Burr Ridge, Illinois, complex. Working for our industry's leading company I saw how a first-class safety culture drove focus and leveraged scale and best practices. I gained more appreciation for process, planning and discipline. Then my phone rang again which led to perhaps my final career and family move.

Based on my prior committee leadership while at Mittler Supply, I was recommended to an individual leading the search for the president & CEO role at the Independent Welding Distributors Cooperative. And, so here I am, privileged to lead the largest group in our industry, IWDC, headquartered in Indianapolis, Indiana.

But to lead means someone is following - how does that happen? Not by title alone. A strong leader is a change agent, able to convey direction, pace, and helping staff to grow along the way. At the core, this is all about business growth as all good things come from growth: pride, industry buzz, dynamic work environment, job opportunities and progression for staff. What might increase your chances to become a success-ful leader? **In addition to business acumen and industry knowledge, leadership success hinges on key behaviors and traits – lesson eight.**

Show through consistent communication and action that you care about the staff and the mission. Lead by example, pick the appropriate time to roll up your sleeves and get your hands dirty. Build trust with your employees, industry partners and customers by always acting with integrity. Limit making assumptions and instead relentlessly consume data, trends and facts. Press yourself to keep asking "what could go wrong?", "how can we improve?", "what could change?" and "why do customer buy from us versus competitors?" Searching for answers to those questions will keep your edge and avoid mental laziness and coasting.

Thank you XO Leaders for allowing me to share my career adventure, catalyzed early on by a globe spin!

# Sandra Lilia

# Velasquez

**CEO & Founder**
*NOPALERA*

## How i dealt with change in my career

I found myself unemployed for the first time in my life at the age of 43. I had no savings, over 80k in student loan debt, and was a single mother to a 13-year old. It was at that low point that I realized the only way I was going to change my future for myself and my daughter was to take different actions.

Up until that point I had dedicated my life to music as the bandleader for the Latin Alternative band Pistolera. Music was my storytelling platform to celebrate my Mexican heritage and bring people together. I thought my purpose in life was to write songs and I dedicated all of my time and energy to building my music career. I had many great opportunities, like opening for Lila Downs, Los Lobos, performing at Central Park Summerstage, The Montreal Jazz Festival, and having my music featured on hit TV shows like Breaking Bad. Compared to many musicians, I had been successful. But music is a challenging life where money is never guaranteed. I always maintained a day-job for health benefits and some semblance of security. Even with the day job, I lived paycheck to paycheck in one of the most expensive cities in the world: New York.

# CHANGE

When the day came that I had no job I reached a low point in my life. For the first time I did not know how I would pay rent. I felt true panic. How did I allow my life to get here?

In retrospect, this moment was one of the most defining moments of my life. Diamonds are made through pressure. And I was under pressure to evolve.

In life, we can choose courage or comfort. We can't have both.

As I stood in my parents front driveway in San Diego, I stared at a familiar plant I had known my entire life: the nopal. At that moment I realized there was a lack of high-end Latina beauty brands on store shelves. As consumers we were all familiar with products that used aloe vera. Why had no one used the nopal as their main ingredient? It was much more abundant and regenerative.

For Mexicans, it doesn't get more ubiquitous than the nopal. It is even on the Mexican flag.

I knew that if I created an irresistible Latina beauty brand centered around the nopal it would galvanize the community. It would help a historically overlooked community – and the USA's largest minority group – feel seen and proud. At that moment I decided I would create an aspirational Latina beauty brand and call it NOPALERA. I wanted to disrupt the historically Euro-centric beauty space that normalized higher price tags for brands with French and Italian names.

For the last fifteen years I celebrated my cultural heritage through music from stages around the world. I knew I had the courage, the passion, and the innate ability to lead.

There were only two problems: I had no money and I didn't know anything about making beauty products.

I enrolled in an online formulation school with my American Express credit card. I called a graphic designer friend of mine and told her my vision. I asked if she could design my brand on a payment plan. Fortunately, she said yes.

I spent a year formulating and building the brand in the quiet. No applause. No one cared except me. I had to get more jobs. Three to be exact. One to pay bills, one to pay debt, and one to fund my brand.

It was a brutal time but it was a means to an end. I stayed focused on the vision.

On November 2, 2020 I launched Nopalera from my Brooklyn apartment. I made all of the products myself for the first year and my boyfriend was my shipping manager. The brand took off right away. Nopalera can be found in Nordstrom, Credo Beauty, and over 400 influential boutiques nationwide.

I appeared on Shark Tank, infamously turned down two offers, and went on to raise 2.7 Million dollars.

I lead a team of seven people now. Nopalera has an engaged community of over 125k followers.

One of the many gifts of changing career paths mid-life is that you can take all of the learnings from past experiences and apply them to your new venture. Music taught me so much about resilience, rejection, and community. Those moments of rejection in my music career were difficult at the time. But what I have learned is that the opportunity lies in adversity.

If everything is always easy and comfortable, you will not grow.

It was only because I was forced to think of a new plan that I did. I had to reimagine my identity and my future and then take actions to step into it.

I am living proof that you are never too old or too broke to learn new skills and change your life.

I am driven by three things: changing my financial life, showing my community what is possible, and making sure my daughter never knows what an overdraft fee is in her checking account.

# Jennifer Lahoda

CEO
*PACIFIC RESOURCE RECOVERY*

## Becoming an Extraordinary Leader: Lessons learned from the frontlines of Change

Leading an organization through change is one of the most challenging tasks a leader can undertake. It is a process that tests the resilience, adaptability and foresight of leaders and their teams alike. Change calls upon us as leaders to be extraordinary; to remain grounded through uncertainty, resistance and unexpected obstacles. Of course, leading during times of change requires basic elements like having a strong vision, building an aligned team and mastering the art of communication. It also requires more nuanced elements, like self-awareness, empathy and the courage to ask hard questions. I have found that learning these nuances comes from the experience of being on the front lines of change.

**Leading through change lesson #1: Self-awareness among top leadership in an organization creates a feedback rich environment which allows teams to thrive through change.**

## Pacific Resource Recovery

CLIENT AND ENVIRONMENTAL PROTECTION

We all know that effective communication sits at the heart of change management. This includes being transparent about the reasons for change, the anticipated impact, and the strategy for its execution. A key element of effective communication from a leader that is often overlooked is self-awareness. As the leader of an organization, if I am not actively aware of my personal internal state and how it impacts the organization, then I will not be an effective communicator. Leaders are humans too and change is hard for everyone. Before embarking on a change initiative, organizations need to have leaders who are willing to understand how the proposed change will impact them and do the work necessary to remain grounded throughout the change process. This commitment to self-awareness is not a one-time event, rather it requires on going practice. Some of the practices I have used throughout my career as a change leader include having a non-negotiable self-care routine, working with a coach to set intentions and identify my personal self-limiting thought patterns and triggers. Each of these practices helps me remain grounded and self-aware, which in turn allows me to communicate effectively.

It's important also to remember that communication is not a one-way street. Leaders need to listen to their team's feedback and understand their concerns. By remaining grounded and self-aware, leaders can more openly receive feedback without defensiveness and adjust as necessary. Transparency in communication builds trust, reduces uncertainty and fosters an environment where employees are valued and heard. This helps in creating a sense of stability in the face of change and makes transitions smoother.

**Leading through change lesson #2: Step out of your worldview as a leader of the organization and into the worldview of the team that you are leading.**

In 2018 I participated in the post-acquisition transition of a company that my family owned for 55 years. We had 80 employees, the majority of whom had worked for us for decades. The transition would last 12-18 months and when finished, the company's operation in CA would be closed. As the HR Director of the company, I was tasked with leading the employee retention efforts – it was imperative that we kept our team as whole as possible because we needed to maintain our sales and production during the transition. It was also very important to us that we were upfront with the employees about the fact that the facility would close and that they would need to find new jobs. There were retention bonus' for those who stayed, but I knew that would not be enough – I also needed to solve for the eventual job loss. With this in mind, I created a plan which included job skills training, resume writing, interview prep and financial planning. I presented the plan in detail to our employees, offering regular office hours and various methods of assistance. Much to my surprise, very few people opted-in to participate.

What I did not consider is that our employees were experiencing an enormous amount of fear and uncertainty. They worried about health insurance, providing for their families and what might come next. Before we could discuss the logistics of "finding a job" they needed tools to process the gravity of this change.

I pivoted my plan and we hired a bilingual life coach who offered group workshops and individual sessions in both English and Spanish. We talked about change management, communicating with family members through uncertainty, grieving the loss of a beloved job and emotionally preparing for new opportunities. Providing this kind of environment to process feelings gave our team the chance to support each other and be supported. They found the gifts that existed in this uncertain situation and they celebrated the many years of service each person had given to the company and to each other.

We eventually implemented logistics plan, but had I started there and not held space for the emotional component, we would have missed out on a very important part of the process. By the time we closed the facility, we had retained 98% of our employees through the entire 18-month transition. Every person who was looking for a new opportunity had one before their time with the company ended. And those who took some time after the closure were offered outplacement resources to use when they were ready.

Stepping out of my worldview as the leader and into the worldview of the team I was leading, allowed me to create the pathway to achieving our goals while supporting the team in a way that had a lasting positive impact.

Author and speaker, Daniel Pink, once noted, "Empathy is about standing in someone else's shoes, feeling with their heart and seeing with their eyes." Extraordinary leaders make this an ongoing practice rather than a destination.

**Leading through change lesson #3: Ask the hard questions and be willing to take meaningful action based on the answers that you receive.**

## CHANGE

The current role I am in has been full of opportunities to lead through change – the most obvious among them being the pandemic. As part of our 2020 annual review, our executive leadership team conducted an equity study to ensure that no employee was more adversely affected than another due to the changes we made to the business in order to navigate the pandemic. In reviewing the data, we were pleased to see that we had maintained equity across all levels of the company and in all categories.

However, there was one trend that surfaced from the data that was not pandemic related: there was a difference in starting salaries for entry level office/desk positions vs warehouse/processing positions – this difference had led to a wage gap trend that was not in alignment with our values. Modern business practice has a widely accepted explanation for this gap: candidates who are college educated have a higher value from a compensation standpoint than candidates without secondary education. For generations this notion has informed hiring practices in companies across many industries.

That said, when we look at what makes our business successful, we need quality candidates to fill both positions. We cannot operate and grow without filling our entry level positions in the office and we certainly cannot operate and grow without filling our entry level positions in the warehouse – these are the folks who process and handle the material that comes through our facility, it is not an easy job. This begs several questions: Why does it make sense for the starting salary of an entry level position in our organization to vary across these departments when the positions are equally valuable to the business? What does the difference in starting pay communicate to our employees about what we value as an organization? Are our hiring practices re-enforcing an outdated status quo?

When the answers to hard questions present themselves, the actions we take as leaders are the most telling to the folks in our organizations. When we recognized this trend in the data, we could have easily justified not taking any action because it is "best practice" across many industries or because our numbers were down due to the pandemic. We also could have decided that the finding was irrelevant or should be addressed at another time because it was not within the scope of the question we initially asked.

Instead, we leaned into the hard questions – our leadership team dialogued and strategized. We ran more numbers and debated the actions we could take that would be in alignment with our company values and goals. When it came time to make decisions the team was in full alignment: we instituted a new minimum wage that is the same for every entry-level position in our company. We also made adjustments to the legacy employees whose positions were impacted by this change. With a two-phase approach, we took meaningful action based on the questions we asked and the answers we received. We communicated to all of our employees our findings and the reasoning behind the new policies. We demonstrated what it looks like to know better and do better as an organization and in the process, we showed our team that they can trust us even in the midst of uncertain times.

Two change-filled years later, the average turnover rate for entry level positions in our industry is nearly 50%, meanwhile our team is thriving, managing big changes and growing with a turnover rate of less than 5%.

Change is full of hard questions – the quality and depth of the questions we ask, the honestly in which we answer them and the actions we are willing to take based on those answers will directly impact the results we achieve in our organizations – it will also inform the legacy that we create through our leadership.

Some of my most impactful lessons have come to me while leading teams through change. I have found that the three lessons shared here hold many universal truths and applications for all areas of life. Leading through change is not a linear process, but an iterative one that requires intentional monitoring, self-awareness and course correction. Even the most seasoned leader with meticulously designed plans will encounter unexpected challenges. Extraordinary leaders see these challenges as opportunities to rise to the occasion. Leaders who can guide their teams through change with this approach will not just survive but thrive in an ever-changing world.

# Edvard
# Philipson

### Principal
### *PHILIPSON BUSINESS CONSULTING*

## Memoirs of an Ex-pat: Facing change as an International Businessman

When people asked me what I wanted for my professional career, I always thought about going *"international."* Having been born to a Swedish immigrant in Mexico, I was always curious about the numerous foreigners that came to visit us from Europe, Canada, and the United States. My father speaks five languages and the food he likes to cook has always been    different from the tasty, local Mexican cuisine. Having family members more than 10,000 kms away who were always sending letters that took at least a month to arrive, was an invitation to discover the world.

In the 80s, moving to a foreign country was not an easy task, inflation and currency fluctuations due to Mexico's unstable economy at the time made it difficult for a young professional like me. But they say that if you have your mind set in a well-defined goal, it's just a question of time until you realize your dreams.

My opportunity came from work. In my late-twenties, I was wor-

king for an international pharmaceutical Company–Eli Lilly--that had an amazing program to develop global talent through an initiative called *"International Sales and Marketing Development Program."* The Program allowed promising young employees to spend time in the United States for 2 to 3 different assignments. The first one, always in Sales. So, with our one-year-old daughter and a second daughter on her way, my then-wife and I embarked on an adventure that took us to West Palm Beach, Florida and then to Indianapolis, Indiana.

For Mexicans, the US is a natural destination, either for work or for leisure. However, going to work for a global pharmaceutical company based in the Mid-West is not exactly easy. I should recognize that Eli Lilly was an amazing Company towards its relocated employees. I remember at least 3 things they recognized as critical:

-   Ex-pat family well-being was paramount. *"If the family does not settle-in well, the employee will not be able to perform well at work."* Therefore, major support was given to our spouses to adapt quickly to their new home.
-   Adapting to a new cost of living. Since you are not familiar with prices and best consumer practices when you move, you will most likely spend more money than you should at the beginning. Therefore, ex-pat employees had a one-time extra month of salary that was granted for "dumb" purchases.
-   Relocation support system. Having someone to explain how and where to buy groceries and medications, where to find a bilingual church, what is the acceptable tip at the restaurant, and so forth.

For my family, there were several challenges we had to overcome:

-   The most difficult and important one was finding an obstetrician that would accept my wife going into her 7th month of pregnancy. Because of liability concerns, it was very difficult to have a doctor's office treat my wife and newborn child. We had to pull all the work connections we had.
-   The other major challenge we encountered was climate, as you may imagine, it never snows in Mexico City. I learned to be extra cautious while driving on ice the day my car spined 3 times in the Interstate 465 highway!

At work, there were several cultural challenges to be faced. Probably the biggest challenge for someone coming from a Latin work culture is Americans' forwardness. In the US, you spend a few seconds socializing at the beginning of a work meeting, but it is usually expected to get straight into business. It is very different from Mexico, where you spend 2 to 3 hours in a breakfast or lunch meeting, socializing before you start addressing the real work!

The other important behavior I had to learn was networking. In the US, there are events especially designed to meet and greet people that will be internal resources or good external connections. You make small talk and engage with other people but what a difficult task it is when you know nothing about the NFL, and much less the statistics of players during the Baseball or Basketball season!

My assignment in Indianapolis was cut short after 2 years, as the Company required me to return to Mexico to start a new Business Unit. My mindset and view of the world was totally different from the young man that I had been before this wonderful experience.

Since then, I have been relocated to 8 different destinations and lived in more than 18 homes. We showed the world to our daughters, and they embraced the wealth and richness of the global diversity and culture.

One of my many destinations was Santiago, Chile. My family and I accepted the assignment without a prior exploration trip. So, we embarked on a plane to the Southern most country in the Americas, knowing very little of the politics, geography, and local culture. I am not sure I would make such a decision today, but the experience was amazing!

Chile was just re-emerging after the Pinochet dictatorship and had recently re-opened diplomatic relations with Mexico. At that time, everything about Mexico was in fashion. People always complemented our *"lovely"* Mexican accent. Nonetheless, I knew very little about banking regulations, labor laws, regulatory requirements for pharmaceuticals, and even less about the fierce competition from the local producers against the global Pharma companies. I had to learn fast, not only to operate but to survive! I reached out to the US Embassy for help and received much support, such that we launched the Eli Lilly Chile affiliate at the US Embassy itself.

I also learned that people (employees and competitors) will take advantage of your limited knowledge of the market. I remember how we bought more costly and fancier cars than needed for the salesforce out of ignorance. I also remember how we lost the insulin government tenders for 3 years in a row due to *"greyish"* competitive practices, that we learned how to neutralize later. The learning curve is steep and you need to quickly process everything.

In retrospective, I can say that succeeding as an ex-pat is tough and demanding. However, the skills and competencies that come with it are invaluable for the future executives and leaders of global organizations. To name a few:

- Learning ability. Adaptation requires the capacity of processing information and deciding on new facts versus the *"way we have always done things"*.

- Flexibility. Behaviors and attitudes are different everywhere and we need to respect and adapt to be successful.

- Building a team and empowerment. There is no way that you can be more efficient in local matters than someone that has always lived in the country, but you can assemble a trusted team of colleagues that you can lead to achieve the purpose you are aiming for.

Finally, I must say that if anyone reading this is considering taking an ex-pat career, there are long term costs that should also be considered. For example, most retirement plans are local and do not consider workers moving into different countries. Make sure you have at least one retirement plan that you can return-to after many years of travelling the world.

The other major challenge is taxes. There are many resources in this field and mutual tax recognition treaties. Still, you should ensure that in the long term you do not end up earning less income by making your own calculations.

Lastly, there is a toll on the family. As you move from one country to another, your children may elect to stay in one of those destinations - either because of friends or due to identity aspects. Make sure that *"home"* is well defined and that some rituals happen every year. Then, everyone will long to get together again!

# Eduardo Rosales

**Founding Partner**
*SOCIALINKS*

## How a soccer-playing poet aspiring to be a businessman, turned into a politician who became a consultant

Everybody talks about change. Tons of books are written on the subject and it's common to hear that change is the only constant. Consultants like me design and use multiple tools to cope with different kinds of changes. Our own bodies, sometimes in a good way, other times not so much, are a clear proof that we are changing every second.

However, we don't seem to be really prepared for this fact. We change with the illusion that it will be the ultimate transformation, the definitive model, the ideal system. The status quo is the default option for all of us. Among all the infinite possible paths for each person and organization, the easiest choice is to go on with the standard procedures. We choose a university, and we usually finish our studies there; we buy some type of vehicle, and the easiest choice is to make a similar decision the next time; we find a decent hamburger stand and we go there every time we crave a burger. Perhaps, most of us would prefer a world

where, for the most part, nothing changed: loved ones that don't die, successful companies that will earn money eternally, a perfect government that finally cares about us.

We don't like change because it is problematic. It distracts us from our core activities, it involves the unexpected use of scarce resources, and the feeling of uncertainty that comes with every change is uncomfortable. We fight for personal, professional, and economical equilibrium, and sometimes change can make some of the systems we have created partially or even completely useless.

Change is inevitable at a certain point. Sometimes, some of the habits we developed for years are no longer leading us to be productive, and the systems we designed to cope with reality are not producing the outcomes they used to. On other occasions, the outcomes are as expected but we are no longer satisfied with them.

Often, it's the context that changes, but we don't, and other times we grow, we change, and the context stays the same. Change, indeed, is the only constant, and my life is an example.

Let me tell you my story:

As any teenager, I wasn't sure about what I wanted to do for the rest of my life. The logical path was to study something practical, related to the family business, such as Business Administration, Finance, or Industrial Engineering. But I knew I loved arts, politics, and sports. My artistic side wanted me to become a writer, and architect or play in a rock band. My political side wanted me to be a social activist or the future President of Mexico. My sports side wanted to score a goal in the Soccer World Cup or win an Olympic medal.

I took the easy way and decided to study Industrial Engineering and be part of the family business, a truck parts shop. My plan was simple: learn tools, work for big companies, and eventually start my own business to manufacture parts for our auto parts shop. I was a good student, as I always have been, especially because I really enjoyed math and engineering courses. Every Saturday, every vacation period, and some days of the week I attended the family business.

In the meantime, I did not forget my passions. I played soccer 2 or 3 times a week, I wrote poems and short stories, I studied French and Italian, I led the youth section of a political party in the opposition, PAN.

The plan kept on working for several years but something did not feel all right. I graduated with good grades, I loved mathematics and processes, and I became a "good engineer". I also managed to work for 2 big companies where I was a young but respected employee with a bright future in the organizational ladder. But the idea of working in a factory or a shop for the rest of my life did not feel well.

The outcomes were as expected, but the plan was incorrect. My advice: It is essential to acknowledge that every decision can be revisited. I decided to take my discomfort as a symptom of something deeper and revisited my original plan.

Unconsciously, I chose an experimental approach: I kept on the same track while tried to walk in the politics path. I did not quit my job in the private sector, but I accepted to coordinate a political campaign during afternoons and weekends. Several months later, I took a position as substitute city councilman and asked for a 6 months leave permit at my job. I even accepted to run for a seat in the local Congress, knowing that it was highly unlikely that I could win, given that the ruling party, PRI, had been in power for nearly 70 years straight.

My party, for the first time in history, won the election and I suddenly turned into a full-time politician. During the "experimental" phase, I had realized that working in something that excites you is very different from having a so-called "good job", so I gladly accepted the change.

My career in politics and public service lasted 15 years. At some point, I should have revisited the plan, but I did not. I assumed I did not have the need because I was working in one of my passions. It's difficult to see the landscape when you are driving.

The first years were in accordance with the new plan. I was councilman in Guadalajara for two terms and I was Congressman for one. I became a very influential politician due to my skills as public speaker and able negotiator. I found good mentors, a loyal and capable team, and I made many friends and allies. I realized that my engineering background was a great advantage when analyzing complex situations and the hard-working ethics inherited from my family was an important asset as an elected official. I was happy, involved in cultural policy, and I discovered a new area of interest: planning. Some of my old abilities from college and the private sector remained: organization, diagnostic skills, strategic approach, processes, but I used them in a different way. I even had the chance to fulfill one of my dreams, to have an Ivy League degree. I went to Princeton University and got a master's degree in public policy. At the end of this stage, after I came back from Princeton, I was appointed Chairman of the State's Planning Agency. It was almost like a dream: a position where I could exercise politics, planning and materialize goods for the general population.

The second part of my public career was almost inevitable. Since I knew "the territory" as chairman of a state agency, I had the proper alliances and I was an already renowned local politician, I became a candidate to lead my party. All my planning skills and my leadership capabilities were set in motion. We mobilized a large group of people and went town after town to diagnose people's demands, local leaders' interests and elected officials' needs. I led a small team that designed a carefully crafted plan to win the election and we succeeded. We easily won over a rival group that had 15 years ruling the party.

I moved from public service to pure politics without acknowledging it. Suddenly, I was no longer designing laws or negotiating budgets for public works, but giving away congress and council positions, creating partisan offices to satisfy political groups and publicly defending the governor or mayors about things I did not even agree with. I became somehow a local figure with power, public attention and what people call "leadership", and I enjoyed it at the beginning. I used, again, my old skills to do my best: to design successful election strategies, to devise optimal negotiation processes, to convey clear and coherent messages. I managed to have the best results for my party in all its history. I was even reelected for a second term as party State President.

But from time to time, I found myself feeling uncomfortable. Perhaps it was the normalization of democracy, my lack of excitement with the daily tasks of politics, or the fact of dealing most of the time with ambitious or untalented people. The thing is that often, I realized that politics did not make me happy anymore, but my team wanted me to keep on going.

So here is another lesson about change: sometimes you know it's time to change, but people around you, don't. Change is not only problematic for the individual or an organization that is committing to it, but also for the system it belongs to. When you are in a leadership position, you play a role in your team members' lives, you help them satisfy their needs and sometimes you take some of the duties they want to avoid. You serve them more than the other way around.

At the end, a change in context gave me a perfect excuse to pivot: my party lost several positions in an election and my internal adversaries used it to organize demonstrations against me. 4 months later, I resigned from my position in the middle of an internal crisis. For several months, I remained as leader of my political group, but my discomfort was so evident that I avoided attending meetings as much as possible and the rest of the team got used to it.

For the first time in my life, I did not have a plan. I knew I did not want to be a politician, but I did not know what I wanted to be.

I kept myself busy to avoid reality. I started a business, but I could not make it profitable. I wrote my thesis to obtain my second master's degree and I applied for another graduate program. I attended meetings and events just to fill my day.

It was a long night: I was 40, working in an environment that did not allow me to leave, and with a lot of insecurities. Doors were closing behind me, and I had not opened new ones.

My college calculus teacher told me once: when you can't solve an equation after a significant amount of time, erase everything and start all over again. That's what I did.

I had to take a long break to realize how my new life should be. I went to Harvard for another master's degree determined to get out of my comfort zone. I took classes with the best professors; I studied subjects I had never taken and attended lectures and conferences on topics I had never heard of. I also realigned with parts of my old self: I got involved in students' politics, I visited museums, I took courses on leadership and innovation, and I played soccer once a week. I immersed in myself to redo my life. To create a new me, I had to remember who I was.

At the end of the 2 years, I knew I wanted to do consultancy on public affairs. I was no longer a politician, but I enjoyed understanding power and its characteristics. I was no longer an engineer, but I felt excited every time I solved complex problems and designed methods to do it. To redesign my life, I used the same old tools: Evaluate my resources, set a strategic goal, and design a plan.

My final advice as a consultant: context changes, people change, organizations change, but it's up to everyone to face it successfully. Don't

## CHANGE

be afraid of change, be afraid of not being prepared for it. Focus on your long-term goals: it may be to improve people's lives, to have a sustainable business model, or to be happy. Then, monitor the context and yourself, draw the path and change what needs to be changed.

Change, in my experience, is more often a blessing than a curse.

# Javier
## Lattanzio

### Director Of Residential Sales & Marketing
*TIME EQUITIES INC*

**M**y story is one about how opportunities and setbacks lead to successful change. Sometimes life does not turn out as we expect and we must build it the best way we can.

I was born and raised in Argentina and started playing tennis when I was 6 years old. As a very successful junior player, I played first division in Buenos Aires and in tournaments all over the world, in France, Spain, and the United States. I jumped to the professional division at 18 and played for over a year, realizing that it was much more difficult than I had anticipated. As a professional tennis player, I went to play ATP tournaments and had to make more sacrifices, such as paying for my own travel expenses to be able to compete. I worked stringing other players' rackets so that I could pay for hotels while traveling for the competitions. After a while, I decided to stop playing professionally and started coaching young kids in Argentina. This coaching job took me to Italy, where I coached young players in Sicily for 5 years before I moved to New York to coach top pro players.

While coaching in New York, I had the opportunity to meet many different people, one of whom became my mentor and gave me the opportunity to work in real estate.

TIME EQUITIES INC.

## CHANGE

Because of a hand injury in the year 2000, I had to stop coaching and started working in the real estate business, which was a drastic career change. I went from hitting a tennis ball all day for 23 years to being in an office almost overnight. It was challenging to adapt to this big change, but I am proud to say that it was a successful move. I worked for 3 years in commercial real estate, where I closed some important transactions. In my debut, with no experience in the business, I managed to rent an empty building on 10th Ave and 30th St, which was 42,000 sq ft, followed by selling the YMCA on 23rd St and 7th Ave.

I am a person who likes to grow. Although my role in commercial real estate allowed me to learn and grow financially, it did not allow me to grow as a person. After 3 years, I saw an opportunity to move internally to the residential department.

On the residential real estate side, our company has converted many rental buildings into ownership co-ops and condos. I wanted to learn the whole process, starting with the offering plans, the pricing, the potential buyers and tenants, and the marketing for the building. So, I started growing in this area by working on the entire process and not just being a broker.

In 2007, I started working in new developments (built from the ground up). For the first time, I had the opportunity to be the sales manager of a brand new building in Jersey City, which was a very successful project. After my project in Jersey City, I was going to start a new development in Manhattan called 50 West Street Condominium, but the financial crisis put it on hold until 2014. In 2014, we launched the pre-construction sales, and I had the opportunity to be the director of sales and marketing, managing my first real team. The project went from the ground up between 2014 and 2017, and we sold many apartments during that period. Through 2017, we started closing the sales of the apartments until 2019.

In 2019, I became the broker of record for my company, which means that I am in charge of all the licenses of everyone in the company. I have a team that manages the residential offerings for sales and rentals, and I now also have my own team in sales and marketing, managing all the unsold shares for condos, co-ops, and high-end rentals. Today, the company is worth $4.5 billion and is an international firm with assets throughout the United States, Canada, and internationally.

I now manage a team of 10 employees, which can be challenging at times due to different personalities and ways of doing things. My approach towards them is to make them understand that every project is important and that each and every project is a priority. They need to be on top of everything all the time, and customer service should be top of the line. Customer relations are what keeps this business thriving. In this line of business, it is difficult to reach the top, but most importantly, once you reach the top, it is challenging to stay there. Mistakes can be costly as they can bring you down.

I have found some similarities and lessons in my two passions:

- **Persistence:**

One of the things that real estate and tennis have in common is the need for persistence. Persistence and the "keep going and going" attitude is the secret to success. Yes, talent is needed for both tennis and real estate, but without persistence, you cannot move forward and succeed.

- **Personal:**

Both tennis and real estate are very personal. Tennis is with yourself, and real estate is with people. Once you enter either an apartment or a tennis court, you leave your problems aside.

- **Experience:**

I also believe that if you have tried a sport professionally in your past life, you will probably succeed in real estate and in any other profession you go for.

I have a lot of valuable experience and I have learned along the way. It is important to recognize the importance of persistence and personal relationships in both tennis and real estate. I have found similarities between success in sports and success in real estate, as both require discipline, hard work, and a competitive spirit. As an advice to all, it's important to continue learning and growing in your field to stay on top and fa e the challenges and opportunities that come your way.

**Roberto**
Bonelli

**Nadim**
Jarudi
*TMAM*

**Martin**
Cabrera
*QUASSAR CAPITAL*

**Bruce**
Cohen
*BRUCE COHEN
PRODUCTIONS*

**Rachael M.**
Kim
*FEMTECH SALON POWERED BY
MY COMMA*

364

# 6. Looking back

**Hans**
Guevara
*EUGENIA INC*

**Luis**
Silva
*AT&T*

**Deven**
Nongbri
*YONDER
HOSPITALITY*

**Gustavo**
Lomas
*MCPU POLYMER ENGINEERING*

# In with the new out with the old?

**Gustav Juul**
Founder & CEO
*AIM GROUP / XO LEADERS*

As some know, I worked closely with the US Navy and Marines for the first long part of my career, almost 10 years. In this article, I want to share with you one of the most important lessons I learned and the implications of what this simple lesson, to this day, means to me. People in the US Navy and Marines Corps are taught to: *"Take care of your men!"*

As you can imagine when you see my salt-and-pepper beard, I have now been part of the business world for over 25 years. There are things that have been wonderful, especially the people I've worked with and the women and men who worked for me. There have also been things I've disliked and things that have made me sad. Still, overall my experience has been one that has enriched me profoundly and which has affected the way I think about how to run my business. The lesson I have learned is: *"Take care of your men!"*.

I am also fortunate to have a wonderful family, and for it to work, I have learned that you have to work on it every day. It doesn't come all by itself. It is a learning experience to be a good father and a husband. What I have learned is: *"Take care of your men! (wife and children)"*.

Over the years, working in different types of organizations, military, business, and family, my understanding of what Leadership versus Management really means, with respect to *"Taking care of your men!"* has changed. There have been times when I aspired to be a better manager and other times when the word *"management"* had become a "bad word" in my vocabulary. At that point, I turned to the term *"Leadership"* and found that that was the only way to run an organization (military, business, or even family). I was wrong in both cases. Now, the way I have come to think of management and leadership, is that they are interdependent. There are certainly key differences between the two and they are both hugely important for success.

**In with the new out with the old?**

There definitely has been a shift in the focus of organizations to create leaders. Leadership has become the new and sexy concept everyone is striving for. I think that it is largely because authors had to have something different to write about, but also because something was missing from running a business. That said, it is simply wrong to think that leadership can replace management.

It is not as simple as *"In with the new and out with the old."* Granted, some specific elements of creating better organizations do not work well when managed, but that doesn't mean that leadership is the magic bullet for everything. Both are important elements, but alone, none can make it possible for an organization to reach its best potential.

So what are the key differences I have found between Leadership and Management? The easiest way I can think of to explain it is through the 4 C's personality model I have created (please see below). For an organization to be successful, it needs to be effective and efficient in the short run, and also effective and efficient in the long run. As you can see, Custodians and Champions fall into the short-term category of Managing and Creators and Caregivers fall into the long-term category of Leading.

## 4 C's Personality Types

4 C's personality types© AIM Group®

Although there are two general categories within Leadership and Management, it is clear that Leaders are focused on creating the plan and that everyone is comfortable with, while Managers are experts in executing and setting the rules for. A leader will ask why, what and whom, with little regard as to the implementation of their grand design, whereas a manager focuses on the questions of how and when, with little ability to see the future or stray away from the decision that was made.

It is, therefore, clear that if an organization is to work effectively and efficiently both short term and the long term, leadership can not work without management as much as management can not work without leadership. Let's explore those differences a bit deeper:

### 1. Differences in Vision

Managers are short-term-oriented and therefore considered practical. They set out to achieve organizational goals by implementing processes such as budgeting, organizational structuring, and staffing. Managers' are bound to the implementation strategies, planning, and organizing tasks to reach the objectives.

In comparison, Leaders are long-term-oriented and therefore considered visionaries. They design the path for the organizations to stay relevant in the future. They are rarely happy with the organization as it currently is and what to change it, continuously, if they were allowed to so. The second aspect of leadership is making sure that everyone's interests are met.

Both of these roles are equally important and require collaborative efforts.

### 2. Organizing vs Aligning

Managers achieve their goals by using coordinated activities and tactical processes. They break down long-term goals into tiny segments and organize the available resources to reach the desired outcome.

On the other hand, leaders are more concerned with what to achieve and aligning people, than how to assign work to them. They achieve this by creating a new vision for the organization and its people in a wider context, creating the possibility of future growth.

## 3. Differences in Queries

A leader asks why, what and whom, whereas a manager focuses on the questions of how, when. As Leaders are visionaries they will thrive on creating change and will have little trouble questioning anything and everything. They will reinvent the wheel every opportunity they get answering the why and redefining what and integrating the who, but will also have a hard time focusing on a new goal long enough for them to implement it.

As Managers are considered practical, they will thrive on stability and have little conflict with something never changing. They crave a well-defined plan for, how the organization wants to reach a goal, by when that goal has to be reached, but will resist changing the goal, even when it is blatantly obvious that it should be changed.

## 4. Operational v. Strategic

In most articles now published, it is said that a manager's role refers to a specific function within an organization's structure and that a leader could be just about anyone. I feel that this is misleading. Everyone in the organization needs to be both leaders and managers.

According to our methodology, everyone has specific functions within the organizational structure with practical short-term goals and responsibilities; this makes them managers in their own right, regardless of what level of authority they have.

Leadership, on the other hand, is a strategic function within the organization. The ownership of the company can not be all-knowing and expected to see every opportunity for improvement. These small and large changes that organizations can make to become ever more competitive should come from any level. Everyone has the responsibility of envisioning a new and brighter future. This does not mean resetting the course of the organization, but it is ultimately the small things that count the most, when you add it all up.

## 5. Deciding v. Implementing

Is it only the Captain that can lead the ship? Well, yes and no. Although there is little doubt that there only should be one Captain who defines the course of the ship, it is also true that he/she will take better decisions when he involves other people in the decision-making process, listening to their point of view on the problems and opportunities that one course of action has versus another and maybe even offered options that were not seen by the Captain.

We can therefore divide up the *"Leadership/Management"* requirements of any type of organization into three very clear areas. Decision-making, decision-taking, and implementation.

- Decision-making should be a collaborative process. It is best served by being cross-functional and it is often a good idea to include key people from different levels. We can call this a multi-person leadership role.
- Decision-taking solely relies on the person who ultimately is going to be responsible for its implementation (next area). This decision should not be based on consensus or a vote and should also not be the flavor of the week or a popularity contest. The decision-taking should only done based on what this person believes is "the best decision that he/she is confident that he/she (the decision-taker) can implement within the organization with the resources that are available to him/her currently.
- Implementing is a Management role where each individual person in the organization has a role, big or small, in making the decision taken a reality. There is a clear break here between leadership and management. An organization cannot have leadership in this part of the natural course of a project. Imagine having a plane in flight changing destinations several times along the way; pretty soon it will run out of fuel. The plane needs to land exactly where it was destined to land when took off. Only after it has landed can we send it somewhere else.

**Stringing a balance**

As the author of several hundred articles, public speaker, lecturer, and co-author of now eight books, the question that always comes up is if there is a difference between a manager and a leader and if that difference really matters. Yes! It matters a great deal. In order to be successful and have the chance to move into greater roles of responsibility, leading becomes much more important than managing. However, you will never have anything the lead if you don't learn how to manage first, and you will soon have nothing to manage if you don't start learning how to lead.

## Conclusion

I travel around the country conducting organizational change programs for corporations. As a team, we help all types of organizations spanning from the public sector and NGO's to family-owned companies. I personally enjoy the latter more because it is much more of a challenge transitioning basically a mom-and-pop shop (even if they have thousands of employees) to a professional organization that guarantees growth and paves the way for a smooth generational transition later.

I always start my projects out by evaluating the Owner and/or CEO of the company we work for. We actually have a vetting panel that interviews the Executive Committee. In most cases, we will recommend doing a two-day workshop called a *"Business Health Evaluation"*. Through that, we will discover what the organization requires and how we can help it reach its full potential. If you are interested in knowing more about our methodology or if you are interested in inviting me to a speaking event, you are more than welcome to drop me a few lines.

gustav@aimsmg.com

# Luis Silva

## Vice President General Manager- South Texas Market
### *AT&T*

## If I knew then what I know now

The elders in society are viewed as possessors of knowledge. These are people that have gained respect through their experience. When I picked this topic to share a few of the things I have learned through 30 years of work, it reminded me of those that came before me and shared their knowledge.

This phrase applies to everything in life. Experience gives you knowledge and it allows you to gain confidence in some cases and in other cases it provides a red alert. The fact that you know the possible outcome in many of these makes you value the situation. Decisions are easier and implementing the different actions or changes give you relative confidence on the outcome. All, when it comes to leadership there are several things I wish I would have known. The following tips and concepts are the most important things I wish I would have known. In no particular order.

Let's start with performing on the job. Most of the people want to gain more money while they grow professionally. In order to get there, you must be good at what you do. It is great to show potential but that needs to be backed up by current performance. In order to achieve the

next step, start by delivering where you are. We tend to forget that those looking at us for a role must use the information at hand, and that is where you stand now. They will use your background, education and communication skills to evaluate your capabilities, but what you are doing today, opens the door. Believe me when I say, *"No one wants a mediocre performer for the next level"*.

This one might sound basic. Every time I was promoted, I thought there was a requirement for me to know what the whole job was all about. What I know now is that there is no expectation for the person to know what to do. There is a normal learning curve and leaders understand that. All you must do is raise your hand and say: *"I don't know"*. Believe it or not, your leader will take the time to explain. All you needed to do, was ask. Amazing concept. I would have saved so much energy and stress by just knowing that. The typical nerves of not knowing, the chase for answers all over the place, all that gone by just raising your hand.

Meetings are great places for networking, and they give us the opportunity to learn about the business. When you go to a meeting make sure that bring 100% of yourself. Take notes, pay attention to what people are saying. The most important thing, write down every question that people ask. Questions give insight on what others are thinking. They tell you what concerns they might have. They show you how much people are understanding the subject. This is one of the most fascinating things, questions provide you with details of how the presentation is going, the subject at hand and what they are doing to fix it. At the end of the day, if you are focusing on what is happening in the meeting, you are not worried about sounding smart or thinking about what to say. Taking your mind off the meeting to self-fulfill with a comment is not worth. Add without missing what is being said.

Adding value is extremely important. Take every task as an opportunity to add value. There are numerous mundane activities in every person's role that can be looked at and improved. Look for those opportunities to improve the day to day. Share what you are doing with your leader and bring them into the fold. We tend to think that innovation only applies to technology and artificial intelligence. Innovation exists in everything that we do and becoming familiar with those tasks and making them better helps show your commitment.

We assume that we owe those ahead of us when we get promoted. The truth is that we owe those behind us. For a company to continue to grow, employees need to build up those behind them so that there is continuity, and the enterprise will keep going for years to come. As a leader never expect anything back when you help someone, the expectation needs to be on what the person that you will help will groom those behind them. This is so simple but so important. The culture of a company depends on this.

Run with problems and walk with great news. Never fear sharing bad news as fast as you can. Sometimes your leader's reaction will not be the best, but the reality is that they will appreciate the fact that you let them know. If you delay informing people of bad news, it will blow up in your face. It is hard but it is the right thing to do. Never hide the issues or try to solve these on your own. The problem will get bigger by the minute.

Be nice to everyone. You never know who you will report to in the future. Every person in the company matters and you should always be the same with every person that works with you and those that do not. Life changes quick and you will be surprised on who will be running the show. Being nice to everyone doesn't cost you a cent, it is the right thing to do, and believe me when I say, *"your days will be so much easier"*.

Never ask some one how they are doing if you are not willing to sit through the story. Do not make that phrase a cliché, it is extremely important. People will share their story when you ask, take your time to listen, be engaged. Do not look at your phone. All you need to do is listen and be engaged. They are not looking for an answer, they want to know that you care. That is key. Asking someone how they are doing and leaving them hanging with the story is rude and it will blow up on your face.

As a leader you need to understand that you are present in your employee's dinner table every night. You chose on what side of that table you are. It does not mean that you just have to be nice and cool, it means that you have to care. People recognize even in hard tough feedback sessions what your intentions are. Those intentions show that you care, even on those tough conversations. You will be in the right side of the table if you do that. The other key point is that you get to do this every single day, so there is always an opportunity to correct any missed step.

Have fun and enjoy the journey. Regardless of the role, we spend way too much time at work. Make sure you always take time to enjoy the moments. I have learned through my years working that we have been more productive when we are engaged and enjoying the tasks at hand. We learn more and we build a better team by having fun.

Finally, when building a Great place to work, don't forget the *"to work"* piece. It is important to build a solid environment with a good culture, but the company needs to be profitable. The to work piece is crucial for any corporation. Good solid results need to be in the forefront, always know the goals, deliver on them and build your culture around that.

If I would have known these things thirty years ago, my work life would have been easier. The reality is that I have enjoyed the journey and loved learning and experiencing these. So maybe, just maybe, learning these on the go as I shaped my career are things that to me were good not to know.

*BRUCE COHEN PRODUCTIONS*

## What is leading all about?

'll start by getting right to the point – if you ask me, leading is all about inspiration and communication. I think that probably applies across all businesses, but I can speak specifically about producing Film, Television and Theater. Many people don't know what a producer does – even my mother never knew how to describe it to her friends at the start of my producing career until she got to spend time on the set and see for herself. She passed away from Alzheimer's at the beginning of Covid, but she played an important role in the development of my leadership skills at an early age, so it feels appropriate to dedicate this essay to her and begin it with that story, especially since it started me on my path to being a producer.

When I was a kid in a Northern Virginia suburb of Washington D.C, a neighbor whom I loved was very active in the local Democratic Party and she had me campaigning door to door for local candidates ... from the time I was 4! I was a precocious kid, I guess, and I'm not sure how inspirational my pitch was but, evidently, I was a pretty good communicator for a four-year-old and my love of politics was born. In 6th grade,

BRUCE COHEN PRODUCTIONS

I decided to run for President of my elementary school. My mother was an artist and had the idea that she could help me silkscreen my posters, which led us to the idea that I needed slogans. Each kid running was allowed to put up 3 posters and ours were *"Cohen Can," "Cohen Cares,"* and *"Cohen's Cool."* I can't remember how many other candidates there were, but I can remember that I was the only one with professional looking posters and coherent messaging ... and I won! This led to my adolescent political career, with its signature silk screen posters, of Vice President and then President of my Junior High School ("Cohen Can" and *"Cohen Can Do More"*) and President of the Sophomore Class and Junior Class in High School (*"Back Bruce" and "Bring Back Bruce"*).

Those elected offices helped me get into Yale, or at least they certainly didn't hurt, which is where I fell in love with film and was inspired to try for a career in the field. While an intern with a desk job in distribution at Warner Bros. right out of college, my co-workers kept telling me that the dream was to find a job on a set – where they made the films and television shows beloved around the world – and I heard about the DGA Trainee program (Director's Guild of America) to train you to be an Assistant Director (AD). I had no idea what that was, so my boss arranged for me to spend a day on the set of *"PROTOCOL"* starring Goldie Hawn and shadow the DGA Trainee. To my delight, I learned that the AD's were the ones who ran around the set with walkie-talkies organizing everything, which reminded me a lot of being Sophomore Class President and I figured if I could put on the Homecoming Dance, maybe I could help organize a film set!

I managed to get into the program and in the spring of 1985, I arrived on the set of my first film as a DGA Trainee, Steven Spielberg's THE CO-LOR PURPLE, produced, along with Steven and the legendary Quincy Jones, by Kathy Kennedy and Frank Marshall. For anyone who doesn't know, that illustrious husband and wife duo are the most recent recipient of the Thalberg Award from the Academy, the holy grail of producing honors, and have, between them, 13 Best Picture Oscar nominations and have produced such tiny, unpopular films as RAIDERS OF THE LOST ARK, E.T., THE SIXTH SENSE, SEABISCUIT, MUNICH, LINCOLN, all 5 BOURNE movies and the 3 most recent STAR WARS movies... or, pardon my French, holy shit. At the beginning of that shoot, I still didn't know what a producer was, but by the end, I was determined to do what they did some day. Kathy's definition of the role, which I have also used to this day is that the producer is the CEO of the company formed to make that film, television or theater project and, as such, oversees every aspect of the production, both creative and financial. Meanwhile, I was the luckiest kid in the most phenomenal candy store, Hollywood-style and Steven, Kathy and Frank at their company, Amblin Entertainment, became my magical trio of mentors. They truly taught me everything I know about producing. They were all about hiring the best people, both in front of and behind the camera, inspiring them with their extraordinary creative vision and then communicating to them exactly what they needed to get the job done.... but not just done... done superbly.

Amblin was like a big family and Steven, Kathy and Frank loved to promote family members who they believed in. I was beyond lucky enough to be one of their many beneficiaries. I was a DGA Trainee, Second Assistant Director, First Assistant Director, Associate Producer and Co-Producer on 6 Amblin productions, including AMAZING STORIES and HOOK, followed by ALIVE for Kathy and Frank's new company, Kennedy Marshall. We filmed ALIVE in the stunning Canadian Rockies and one day on the set, Kathy walked over to me and announced that she had spoken to Steven back in Los Angeles, that Amblin was getting ready to shoot the live action version of THE FLINTSTONES that summer and that I was going to produce it. This seemed insane to me! They knew full well that I hadn't produced a film before – how would I know what to do and how to do it? Kathy, in her inimitable style, basically told me I was being a wuss, that I was ready to produce and that was that. The three of them had certainly tried to teach me by example that true leaders inspired with great vision and communicated with great clarity and, it turned out I had, in fact, been paying attention.

I think I would say that one of the funnest ways I got to practice my producing skills on my first feature was for the arrival on set of person playing Fred Flintstone's mother-in-law, Pearl Slaghoople, the legendary Elizabeth Taylor. THE FLINTSTONES turned out to be both her return to the silver screen after a several decade absence and the last film she ever did, but no matter how you slice it, to this gay kid from Falls Church, Virginia who found himself now producing movies for Steven Spielberg, it was a VERY BIG DEAL... and I leapt into action. My goal was to produce her return to the movies in a manner befitting her magnificence and to accomplish that, for starters, I selected and purchased an elaborate series of start gifts, thanks to a personal check from Steven, at her favorite store (it was a Hollywood legend that she expected elaborate gifts at the start of each production which she confirmed for me at her costume fitting by whispering in my ear *"Cartier, dahling"*). On her first day of filming, I had her trailer filled with purple flowers (famously her favorite color) and had a purple carpet put down for her entrance back on the soundstage after all those years, in a scene right out of SUNSET BOU-

LEVARD. As the piece de resistance, I had learned that when she was a contract player in the early sixties on the Universal lot, where we were filming, the entire crew wore dress shirts and ties to work every day and so I communicated to our crew (see what I did there?) to please do the same for La Liz's first day. And when she walked down the purple carpet onto the stage, holding onto my arm, and saw the whole crew applauding her historic return in shirts and ties, she burst into tears.

Twenty-nine years later, I am currently in production on my 16th film as a producer or executive producer, including AMERICAN BEAUTY, BIG FISH, MILK, SILVER LININGS PLAYBOOK and the upcoming RUSTIN. I have produced television series, mini-series and specials, including PUSHING DAISIES and THE ACADEMY AWARDS, the Broadway musical version of BIG FISH, co-produced two Broadway plays, THE INHERITANCE and SLAVE PLAY, as well as producing     countless live events, award shows and fundraisers, protests, marches, parties and memorials, because I believe EVERYTHING needs a good producer, especially if they are bringing their vision and communication skills to the table.  I hope I have been a credit to the producing profession, I hope my projects have made audiences around the world laugh and cry, I hope they have maybe even changed the world a little, but most importantly, I hope I have made Steven, Kathy and Frank proud.... and, of course, my mom.

*Hans*
Guevara

## CEO & CO Founder
*EUGENIA INC*

## A letter to a friend

*Hey there,*

I still remember the first time I entered your life. Your parents sent you to a good school outside Mexico City, and you were friendly but a bit shy. We soon noticed that something was going on. The school staff would often pull you out of class, and you'd wait outside until your parents came to pick you up. All you wanted was to go home and see your grandfather, your best friend.

After a couple of years, we figured out what was happening. It scared us because we realized there wasn't enough money to pay for the school, or even for gas to get there, and sometimes we couldn't afford to eat. But your parents were doing their best to fix things. I remember you wanted to help, but there wasn't much you could do. Sometimes you were frustrated with me, but I couldn't change the situation.

You always loved watching how movies were made with your dad, and you were curious about technology. We had good times as a family, with mom, dad, your brother, and your grandfather, all living

EUGENIA

together and helping each other move forward. Your parents would say, *"Family is the most important thing, and together we can achieve great things."* I always admired that, even when you lost your best friend. The family stuck together, and your father said, *"No matter what, never give up."*

It might sound nice and easy, but I remember you struggled a lot. Sometimes you tried so hard, but it felt like you were getting nowhere. I told you to give up more than once, but you never did. You always said, *"Never give up."* You worked two jobs while studying at the university, chasing your dream of starting your own company to help your family. I remember telling you to calm down and take a break, even when you crashed the car because you fell asleep on the highway. Thankfully, nothing serious happened, but you were angry with me, and I couldn't understand why.

By your twenties, you had already worked at different companies, and you were the creative director of a prominent company. I kept telling you that you weren't ready, that you were too young, and people wouldn't believe in you! I remember some of them even quitting, saying they wouldn't take orders from a young guy. I warned you, but you just kept repeating, *"Never give up."*

After some time, your wise old colleague, Plinio, told you, *"When I first met you, I thought you would quit this job. But you proved me wrong. I see your passion. Start your own business, and if you do, I'll trust my son and my wife with you. In ten years, you'll hire me. You just need to believe in yourself."* To be honest, I was scared when I heard that, but for the first time, I was on your side. It was time. Let's do it.

You went to your friends Carlos and Gerardo and told them, *"It's time to start our own business."* You were completely convinced and willing to invest all your time and money to make it happen. I saw your commitment, and you were happy.

The first two years were tough, but let's face it, starting a motion capture company in an underdeveloped market didn't make much sense. You were putting in so much effort, but there were no visible results. I remember all those comments from friends and family, telling you to stop doing foolish things and go back to a *"real"* company. It was painful, and for the first time, I saw you deep in thought. I thought you were going to give up. Even Gerardo, co-founder, decided to leave and take another job, leaving only Carlos and you. You lost all your savings and had to support your family financially. I kept pushing you to quit, but you simply responded, *"Never give up."*

But after six long years, my friend, you did it. You became the leading motion capture company in all Spanish-speaking countries. I felt so proud, although I never actually told you. We celebrated a lot because you finally could support your family and find some peace.

That's when we truly understood the wisdom of your dad's words, *"Family is first."* We realized that family isn't just about blood relations but also about those who love and support you unconditionally. Remember when your mom felt ill and the health insurance couldn't cover her expenses? You ended up with a huge debt at the hospital, and to make matters worse, you lost a legal battle with the government. I remember how scared you were. You spoke to Carlos, your friend and co-founder, saying, *"The hospital debt is enormous, and we also have to pay to the government. Both need to be settled in the next few weeks, and maybe the company won't survive."* And he simply replied, *"If we go bankrupt but your mom is still alive, then let's go bankrupt."* That's when everything fell into place — *"Money comes and goes, but family is always first."* With the support of our family and friends, we managed to restore your mom's health and save the company.

After being an entrepreneur for ten years, over 5,000 people have learned motion capture, and more than 100 individuals have worked with our companies. You're finally able to support your family and help others in an industry you've loved since your youth — the cinema industry.

I'm genuinely thrilled that you've found your purpose and are making an impact with your ideas, helping those around you. As you always say, we can have dreams, but surrounding ourselves with the right people is what makes them come true. Act well, do good, and you'll never be alone.

We've been together for 35 years, and I know I haven't always been the most positive person. I've been scared to make decisions and often fought with you. Sometimes, I was trying to protect you from suffering or reliving difficult times.

New challenges lie ahead, like virtualizing humans for the cinema industry. It sounds ambitious, but I finally understand that working together will help us achieve even the most impossible goals. Let's do it and never give up!

Even though we are the same person, I wanted to write this letter to take a moment and reflect, to look back and be grateful and proud of who we are, who we've become, and who we aspire to be.

So, thank you for walking this path with me. With gratitude, Hans Guevara.

## Reflection

I decided to write this letter to myself as a reflection on some moments I've experienced throughout my life. These experiences have shaped me into the person I am today and have helped me find my purpose.

This analogy illustrates how we sometimes get frustrated with ourselves for not doing more or feel anxious about the decisions we've made. It also highlights those precious moments when we should pause, appreciate our achievements, and express gratitude for the people who are a part of our lives.

Life often introduces us to different types of people. It's important to be wise in choosing who we spend our time with because time is the most valuable thing anyone can offer. Give it to those who deserve it, and most importantly, give time to yourself.

Invest in self-improvement. We all have our demons from the past, and sometimes, they can be a heavy burden to carry. However, it is up to us to decide whether we want to befriend them and accept who we truly are. Every experience we have had, good or bad, has shaped us into the person we are today. Knowing ourselves is the first step in finding our purpose, and once we find it, we should never give up.

Remember, progress happens step by step, regardless of its size. Difficult times may be challenging, but they also provide opportunities for growth. Sometimes you win, and sometimes you learn, but you never truly lose.

Many people dwell on the past and worry about the future, rarely focusing on the present. So, whatever you're doing, make sure to enjoy the present.

Trust yourself, stay true to your purpose, and never give up. With determination, resilience, and gratitude, you will continue to make a positive impact and create a meaningful and fulfilling life.

Feel free to write a letter to yourself.

# Rachael M. Kim

## CEO and Femtech Ecosphere Builder
### *FEMTECH SALON POWERED BY MY COMMA*

## You Gotta Be

Growing up as a 2nd generation Korean-American between the lush, gorgeous west coastline of Washington State and the majestic snow-capped views of Mt Rainier, I rarely saw anyone who looked like me. I was one of five Asian students throughout elementary to high school—accounting for less than 1% of the student body population. My community was a predominately, white farmland suburb of Seattle, WA known for the Olympic gold swimmer, Megan Quann, and its annual fair. And while I grew up in the backdrop of a homogenous metropolis, I recognize that I always had entrepreneurial sparks since the beginning.

From teaching violin lessons at the tender age of nine (at the encouragement of my teacher as I was concertmaster of my school) to building a business line that made my previous employers millions as an intrapreneur—I knew that I would always have something that was mine someday—I simply did not know what or how. After my own health scare in my early 30's working for a global consultancy firm in London, I solo backpacked across 4 continents and saw the need to propel innovation and equity for women's and nonbinary healthcare.

The Femtech Salon

Upon my return to the States, I started a femtech startup which over three years during COVID, pivoted into My Comma and the Femtech Salon. My Comma is an organic period care subscription platform amplifying women and BIPOC led brands to power new daily routines while Femtech Salon is a pre-accelerator for femtech founders to amplify them by creating a more connected ecosystem to thrive.

With the recent gold rush and investments into women's health, my growing health awareness at age of 37 prompted another health discovery—I have been an undiagnosed neurodivergent my entire life. Looking back, the acknowledgement of my condition provides so much clarity to my amalgamated experiences. What I didn't realize until now is that I naturally coped with anxiety and stress through my immersive love of music.

And so it is through music I impart my thoughts on what I wish I knew then what I know now. I first heard this song in elementary school and I remember that I didn't think much of the entire song—just the kitchy head bop to the *"you gotta be"* chorus line. However, after 29 years since the song's release, I came across it again as an *"empowering song"* to add to my spotify recently and these lyrics made my neurodivergent, entrepreneurial brain come to life.

You Gotta Be by Des'ree with entrepreneurial musings from Rachael Kim's neurodivergent brain.

| | |
|---|---|
| *Challenge what the future holds* | *Startup life is endlessly shifting—mental agility is your superpower* |
| *Try and keep your head up to the sky* | *Stay positive, celebrate the small wins, it's not about being perfect* |
| *Lovers, they may cause you tears* | *Time will show you those around you who may not support your or believe in you* |
| *Go ahead, release your fears* | *Every glorified leader on Earth has fears—those who succeed embrace them to understand themselves leave legacies* |
| *Stand up and be counted* | *Share your story everywhere—you never know what effect it might have on someone to change their life* |
| *Don't be ashamed to cry* | *Embrace your EQ, allow yourself to feel, and know that you should not make key decisions with heightened feelings* |

| | |
|---|---|
| You gotta be | True and self-aware |
| You gotta be bad | And find other baddies just like you too |
| You gotta be bold | Put yourself in places and situations to enable opportunities you would have never otherwise realized |
| You gotta be wiser | Always be in a growth and abundance mindset |
| You gotta be hard | In maintaining your personal boundaries |
| You gotta be tough | In consistently communicating to your stakeholders who are a part of your journey |
| You gotta be stronger | From showing gratitude in being able to pursue your passion |
| You gotta be cool | In knowing when to act |
| You gotta be calm | In how you work with others even when the world is in a frenzy |
| You gotta stay together | Build the culture you've always wanted with the people you value and respect |
| All I know, all I know, love will save the day | Love and grace for yourself are going to get your through every hard decision |
| Herald what your mother said | Keep the core values you hold dear |
| Read the books your father read | Learn one new thing every day |
| Try to solve the puzzles in your own sweet time | You may see others succeed in startup world before you—just know that how you are solving a problem with your company is your own unique path at your own pace—also recognize that timing is important too |
| Some may have more cash than you | Don't worry about competitors—take stock, be different, and keep moving |
| Others take a different view | Gather your team of diverse advisors and team members |
| My oh my, eh, eh, eh | Incorporate play and fun into work as much as you can |
| ... | |

| | |
|---|---|
| *All I know, all I know, love will save the day* | *Build community around what you love will also anchor your sanity* |
| *Time asks no questions, it goes on without you* | *Seize the right opportunities and gravitas in front of you and assume you will never get a second chance* |
| *Leaving you behind if you can't stand the pace* | *Constant indecision is the ultimate killer of all organizations* |
| *The world keeps on spin-ning* | *There is a world outside of your micro-cosm, always step out to see the bigger picture* |
| *Can't stop it if you tried to* | *Acknowledge what is in your ability to control and what is not* |
| *The best part is danger staring you in the face, oh* | *Choose to be motivated when threats surround you* |

And while the song goes on…these are my cumulative learnings culti-vated over a lifetime. Granted, even knowing the above is not the same thing as living it—so I encourage you to get ready for your own adven-ture and truly live.

*Youtube video: https://www.youtube.com/watch?v=WRUwSk9UTrA*
*Look for it in Spotify: Des'Ree "You Gotta Be"*

# Gustavo Lomas

## North America Marketing and Sales Director
### *MCPU POLYMER ENGINEERING*

## Management versus Leadership: What I have learned along the way

Could it be that these two trends should be confronted? Many people have talked about this topic, and the title of this article indicates that perhaps the two roles are opposites. From my point of view, however, they are complementary roles, both equally necessary in an organization. They are two sides of the same coin that represent equally important functions that cannot survive without each other. They enrich and strengthen each other and that in fact interweave the personality of a team, company or society according to the way in which they develop and perform.

There is no doubt that since we were young, we have been taught that we must be leaders, that we must develop skills that allow us to lead our lives and those of others into the future. We must create a vision, inspire others, and in some way influence society or the organization in which we participate. But little is said about the managerial or directive skills that are equally necessary. They are reviewed from a very theoreti-

cal point of view, and professionals are left to learn them on a daily basis and to perfect them in postgraduate courses in a more technical way.

I truly believe that in this country we need to develop both skills in a more serious way. The subject of leadership or management tools taught in universities presents it in a very general, theoretical and to some extent in a terse way, without putting the knowledge into practice. Recent graduates often think they already have all these skills by the mere fact that the "subject" was in their study plan. We need to get involved with the new generations of employees and create a new way of living these two roles simultaneously and that once and for all they understand that both are equally important when it comes to developing plans that take organizations to another level.

For me being a leader in the field of marketing is exciting. At first, only one word resonated in my head: Influence. In marketing there is a lot of discussion about influencing audiences and potential clients to get them to carry out actions that, in one way or another, contribute to achieving and reaching the goals that have been planned. So as soon as I started to hold senior-level positions in companies, I only had in mind the notion that I would influence both internally and externally. Almost immediately when I started preparing for these roles another thought came to mind: Inspire. Should it be only on a professional or also on a personal level? What should I do first, influence or inspire? Will I really be able to do it or where can I learn to do it? In short, a lot of questions came to mind and although I did not show any concern about it, inside I felt an overwhelming need to know how to do it. I already considered myself a good leader, based on what I had learned in theory at my university and in my postgraduate studies, but was that all I needed to know and simply apply it?

It was there that I learned my first real lesson in leadership, which went hand in hand with management. I had been forging the whole idea of being a good leader, a good manager, a good director around myself and not around others. And that had been my mistake. The reality of a good leader is that it exists in relation to others, and it is in others that it takes on its true importance. So I completely changed the focus and became more humble. I began to see each of the people who reported to me at that time as a potential leader, which completely changed everything for me.

I realized that many of the people in positions of influence with whom I had had the opportunity to work had made precisely that mistake: they had been exercising their leadership position from a very personal perspective, often seeking only their own benefit and that is precisely why I had originally followed that trend. I managed to completely change the game and began to be interested not only in achieving and surpassing my company's established goals and objectives, but I began to be interested in the goals, objectives, even the dreams of the people who reported to me. The next step was that I tried to align both sides in a common vision that included the company's goals but that in some way also contributed on a personal level, elements for my team to advance in steps to achieve their personal goals and objectives.

The process was long, taking me several months in which on weekends I studied ways which I could align them. It even led me to redefine roles and job descriptions and also to realize that I had to work more on the development of my team on both a professional and personal level, creating "soft skills" that we were lacking. It was the first time I found myself changing the sense of direction and leadership in an organization. The challenge was even greater because it was not only about doing it in Mexico, but at a Latin American level, with a team of fifty people under my responsibility. In addition, the challenge increased when I discovered that within the same organization there were differences between the marketing teams in each country. This became a titanic task that could only be solved by getting to know the team well and exposing how their personal goals could be aligned with the goals of the organization. After almost six months, we found ourselves with a marketing team of fifty people with more than fifteen nationalities working with common goals and objectives. We were highly motivated, mostly self-directed and with a huge drive to improve ourselves.

I must admit that the first experience was quite overwhelming and that it cost me a lot of work. However, it opened the doors to a work model focused on people. I realized that as directors or leaders, we forget that we have a huge responsibility that goes beyond inspiring or influencing. Our responsibility is also to train people, not only professionals, but people. The individual is a fundamental part of society and many company executives have forgotten that if the individual is not well, then the organization is not well.

Something that has evidently helped me to be able to replicate this model in my work has been precisely to understand that I am with individuals. As the word implies, each one is different, so we must try to understand them to help them align their personal purpose to the objectives of the company. That is where I have noticed that I have really come to inspire people. When I am more empathetic with their situations and humble in wanting to learn from them, when I make connections with my team and assign responsibilities and tasks according to the skills that I have detected in them, that is when people start to get inspired and seek alignment.

One of the most important points that I must emphasize is that in leadership or management roles, you have to be highly empathetic but also extraordinarily creative. We must look for new ways of doing things based on what we have been doing. I believe that by being creative we become much more open to new options and encourage the intellectual development of our collaborators. I especially love this point because it is where an individual has the opportunity to develop. It is true that overseeing companies is an enormous task. For the right personalities, however, it is more than a job, it is a delight. And for me that is the secret of success: Find the pleasure in what you do and if you add to that the fact that it leads you to be creative, empathetic, humble and to develop people, then I think you are highly blessed because you have the opportunity to really bring about a transformation in the society or country you are in. That is one of the best things that can happen to you, if you are in charge of a team, do not forget your responsibilities towards individuals, on the contrary motivate yourself knowing that your experience alone can change the world. I invite you to reflect on this and to always keep in mind that the roles of leadership and management go hand in hand and must create such a synergy that the organization is revolutionized when a person with these characteristics begins to work with them.

I like to say that the future of this great nation is in our hands, but I think it is more accurate to say that the present of our nation is what we have right now in our hands, and that our constant actions are what will dictate that future, therefore we must assume a leadership role immediately, not only in organizations, but in communities, groups or families. There does not have to be only one, as these responsibilities can be shared, but I urge you to be that agent of change. Are you ready? If not, then prepare yourself even more and if you already are, go ahead.

# *Roberto*

# Bonelli

## Freelance Movie Maker

## When in Rome, be water.
**(and for those who don't know Bruce Lee, that means adapt!)**

In my time as a Production Designer for movies, I have had a great deal of challenges leading different crews to create the sets and dressing for movies big and small. However, in my eyes, the true leadership challenges I have had, have been the times when I was sent abroad to design commercials with different local crews. Commercials are produced very differently than movies. Not even on major commercials, such as spots for the Superbowl, does the Production Designer get to bring his favorite crew but will have to work with what is available locally. Most of the time very competent people, but because of the short timeline for these commercials, there is not enough time to really get to know one another before the project is deep in its crucial phase, and it might be too late. As a Production Designer, apart from being creative, it is essential to inspire and lead people to realize the projects, and the less time you have, the harder it is.

I know that the film industry is a very specialized world, but I also feel that basic management can be applied to other industries. Based on my experience, these are the five steps to follow to lead a group of

people that you have never met and that you will only be leading for a short while.

1.  Break the ice.
2.  Adapt to the local way of doing things.
3.  Be clear.
4.  Lead by example.
5.  Don't trust the translator.

Before we go into details, here is first is a little outline of how we make commercials:

Once the job is awarded, I get sent the director's treatment and info on the country where we will shoot the commercial. That info is usually the available locations, budget, and available crew. Together with the director, we select the best locations we want to see once we get there. Then, I chose two key collaborators from a list of proposed Art Directors and Set Dressers. If I am really lucky, someone who if have worked with is available, but in general, I have to choose someone new. If I am unlucky, there may not be qualified options available. Before arriving in the chosen country and meeting my new crew, I might have had a kick-off call or a video meeting, but that's it, and by the time we get to sit down together, there are two to three weeks until we start filming. Considering we need to design sets, have them approved by the director and the advertisement agency, and then build them, time is usually really against us.

So, my newly hired local Art Director and Set Dresser will already have their own assistants, but since we usually shoot in multiple locations, I do have a lot of direct contact with all of them. Often, a Set Dresser assistant will pick me up to scout the Prop Houses while the Set Dresser visits stores and the art director starts the construction of the sound stage.

So, how do I get all of these people to work optimate?

### 1. Break the ice
Share a personal side of yourself and not just the professional you. Open up a little. You don't have to lower your professional guard, and you shouldn't come across as fake or unserious but find a balance where you can be professional and open at the same time. Getting through in a sincere way can be vital for running a group with people you have just met. Don't just share our success stories but share difficulties you have had on previous projects. Your key people should

feel they can share problems with you instead of resolving them be-hind your back. You telling them to do so is not a guarantee that they will actually do it, but if the ice is broken, you stand a better chance of them trusting you. I usually tell them that I can help solve their problems. For instance, it sometimes happens that there are budget issues. The local crew will most likely prefer not to provide what you have asked for rather than going over budget since they have the financial responsibility and need to stay on good terms with the local production company. It is, therefore, essential that you are part of resolving those issues to get what you need.

## 2. Adapt as much as possible to the local way of doing things.
The structure of any Art Department can be set up in many ways. I believe that it is not a good idea to impose methods but to figure out together what fits the project best. Ask your local key crew to explain the planned setup. It is not a bad idea to explain how things are usually done in the U.S. and, indeed, in other parts of the world, but if they have objections, I recommend listening and adapting. Nor-thern America and Europe usually have smaller but more specialized crews, while countries with smaller film industries will often just add more assistance to compensate for the lack of skills. In certain cases, it is better to sub-hire providers to take care of parts of the job be-cause there is skilled labor in every country, but they are not always in the local film industry.

An example of this is a staircase. It can be built of wood, metal, con-crete, or something else. So, if it turns out that there is a great local tradition for carpentry, then that is probably the best way to go. Of course, you should not let your assistants bully your vision or ideas, but maybe they can be adapted to a way your crew feels more com-fortable with. If you do need to put your foot down and insist, do it. Be firm but fair and show them that you were open to suggestions but feel strongly that your way is the correct one in this case.

Its kind of goes without saying, but I will say anyway since part of my philosophy is not to take anything for granted: You have to follow the laws of where you are working. Labor laws are different. Most important, you have to adapt and respect the agreed working hours of the place you are in.

And don't complain about petty problems. Not everything is like home, and we sometimes get spoiled by the excellent service we get in certain places. You are there for work and not on holiday. You need to keep your comments to important work-related issues. Then your comment will be more effective.

### 3. Be clear (and don't use slang or abbreviations).

Make sure that your crew has understood their responsibilities and deadlines. Be crystal clear about what is expected from them and ask them if they feel they have the foundation to deliver. Let people know that you expect some misunderstandings to happen but that everyone should make an effort to be clear to keep them to a minimum. A small example is not using abbreviations or expressions that are not common worldwide. Nowadays, so much of our communication goes through text messages, which are often read at a glance while performing another task. Being clear and not leaving room for interpretation is very important. Take the time to write properly. Do not just forward e-mails but cut out the important information from the long chain you may have received and re-send only that part. I know this sounds banal, but you would be surprised how many producers and directors apply the forwarding of e-mails without further explication. Even though you understand it, you should not take the risk of your team members misunderstanding it. If you send your key people clear information, they will most likely pass it on in a clear way down the chain.

Also, let them know that there is no such thing as a stupid question. Your crew should feel confident enough to ask you questions, even ones they have already asked you. Film-making is very abstract and subjective, so the same question can have a new perspective once the process is a little more advanced.

### 4. Lead by example.

I find that it is essential that you are first in line when it comes to pulling the load. To make a commercial, the crew almost always works as long hours as is legally permitted. It is important that they see you do the same; otherwise, they will most likely opt for quicker solutions rather than better ones. Don't arrive at the office hours after your crew. Even though you might be up late doing some kind of work, it is important that you are present and available during the hours your crew work.

Ideally buy the crew lunch (something fast but very good) and don't disappear for long lunches while the crew is waiting for info or feedback to continue their work.

Make a big effort not to be late to meetings and let your team know in time if it is inevitable.

Let them know that you are always available if doubts occur. Waiting to make important decisions can affect your crew's workload and, indeed, morale as well. Making hard decisions is your responsibility and the biggest reason that you are in charge. If you are indecisive and look nervous about it, you will have a hard time leading our crew. If you genuinely have a doubt about something, you could consider asking your key people what they think but just keep in mind that you are the person closest to the director and probably know better what is right for the project. It's not about personal taste but was is right for the project. In fact, if I decline suggestions from my crew members, I say: 'it is not right for this project.' I then thank them for that suggestion and encourage them to keep suggesting.

5. **Don't trust the translator.**

Another thing to be aware of is that things get lost in translation. If you are in a country where you don't speak the language and have to use an interpreter, you should never trust that your message has gone through. The interpreter is usually specialized in language but not in the specific field that you are talking about. Therefore the communication should be as direct as possible. In the case of film design, we use plans or simple sketches. Paint and texture samples. I remember using an interpreter to communicate with a Chinese scenic artist who was painting a set. The painter was very good, and the translator spoke English very well, but the translator had never worked in an art department before. I didn't have the time to educate the translator, so I tried to communicate as directly as possible with the painter, only using the translator for specific keywords. It was not without hickups, but it was surprising how well it worked.

# Cabrera

### Founding Partner / Chairman of the Board
*QUASSAR CAPITAL*

## Finding my balance...

For many people hearing the word balance is very easy to say but it is difficult to apply and it is essential to be calm, aware of our decisions and our actions in order to be fulfilled.

It is a balance in which things are not all black and white, but there are a number of colors that we must balance in order to have fullness as individuals.

Currently we are vulnerable to various demands of society that set standards of personal and professional success, in which we also demand ourselves to meet these superficial requirements and often neglect the balance that will give us satisfaction in the long term and develop us as people.

There are managers who work exhausting hours that come to diminish their quality of life as they often put on their person and often on their health the fulfillment of organizational objectives, students who demand more than the account thinking that a number describes their

intelligence and employees who forget about their person to meet the needs of a company; in all these cases it is wrong because there must be a balance both in our person and in our objectives either professional or academic and that harms both our mental health and our person.

*"Companies are made by people and the development of the same depends on the achievements of each of the employees who are the reflection of the balance in their life both inside and outside the office."*

The year 2012 when I sat down with my partners who shared the idea of creating a leading hedge fund in the United States we had a very clear objective, which was to be able to create a company that would never lose the perspective that it was going to work thanks to our people and those same people had to share our passion for what we do; that is how Quassar Capital was created.

As time went by, we started to have private investors, later with large companies, then we managed to have transnational companies as investors and later we became advisors in financial matters for different governments. Our people accompanied us and, as I said at the beginning, we evolved. Quassar Capital became a person with its own objectives, but also with its own strengths and weaknesses that demanded greater commitment from each one of the collaborators who functioned as a big family.

The year 2020 arrived and Quassar Capital employed a little more than 150 people in the New York and London offices, we had approximately 57 billions in assets under management and we were considered by Global Finance magazine in London as one of the 25 most influential hedge funds in the United States.

The company demanded more time and commitment on the part of all the collaborators that we considered were remunerated according to their work. It was in May of 2020 when in a meeting with the entire Finance Committee we realized that we were gradually losing the original idea for which Quassar Capital was created because our people, who were among the best in the industry spent more time in the office than at home, at that time was when we approached our compliance coach and decided to measure the satisfaction of each of our employees regardless of position, whether they were interns, managers and management team.

The results were interesting because they were all satisfied as they had a very high sense of belonging and felt part of what Quassar Capital represented, they were completely satisfied regarding their economic remuneration but many of them had families, some of them had planned to do an MBA or additional studies in a University that we had a collaboration agreement, many had stopped attending the gym that was near our office and with which we had an agreement, at that moment was when we launched the initiative *"Quassar take a break"* #quassartakeabreak.

This initiative was basically going to focus on 3 key points:
1.- Teamwork
2.- The employee as a person
3.- Fulfillment of short term objectives.

Divide the activities of all departments so that they can begin to identify priorities (first what is urgent and second what is important), being a hedge fund that operates in the main stock exchanges in the world, invest in more personnel to reduce workloads in the teams and formalize work schedules for all employees depending on the market they operate in, This is summarized in more free time so that employees can dedicate time to their personal lives and this will be reflected in the satisfaction of all employees, since they will have a balance between their personal and professional lives and better results will be obtained in the short term, since this will avoid employee dissatisfaction.

It worked, by the end of the year 2021 we reduced staff turnover considerably, we currently have $68 billions in assets under management and we appeared in the ranking of the Global Finance magazine of London in the position No. 19 of the 25 most important Hedge Funds in the United States and we have an operating effectiveness of over 93%.

We learned that as a company having a balance is not a choice, it is imperative for us to grow, it is necessary that our people can feel satisfied both in their personal and professional lives because thanks to their dreams, goals and personal objectives we support them to achieve well-being and be complete people.

To have a balance as people is to seek that balance between the ego and our being, both our personal and professional life and in the professional life both the values of the company and our values learned at home.

Finding balance is not easy because it is not rigid or static, it evolves as we live and daily circumstances complicate it and make it dynamic, it keeps us in a constant process of adaptation as it evolves and also requires us to find a balance between our feelings and thoughts.

# *Nadim*

# Jarudi

**COO**
*TMAM*

## The truth

almost feel like this is one of those AA meetings. You walk in, look around at all these strangers and end up choosing a chair near the exit. No one talks to one another, but you know that misery loves company. The silence is broken by a man that looks well into his 40s but is actually only 32 (you ask yourself *"I wonder what shit he's been through?"*). he welcomes everyone and congratulates them on taking the first step; admitting that you have a problem and seeking help.

We go around the room and everyone introduces themselves... *"hi, I'm james and I'm an addict"* and the room echoes *"hi james"*. Then it's my turn... *"hi, I'm Damian (name changed for obvious reasons) and I am an addict"*. So, what is my addiction? This has nothing to do with drugs or alcohol. This boils down to this relentless feeling of being able to build something better than someone else.

*"Hi, I'm Damian and I am an entrepreneur."*

Everyone has a drug of choice; may it be AI, fintech, ed-tech, data... the options are endless like a kid in a candy store. We all jump in blindly because entrepreneurship and the startup world are glorified and romanticized.

We all think we will become instant millionaires.
Our own bosses.
And have an unchecked amount of clout.

What more would anyone want to ask for? For me, it was the truth. No one told me the truth before all of this started. So, to all the aspiring entrepreneurs out there, this is my truth to you. Don't think of this as a deterrent but more so the fine print in the terms and conditions of becoming an innovator. A disruptor. An entrepreneur.

So, my story started over three years ago, and just like everyone else's, I couldn't stand the corporate world anymore and thought that I was capable of doing something on my own.

I jumped.

I left a high paying job in the Gulf to a nominal salary of zero. I don't want to call it regret, because you shouldn't regret anything in life. Before jumping, you need to be ready to accept the fact that you are stepping into a world of endless financial instability. The uncertainty of where your next paycheck will come from, if it will cover your basic needs and all the pitfalls associated with it.

I took my corporate paycheck for granted, just like a lot of you do too. That constant expectation that on the 25th of that month, you get a text from your bank saying that your salary has been deposited which then gets uncomfortably replaced with an unwanted conversation with your co-founder/employees that you can't pay salaries this month (or even next).

Our first advisor used to ask our potential employees one question *"do you have at least one-year salary saved up?"* If they said no, that was the end of the conversation. Wise words, a little too late for me.

You start seeing your friends around you enjoying life, talking about a raise they got at work or that trip to Croatia they just came back from. You start becoming a hermit. A life of saying no to a lot of different things. Digging yourself deeper into a hole only to discover who your true friends are, and in some cases, your true love (corny I know but that *"through thick or thin"* statement really rings true).

To be a *"true"* entrepreneur, you also begin to read/subscribe to blogs on medium and articles on TechCrunch, Inc., Entrepreneur to name a few. Never do any of the articles actually talk about failure or even so what all this does to your emotional stability. I came into my startup with the same excitement and passion as the rest of you. We know we built a great thing, we even started to win awards and the media publicity was great (if you're impressed by this, stop reading). But nothing prepares you for your first no and the subsequent no's. There was this one post on Medium which talked about the state of depression this one entrepreneur went into. But just like everything else in life, you think you're invincible. I sit here writing this to you with a prescription for anxiety and depression. This is real and what you are going to put yourself through is very real. The life of a hermit, the life of saying no, the life of hearing no's all begins to take a toll on you and will affect your health. There are side effects to entrepreneurship; some may experience sleepless nights, loss of appetite, impatience, etc...

My biggest fault was that I internalized everything and defined success incorrectly. So, who defines success? You know on the first day of our startup we were asked what our exit strategy was. We hadn't even started, and people wanted to know how we were going to finish. Was success defined publicly by raising millions in your Series A? exiting to a western company? We obviously know what the media likes to write about, but is that your success? You need to define your own success. A quote that resonated with me was "a billionaire is not a person who has a billion dollars but more so someone that has changed a billion lives." We knew we had the product to do that but we didn't set up milestones (quick wins) along the way.

Your first customer, the first time they used your product twice, the organic leads. Don't ever take any of those for granted. Relish in those negative reviews; they write them because they believed in your product enough to write something cause they wanted it to be better. Once you begin to focus on you, on your wins, on the product and blur out the rest... everything will slowly fall into place. Just know one thing, your success is not tied into your company's success. If the company fails, it does not mean that you failed or you're a failure. You tried something millions of others couldn't do. You may not see it now (to this day, sometimes I don't) but you will.

So, this story could have gone in two directions; positive or negative. One implies that everything fell into place and the above was reminiscent of a time passed or the total opposite.

No money.

Chicken vs. the egg dilemma.
Doctor visits.
Disintegration of working relationship.
Burn out.
Faded passion.

Let's not define this as failure but more so your acceptance of the status quo and knowing when to move on and not regret anything. You should, or will become, mature enough to see the silver lining in the rollercoaster experience you put yourself through. The peaks of potentially generating millions in revenue to the troughs of the third failed acquisition offer. You will have the odds stacked against you in a copy-cat ecosystem that questions innovation and overly charges you for your existence.

*"Fail mindfully. Be aware of the lessons learned. And be aware of the responsibility to share those learnings with the world."* - Leticia Gasca

So, do you accept these terms and conditions?

# *Deven*

# Nongbri

### Advisor
### *YONDER HOSPITALITY*

## If I knew then what I know now

Having worked in multiple industries across different continents and in a number of roles, both leading organizations and individually contributing to different companies' successes, I've come to appreciate my family, my community and my career even more than I did when I was just striking out on my own.

What advice would I give to my younger self that might help ease some of the anxiousness that I often felt in different situations? What guidance might have helped me make better decisions at key points in my own life?

There are certainly lessons learned and life suggestions I could pass along, but it might be more useful to share some of the *"hard realities"* that only come with experience...and some reflection.

### Most of your friends are probably just acquaintances

How many of you have over one thousand connections on LinkedIn?

Yonder
ESCALANTE

Three thousand? Five thousand? That's a wonderful thing, making all of those links and connections to help advance your career, but how many of those people do you actually know? How many of those folks can you pick up a phone and call today?

Probably not one thousand, or even five hundred. Your collection of connections is most likely made up of many hundreds of people you may have only met briefly in person (or at all) from a conference or even at a company gathering. These folks aren't going to be there when you need a reference, a potential good word about your work or even a shoulder to cry on.

Your true friends are probably on a GroupMe or text thread that's at least a decade old, and the conversation continues despite people living on different continents, in different time zones, getting married, having kids, getting divorced, suffering the loss of a family member and surviving the pandemic together (at least virtually).

Your true friends are there to help, support and celebrate the highs and the lows of work life and personal life, and - this is key - they need or want nothing in return. They are there for you, and you are there for them. They are your real friends, and the earlier you can identify that handful of people, and support them and keep the lines of communication open, the richer your life becomes.

**You may only see your loved ones a few more times**

Our immediate family experienced a wave of untimely passings during and after the pandemic that took all of us by surprise. Upon reflection, though, most of these deaths could have been expected had we looked a little more closely at each persons' circumstances.

Poor health played a defining role in each case, so we rightly could have expected premature death as a possibility, but instead we focused on living our lives and not calling or visiting as often as we could have, in the belief that we'd *"see them at Thanksgiving"* or the next holiday.

The reality is, especially for Millennials and Gen Xers living in different cities (states or countries) from their parents and other extended family, those visits and *"next holidays"* are but a couple of times a year. And with the average lifespan falling to 77 years in the US, the math may not look good for many people.

Let's say you're living in Chicago but your 70 year old parents are still on the east coast. You get together every summer and then see them over winter break, so twice a year gatherings. When you do the math, you and your family will see your parents just 14 more times. Obviously, these are averages, but you get the idea.

Find ways to prioritize quality time with your family and (real) friends. You are actually giving yourself and your loved ones the gift of presence, and you won't regret this kind of action.

## You never quite know what you want to be when you grow up

There's a belief that you should know what you want to do with your life by age 20, and this is simply a lie. My own path was a little different, as I knew as a 14 year old I wanted to be in marketing, but doing what, I wasn't sure. And I certainly didn't know how to get there, even as a college student.

But I've known other folks, good friends and colleagues, who've spent years stressing out over a lack of a clearly defined path both in school and in the workforce.

I've come to know now, having worked in the community, on boards and in numerous private and public company settings, that the most successful people only have the faintest idea what they want to do. They just ask great questions to identify opportunities, and have a bias for action that has allowed them to capitalize on the opportunities they identify. And then they go and do.

If you have a bias for action, and ask the right questions, you'll be fine.

## Real and truly useful hacks are few and far between

Despite the popularity of *"life hack"* channels on Instagram or Tik-Tok, there are very few shortcuts that truly provide the results you think you want (or need).

If anyone tries to sell you the latest hack, you should run away as fast as you can. In my own case, it seems that AI hacks are fast becoming fodder in my Twitter feed: ChatGPT prompts for sale everywhere I scroll.

The only (mostly) successful hack is painful, relentless consistency. It's not easy, but it works. You. Can. Do. The. Hard. Things.

## (But...) Hard work and consistency aren't always enough

There's a common phrase in some sales circles, *"Hard work beats talent when talent doesn't work hard."* You may have seen this on motivational posters at the office or in someone's email sign-off, and it was a bit of a mantra for the *"hustle hard"* generation of the early 2000s.

But things actually don't work out every time you've got something big to do. It's just the way things happen, despite our most positive intentions. Do your best, but don't blindly assume it's always going to be enough.

Hard work and consistency will always give you a shot, but sometimes you're just going to get beat. If you lose, make sure it's because the other person is simply more talented than you.

Never beat yourself, and know that your hard work and consistency gave you the best chance at realizing an opportunity. It probably doesn't hurt to ask those great questions, too.

## The world is definitively not fair

There is plenty of uncontrollable luck that eventually impacts our lives: Where we are born, to whom we are born, and the circumstances of our early childhood all have an outsized impact.

Bad people win and good people lose—all the time. The pandemic showed us as much, no matter where we were in the world.

But within that dark context, there are bright spots: The opportunity playing field is leveling. The Internet and access to technology is opening up the planet so that people everywhere can get chances to grow and contribute.

The world may never be truly fair, but it will always belong to those who make the most of what they have before them. Keep your eyes open to opportunities, have your good questions at the ready and keep that bias for action.

## Be action oriented

Speaking of action, this is something that caused me a great deal of stress early in my career. I was always the guy taking notes, not saying a whole lot in meetings because I (wrongly) thought I had nothing to contribute. I was new, right out of school - what could I possibly know?

That's exactly the mindset that held me back at the start of my career, and it's one that I look for in new hires and younger teammates so I can try and help them get past it, and really unlock their potential.

If you can adjust your natural tendencies to favor action, you'll find that you'll get that experience and will actually have something real to contribute. You will probably do or say the wrong thing more than a couple of times, but you can learn from most of those kinds of mistakes, so it becomes a net positive.

If someone did a great job on a team project or helped you in any way, recognize or thank them right then and there, and don't wait for the *"right time."* Regret is more painful than failure, so when in doubt, just do.

## Conclusion

Developing an awareness of these *"harsh realities"* has allowed me to improve my decision-making and make life changes that have unlocked new growth and progress in both business and at home.

My hope is that others can think (but not too deeply) about each of these truths, and determine if they apply to their own businesses or personal lives.

Printed in the USA
CPSIA information can be obtained
at www.ICGtesting.com
LVHW021425220324
775249LV00032B/654